The Art of Preaching
Old Testament Poetry

Steven D. Mathewson

Baker Academic
a division of Baker Publishing Group
Grand Rapids, Michigan

Published by Baker Academic
a division of Baker Publishing Group
Grand Rapids, Michigan
BakerAcademic.com

Printed in the United States of America

Library of Congress Cataloging-in-Publication Data
Names: Mathewson, Steven D. (Steven Dale), 1961– author.
Title: The art of preaching Old Testament poetry / Steven D. Mathewson.
Description: Grand Rapids, Michigan : Baker Academic, a division of Baker Publishing Group,
    [2024] | Includes bibliographical references and index.
Identifiers: LCCN 2024013518 | ISBN 9781540967626 (paperback) | ISBN 9781540968364
    (casebound) | ISBN 9781493447725 (ebook) | ISBN 9781493447732 (pdf)
Subjects: LCSH: Bible. Ecclesiastes. | Poetry—Religious aspects—Christianity. | Preaching.
Classification: LCC BS1475.52 .M275 2024 | DDC 223/.806—dc23/eng/20240522
LC record available at https://lccn.loc.gov/2024013518

Cover art: *As Pants the Hart* by James Jacques Tissot / Private Collection / Bridgeman Images

Baker Publishing Group publications use paper produced from sustainable forestry practices and postconsumer waste whenever possible.

24 25 26 27 28 29 30   7 6 5 4 3 2 1

To
Ron Allen
Mike Boyle
Gerry Breshears
Don Carson
Scott Manetsch

These faithful servants have all played a significant role in my development as a pastor, preacher, teacher, and follower of Jesus Christ. I am grateful for each one of them and for their mark on my life and ministry.

Contents

Illustrations

Figure

Tables

Acknowledgments

It is a privilege to thank and acknowledge those whose help, encouragement, and support have enabled me to write this volume. I am forever grateful for each one of them.

First, I thank my family. The love of my life, my wife, Priscilla, has supported my compulsion to write and has never once complained about the sacrifice of time needed to complete this book—or the others I have written. Our children and their spouses have been great encouragers too and have frequently asked about the book's progress. So here is a shout-out to Erin and Manny DeAnda, Anna and Grant Vander Ark, Ben and Nicole Mathewson, and Luke and Janzyn Mathewson. Our grandchildren have been a great joy to us, and I have always been happy when one of them "interrupted" me while I was working on the book. Thank you to Blake, Kolby, Gabriella, Miles, Madden, Halle, Taryn, Jacob, Mila, Jameson, and Dakota. I love them dearly. Also, I want to acknowledge the support I received from my siblings, siblings-in-law, and their spouses during the months I wrote this book. They were encouragers during some challenging days. So, thank you to Dave Mathewson, Mark and Kim Mathewson, Kevin and Ellen Mathewson, Andy and Teresa Perkins, Sam and Joy Perkins, Cal and Miram Leavitt, and Tom Perkins. My brother-in-law Sam unexpectedly passed into the Lord's presence during this project, and we all miss him deeply.

Next, I thank friends who have encouraged me along the way. Dave Goetz has helped me grow as a writer—perhaps more than anyone else. He has been a great fly-fishing partner too. Dave and his wife, Jana, are "friends to ride the river with," as Western writer Louis L'Amour liked to say. Dwain and Sharon Tissell have been gracious to open their home to me whenever I am in Portland to teach at Western Seminary. They are the best! Dwain and I have had many rich conversations about Scripture, theology, preaching, and writing. Lance Higginbotham, a fine Old Testament scholar, has taught me a lot about the wisdom themes in the Torah, and he has been a supportive friend in challenging times. The members of our small group deserve thanks for their many acts of kindness over the years: Phil and Sara Anderson, Paul Carlson, David and Cindy Naftzger, Mark and Pat Scales, and Joe and Mary Swinski. I am also grateful for our friends Paul and Shannon Metzger, who have showered us with so much love and care. And what more shall I say? I do not have time to tell about how others have helped and encouraged me along the journey of writing this book. These friends, writers, and scholars include Chris Brauns, Brian and Amy Cope, Chris Dolson, Lee Eclov, Kevin Kneeshaw, Michelle Knight, John Kwak, John Ramer, and Taylor Turkington.

Also, I thank the team at Baker Academic for their expert guidance throughout this project. I am grateful for Jim Kinney, who first suggested the topic of this book as a follow-up to my previous volume, *The Art of Preaching Old Testament Narrative*. Jim is an incredibly gifted editor and a wise man. James Korsmo has done a fantastic job as project editor. We discovered along the way that we both have family members in Montana's Gallatin Valley who know one another well! I have also appreciated the skills of Paula Gibson, Anna English, and freelance editor Robert Maccini. All of these folks are exceptional at what they do.

Furthermore, I hear the voice and wisdom of my esteemed mentor and friend, the late Haddon Robinson, whenever I write anything about preaching. I will always be grateful for his imprint on my life and ministry.

Finally, I want to thank the "influencers" to whom I dedicated this book. Each one has had a profound influence on me, helping me grow as a pastor, preacher, teacher, and follower of Jesus Christ. Each one deserves their own dedication, but I may not get the opportunity to write enough books to make it happen. So, I have opted for a multiperson dedication.

Ron Allen was my beloved Hebrew professor. His courses on Psalms, Proverbs, and the theology of the wisdom writers instilled in me a love for Hebrew poetry. I am happy that, in his early eighties, he is still teaching Scripture around the world.

Mike Boyle was pastor of the church where I served as a pastoral intern the summer right after Priscilla and I were married. Mike and his wife, Mel, were great mentors, and Mike has become a lifelong friend as well as someone I still turn to for wise counsel.

Gerry Breshears has mentored more pastors and Christian leaders than anyone I know, and I have been blessed to be one of them. Gerry took an interest in me when I was one of his seminary students and when my wife, Priscilla, and I were members of the local church where he served as an elder. Now he is a friend and colleague at Western Seminary. And I am still learning from him.

Don Carson influenced me deeply from a distance for the first two decades of pastoral ministry. His writings and conference ministry taught me much about studying and proclaiming Scripture. Then I became senior pastor of the church where he and his wife, Joy, are members. Don has been my pastor as much as I have been his, and he and Joy were a great encouragement to Priscilla and me (and to my adult children) during a particularly difficult season of ministry.

Scott Manetsch and his wife, Cathy, have been wonderful friends for the past fifteen years or so. Scott has always provided enthusiastic support for my writing projects, as well as for my pastoral and teaching ministry. He is truly a Proverbs 27:17 friend, and I look forward to meeting him every other week for breakfast.

Most of all I am grateful to the triune God, who has been my shepherd all my life to this day and whose goodness and loyal love pursue me all the days of my life. He is worthy of all honor, glory, and praise.

Abbreviations

BHS	*Biblica Hebraic Stuttgartensia* [Hebrew Bible]
CSB	Christian Standard Bible
ESV	English Standard Version
HALOT	Koehler, L., W. Baumgartner, and J. J. Stamm. *The Hebrew and Aramaic Lexicon of the Old Testament.* Translated and edited under the supervision of M. E. J. Richardson. 4 vols. Leiden: Brill, 1994–99
HCSB	Holman Christian Standard Bible
KJV	King James Version
LEB	Lexham English Bible
NASB	New American Standard Bible
NET	NET Bible (New English Translation)
NIV	New International Version
NJPS	*Tanakh: The Holy Scriptures: The New JPS Translation according to the Traditional Hebrew Text*
NKJV	New King James Version
NLT	New Living Translation
NRSV	New Revised Standard Version

Introduction

This is a book for people who preach and teach Scripture. Specifically, it focuses on Old Testament poetry—Psalms, the wisdom books, and Song of Songs. But let us back up one step. Before we can preach and teach Scripture well, whether it's poetry or any other type of literature, we must read it well. We must become the kind of readers we want our listeners to become. In his novel *East of Eden*, John Steinbeck describes the kind of reader I want to become. He does so by contrasting two of his characters: Samuel and Tom Hamilton, a father and son. Steinbeck writes, "Samuel rode lightly on top of a book and he balanced happily among ideas the way a man rides white rapids in a canoe. But Tom got into a book, crawled and groveled between the covers, tunneled like a mole among the thoughts, and came up with the book all over his face and hands."[1] Samuel hurried through a book, while Tom engaged with it deeply. Samuel's reading was superficial. Tom's was thoughtful.

These approaches reflect two ways of reading Holy Scripture. Years ago I floated both the Yellowstone River (south of Livingston, Montana, in Yankee Jim Canyon) and the Snake River (near Jackson, Wyoming) in a raft. On both floats, our raft zipped through some Class III rapids. The experience was exhilarating but short-lived. I felt an immediate sensation, yet I did not return to it or ponder the experience. I moved on. Sometimes, I read Scripture like that. I hurry through it. It may produce an immediate sensation, but then I am on to the next paragraph or chapter, or even on to the next task or experience in my day. Yet there are times when I crawl and grovel and tunnel through a biblical text. I pay attention to its poetics.

1. Steinbeck, *East of Eden*, 280.

I look up a word. I try to untangle a difficult grammatical construction. And I make connections with other texts of Scripture. Then I ponder it for a day or a week. This is what it takes to read and preach Scripture well—and to teach our listeners to do the same.

Yet there is another dangerous, even deadly, approach to reading. Earlier in *East of Eden*, John Steinbeck says this about Liza Hamilton, who is Samuel's wife and Tom's mother: "And finally she came to a point where she knew it [the Bible] so well that she went right on reading without listening."[2] I find that frightening. While Steinbeck portrays Liza as a reader who never studied or inspected Scripture, there are crawlers and grovelers and tunnelers—in the Tom Hamilton mode of reading—who still end up where Liza did. They read without listening. In the Old Testament, or Hebrew Bible, the call to listen is a call to obey. Indeed, one of the main ways that the Hebrew Bible expresses obedience is with the words "listen to the voice"—the verb שָׁמַע (shamaʿ, "listen") plus the preposition בְּ (be, "to") plus the noun קוֹל (qol, "voice").

When it comes to preaching and teaching Old Testament poetry, we must begin by remembering that we "are dealing with God's thoughts." Therefore, "we are obligated to take the greatest pains to understand them truly and to explain them clearly."[3] And we must carry out this task as those who listen to God's voice and respond to it—what James 1:22 describes as "doers" of the word, not simply "hearers."

Admittedly, trying to understand and proclaim the poetic texts of the Old Testament might seem painful. We are often uncertain how to preach the highly emotive poems in Psalms, the one-liners in Proverbs, the tedious conversations in Job, the esoteric observations about life in Ecclesiastes, and the confusing love poems in Song of Songs. It is likely that we bring many questions to our task.

In the book of Psalms, how can we preach with poetic flair rather than flatten out the vivid poetry into something that sounds like a bland lecture? How can we help readers feel the emotion of a psalm rather than simply describing it with literary labels?

In the book of Proverbs, should a preaching text in chapters 10–29 consist of individual proverbs grouped around a particular topic, or is it possible to preach a particular section such as 10:1–16 or 25:16–28? How

2. Steinbeck, *East of Eden*, 42.
3. Carson, *Exegetical Fallacies*, 15.

can a preacher proclaim Proverbs 31:10–31 when women in the congregation are ready to scream if they hear another sermon on "the ideal wife"? Or might this text apply to men as well as women?

In the book of Job, what can we say about suffering, since the book is not a treatise on why the righteous suffer? What question does the book of Job answer? And what do we make of Job's confession, "I know that my redeemer lives, and that in the end he will stand on the earth" (19:25)? Practically, how many Sundays should a pastor devote to working through the book?

In the book of Ecclesiastes, what in the world (or "what under the sun"!) is the meaning of הֶבֶל (*hebel*), the Hebrew word translated as "vanity," "meaningless," or "futility"? What do we make of the polar extremes in the book? Sometimes it seems cynical and pessimistic, while other times it encourages its readers to enjoy life.

In Song of Songs, are we reading a collection of love poems with no plot or a love song with a developing story? And how are we to understand Solomon? Is he a noble, idealized lover, or is he a villain or intruder?

But the issues run deeper. What do we do with imprecatory psalms that sound repulsive and vindictive? What exactly is wisdom, and can we distinguish biblical wisdom from the wisdom traditions of Israel's neighbors? After all, parts of Proverbs 22:17–24:22 appear to be lifted from an ancient Egyptian text. Furthermore, how do the books of Proverbs, Job, and Ecclesiastes fit together when they offer such differing perspectives on wisdom? When we preach Song of Songs, do we present it as an allegory of God's love for his people (Israel or the church), a marriage or sex manual, or simply a celebration of the beauty and power of love? Also, how do these books fit into the larger story of Scripture, whose hero is Jesus? Finally, how can we proclaim these books in a way that is faithful to their literary strategy while connecting with listeners who often prefer biblical truth packaged in bullet-point lists?

My reason for writing this book is to help you preach the poetic texts in the Old Testament just as I tried to help you preach narrative texts in *The Art of Preaching Old Testament Narrative*. Specifically, I'd like to provide help in two ways. First, I want to make the best scholarship and thinking about the messages of these books accessible to preaching pastors, pastors-in-training, and anyone else who is serious about teaching Holy Scripture. Second, I want to provide some preaching strategies that are faithful both to the text (particularly its shape) and to the listeners (who may or may not have a taste for the kind of literature found in these books).

My prayer is that when you finish reading this volume, you will feel more motivation than intimidation when you think about preaching the poetic books and texts of the Old Testament. Please join me on this journey.

1

Preparing to Preach
Old Testament Poetry

Numerous pastors have confessed to me over the years that they do not like poetry. The same is true for a lot of our listeners. At least that is what they claim. Whenever someone tells me about their dislike for poetry, I ask them what kind of music they like. The responses range from "the old hymns" to "Taylor Swift" to "Michael Bublé." Then I observe that the lyrics to the songs they like are poems—whether Robert Robinson's hymn "Come, Thou Fount of Every Blessing" or Taylor Swift's hit "Anti-Hero." The point is, if you like music with lyrics, you already like poetry! While it is an overstatement to say that the book of Psalms was the "hymnal" of ancient Israel, the psalms are songs as well as prayers.[1]

Even if you like the book of Psalms and other poetic books or texts in the Old Testament, you may feel a bit uneasy preaching them. A lot of our listeners, especially the boomer generation and those who grew up in evangelical churches, like the plain facts. They prefer the direct approach

---

1. According to Bruce Waltke, "The praises of the Psalms . . . were intended to be sung to musical accompaniment. . . . Psalms are prayers of petition and praise expressed in music and poetry" (Waltke and Zaspel, *Psalms*, 4–5). Of course, the collection of 150 psalms we have today did not take shape until later in Old Testament history. Thus, Israel did not have a "hymnal"—at least until much later in its history. Also, note that although Waltke and Zaspel's book is a joint effort, "the bulk of the work was done by Bruce over many decades" and is based "primarily on his lecture material" (xvii). Thus, when I share quotes or comments in the main body of my volume, I simply refer to Waltke rather than Waltke and Zaspel. This is in no way meant to slight Zaspel for his admirable work. It is simply a reflection on the source of the content.

of discourse. I have found this to be the case when preaching to everyone from ranchers and miners to chemical engineers and CEOs. Listeners like bullet-point lists. Those who grew up in the church have likely been fed a steady diet of parallel, alliterated outlines. So even when we preach poetic texts, we are tempted to mash the contents into a neat outline like this:

I. The call to praise
II. The character of praise
III. The cause for praise

While these kinds of outlines are clear, they subdue or even squeeze out the poetic elements of a passage in order to "get to the truth." They may help preachers proclaim Bible-shaped content, but they fail to help preachers proclaim a Bible-shaped way. In order to understand fully what Scripture says, we must pay attention to how it says it and then shape our sermons accordingly. Helping you do this is the purpose of this volume. I want to help you feel confident rather than conflicted when preaching the Old Testament books and texts.

Where We Find Poetry in the Old Testament

Jan Fokkelman observes that "roughly one third of the Hebrew Bible consists of poetry. I call that quite a lot."[2] Where does poetry show up in the Old Testament? Everywhere! Poetry appears as early as Genesis 2:23 in Adam's outburst of praise over God's creation of the woman:

This! Finally!
    Bone from my bones.
    Flesh from my flesh.
This one, she will be called "woman,"
    because from man
    this one was taken.[3]

---

2. Fokkelman, *Biblical Poetry*, 1. Fokkelman arrives at this percentage by first noting that the standard edition of the Hebrew Bible, *Biblia Hebraica Stuttgartensia* (fourth edition), consists of 1,574 pages and that 585 of these pages contain poetry, thus 37 percent. Then, he lowers the figure to one-third to account for these pages containing more white space than pages with prose.
3. My translation. English translations (including the NIV, ESV, CSB, NASB) typically format this verse into four lines. The Hebrew Bible (*BHS*) formats the verse in two lines, with each

It is easy to spot poetry in the Old Testament because our modern English versions put poetry in lines rather than in paragraph form. Although the oldest Hebrew manuscripts of the Old Testament—the Dead Sea Scrolls—do not format poetic statements in lines of verse, our modern editions of the Hebrew Bible (such as the *BHS*) and our most recent English translations (such as the NIV, CSB, ESV, NASB, NRSV, NLT, and others) do so.[4] You can ask your listeners to compare Genesis 2:19–22 with 2:23 to see the difference. Or have them compare a page from Psalms with a page from Judges. Tell them that a quick glance at the formatting of a page will indicate whether they are reading prose or poetry.[5]

As you continue reading the narrative and discourse sections of the five books of Moses and then the historical books, you will discover that poetic texts show up in prose at climactic moments in the storyline of the Old Testament. Here some prime examples:

- Jacob's blessing of his sons (Gen. 49)
- The Songs of Moses and of Miriam (Exod. 15:1–21)
- The prophecies of Balaam (Num. 23:7–10, 18–24; 24:3–9, 15–19, 20–24)
- The Song of Moses (Deut. 32:1–43)
- The Song of Deborah and Barak (Judg. 5)
- Hannah's prayer (1 Sam. 2:1–10)
- Samuel's rebuke of Saul (1 Sam. 15:22–23)

What you learn in this volume will help you understand and proclaim these marvelous songs and prayers, which are scattered throughout the narratives and discourses of Genesis through Esther in your English Bible.

---

line containing three subunits. My translation reflects this approach. The Jewish Publication Society's English translation, the NJPS, casts the verse in five lines. Its structure is similar to mine except that it combines the final two lines into one.

4. The KJV (1611) and its revision, NKJV (1982), are exceptions. They structure the poetic verses or texts of the Old Testament in paragraphs rather than lines. I will explain the reason for this in my discussion of the poetic feature called parallelism (below).

5. However, not everything laid out in indented individual lines of text is a poem. Our English versions sometimes use lines of texts for things such as genealogies or lists of descendants (Gen. 10; 1 Chron. 1–9; 15:5–10), census lists (Num. 26:5–50), stages of a journey (Num. 33:3–39), and lists of leaders or warriors (Num. 34:19–28; 1 Chron. 11:26–47).

However, the focus of this volume is on the group of books in the Old Testament known as the poetic books: Job, Psalms, Proverbs, Ecclesiastes, and Song of Songs.[6] We will begin with the book of Psalms—the collection of songs and prayers of Israel's leaders, kings, and musicians. Then we will explore the wisdom books—Proverbs, Job, and Ecclesiastes. I am intentionally referring to these as "wisdom books" rather than as "Wisdom literature" out of sensitivity to a current debate. Hebrew Bible scholar Will Kynes has written an "obituary" for Wisdom literature, arguing that the category originated in the rationalistic, secular, skeptical worldview of mid-nineteenth-century scholarship.[7] His main concerns include the need to root wisdom in the fear of the Lord and Israel's special relationship with him; the need to recognize the presence of wisdom themes throughout the Old Testament law, historical books, and prophets; and the need to appreciate the different literary genres in the books of Proverbs, Job, and Ecclesiastes.[8] Like Tremper Longman, I do not object to the term "wisdom literature" when it is used in a broader sense than the older, outdated view of genre to which Kynes objects.[9] However, in light of the debate, I prefer to speak of the wisdom books or wisdom texts of the Old Testament rather than lumping them together as wisdom literature. Perhaps it goes

6. Fokkelman says that the "books of Psalms, Proverbs, Song of Songs, and Lamentations consist exclusively of poems, the book of Job almost exclusively." He notes as well that the books of Isaiah and the Minor Prophets were "also largely written in poetry" (*Biblical Poetry*, 2). However, we will not consider the Major and the Minor Prophets (as they are called in English Bibles), since they are worthy of their own study. See my comments later in this chapter. Fokkelman does not include Ecclesiastes in his list, although I believe it is highly poetic, even if not exclusively.

7. Kynes, *Obituary for "Wisdom Literature,"* 1–22. See the concise summary of his view in Kynes and Kynes, *Job*, 9–11.

8. It should be evident when reading the three wisdom books—Proverbs, Job, and Ecclesiastes—that they employ different kinds of literary approaches. This is in contrast to "narrative literature," for example. Though books like Genesis, Judges, Ruth, and Samuel have different purposes, convey different (though consistent) messages, and record events from different eras, they all share the same basic literary conventions and can thus be grouped as narrative literature. See Mathewson, *Old Testament Narrative*, 41–85, 88. See especially there the summary or narrative features in table 8.1 on p. 88. These apply across the board in Genesis, Judges, Ruth, Samuel, and so on.

9. See the helpful appendix "Is Wisdom Literature a Genre?" in Longman, *Fear of the Lord*, 276–82. Here is Longman's view on genre: "Genres are texts that are grouped together because they share similarities. These similarities may be formal, structural, or based on purpose or content. Genres are not categories that fall out of heaven but are constructed because authors write with similarities to other writings, and readers are able adequately to understand the writing of authors because they know 'how to take' their words based on their recognition of a text's genre and their previous reading experience. In a phrase, genre triggers reading strategy" (278).

without saying, but there is no need to split a church over this, nor is there any need to bring this up in a sermon.[10] Finally, we will turn to Song of Songs, a book of love poetry. It still uses poetic devices, yet the book as a whole works differently than Psalms or wisdom books.

There is another major collection of books in our Old Testament that primarily employs poetry: the Old Testament prophets.[11] Eric Tully points out that one of the "persuasive" strategies of the prophetic books is "the pervasive use of poetry."[12] So the insights in this volume on preaching Old Testament poetry will be useful when studying and preaching the Old Testament prophets. They use other literary forms and strategies as well, such as sign acts, parable and allegory, disputation, and vision reports.[13] The Old Testament prophets are worthy of their own volume on how to preach them well.

Some Thoughts about Preaching Scripture

Before we explore how Old Testament poetry works and apply this to how we preach it, we need to think a bit about the task of preaching. To lay my cards on the table, I am committed to expository preaching (at least the kind I describe below), and I believe that Tim Keller's conclusion in 2015 is still spot-on for today: "The sermon form is not dead, and many predictions of preaching's imminent demise now feel dated."[14] Of course, I agree with those who say we need to do more

---

10. I am quite sure that Will Kynes would agree with me because he is warm and gracious in his writings, and those who know him assure me that he is the same in person. So my statement is not aimed at him. It's a reminder to preachers (like me) that we must be careful about bringing up scholarly debates in our preaching. Rather, we will take insights like those of Will Kynes and be careful to help our listeners understand that wisdom is rooted in the fear of the Lord, is a theme that can be developed in various kinds of literary genres (given that Proverbs, Job, and Ecclesiastes work differently on a literary level), and can be found in places other than the so-called wisdom books (e.g., in wisdom psalms and even in texts like 1 Kings 4:29–34).

11. In the arrangement in English Bibles, the prophetic books consist of the Major and the Minor Prophets—a distinction based on the size of the books, not on their importance. In the Hebrew Bible's classification, these books are referred to as the Latter Prophets (as opposed to the Former Prophets, which include Joshua, Judges, Samuel, and Kings). The Latter Prophets include "the Twelve"—the books that we classify as the Minor Prophets.

12. Tully, *Prophets*, 128.

13. See Tully, *Prophets*, 111–31. Of course, there is limited use of parable and allegory in the Old Testament poetic books, particularly Song of Songs.

14. Keller, *Preaching*, 95.

than preach if we are going to make disciples and unleash our churches on mission. Yet we cannot afford to do less. The church rises and falls with its preaching.[15]

After preaching regularly as a pastor for thirty-seven years, and after teaching preaching in various Bible colleges and seminaries for the last twenty-five years, I have observed at least eight characteristics that make for an effective expository sermon—one that works its way through a biblical text, exposing its argument, and relating it to listeners' lives.[16] I agree with Haddon Robinson that expository preaching is more of a philosophy than a method. So here are my eight characteristics of an effective expository sermon. Perhaps these will encourage or challenge you in your own preaching. At the very least, they will help you understand the convictions I bring to the task of preaching the poetic books and texts of the Old Testament.

1. Accurate

Good expository preaching is faithful to the text. It accurately handles the Word of truth. This seems like a given, but what we assume ends up being taken for granted. A good sermon is grounded in rigorous exegesis of the text. In a day when the Bible gets treated as a book of sayings, an effective expository sermon reflects an effort to track the argument of a text and to understand it on its own terms. It reflects careful, prayerful reflection on the biblical text, as well as thoughtful interaction with the insights of other interpreters throughout the centuries.

2. Clear

It's impossible to overrate clarity when it comes to preaching. If your sermon is too complex, or if you ramble without connecting your thoughts, your listeners' minds will wander. Thankfully, there are tools to help you preach with clarity. One of the main tools is the identification of the big

---

15. As D. A. Carson observes, the "Bible sometimes envisages other forms of oral communication. . . . Yet in the oft-repeated 'Thus says the Lord' of the Old Testament, or in the proclamation so common to the New Testament, there is an unavoidable heraldic element—an announcement, a sovereign disclosure, a nonnegotiable declaration" ("Twenty-First-Century Pulpit," 177).

16. Carson says, "Exposition is simply the unpacking of what is there" ("Twenty-First-Century Pulpit," 176).

idea of the passage you are using. Of course, any biblical text contains multiple ideas. But there is usually a controlling, central idea—a peg on which everything else hangs. The problem with unclear sermons is not that they contain too many ideas but that they contain too many *unrelated* ideas.[17] Another tactic that helps with clarity is a simple sermon structure. It is best if you have two to four main movements—that is, modules of thought—in your sermon. These movements will be reflected by the main points in your outline. If you have more than two to four main points, your sermon will be too complex to follow. When you have too many main points, you do not need to eliminate some. Rather, group some of them together. Ideally, your two to four main points will track the flow of thought of the passage. Also, as important as your outline is, your listeners do not need to remember it. Your outline resembles a skeleton. You need it for strength and mobility, but no one needs to see it. Finally, transitional statements or paragraphs are worth their weight in gold. Listeners need to follow the logic or argument or flow of thought in a passage. We need to help them do that.

3. Compelling

A sermon can be clear but boring. There are several factors that contribute to a compelling sermon. One is the preacher's passion for the text. This is connected to being Spirit-empowered (see characteristic 6 below). A good introduction helps as well. While a good introduction needs to be as brief as possible, it must create interest, raise a need for the sermon, and orient listeners to the text. When our introduction is finished, we want our listeners to think, "I want to listen to this sermon. I *need* to listen to this sermon."

17. The dean of the "big idea" approach to preaching is Haddon Robinson. His classic textbook, *Biblical Preaching*, makes the case for and explains the formulation of a sermon's big idea (15–26). For a defense of the "big idea" approach to preaching, see Mathewson, "Let the Big Idea Live!" Timothy Keller offers some cautions about the "big idea" approach, noting that it can be applied too rigidly and that it is not easy to discern a clear central idea in some Bible passages (*Preaching*, 42–43, 249–51)—cautions with which I believe Haddon Robinson would agree. Yet Keller still counsels preachers to "know the main point of the author"—that is, to "identify the main thrust and message of the text for the original hearers" (68). We should note that Haddon Robinson's approach accounts for biblical texts in which multiple ideas seem to be "central." In this approach, the "complement" of the big idea consists of multiple items. Robinson calls this "A Subject to Be Completed" arrangement (*Biblical Preaching*, 85–86).

Another factor is a preacher's ability to answer the questions that listeners will raise. Haddon Robinson is especially helpful here, encouraging preachers to ask three developmental questions:[18]

1. Explanation: "What does this mean?"
2. Validation (proof): "Is it true?"
3. Application: "What difference does it make?"

We are trying to anticipate where our listeners need explanation, proof, or application. This keeps us from overexplaining, ignoring objections our listeners are likely to raise, and failing to help them see how to respond to what God is saying in his Word. Note that there is a logical order to these questions. You cannot apply what you do not accept, and you cannot accept what you do not understand. The second question has become even more urgent in our late-modern culture. Haddon Robinson often referred to this as "the C. S. Lewis question." I like to describe it as "the Tim Keller question" because Keller did so well at anticipating and dealing with the doubts and objections of his listeners.[19] This does not mean we have to raise these questions sequentially in our sermons. Rather, they are tools to help us determine what to include and what to omit in our sermons.

A final factor that contributes to a compelling sermon is sermon length. My suggestion for the length of an expository sermon is thirty to thirty-five minutes. It takes time for thought to form. Yet, it is often true that "less is more." My suggestion relates not so much to our listeners' attention spans as it does to the value of being concise. Honestly, I have heard very few (if any) sermons lasting forty to fifty minutes that would not have been more effective at the length I'm suggesting. Furthermore, the few (I hope) sermons I have preached that exceeded thirty-five minutes would definitely have been better had I trimmed them down to a half hour or so. The place to redline your sermon content is typically in your introduction, your illustrations, and in your explanation of key details in the text. Repetition is helpful to a point, but too much repetition bogs down your sermon.

18. Robinson, *Biblical Preaching*, 49–69. Although Robinson suggests asking these questions of both the text (as to what it is doing) and the listeners (anticipating what questions they will ask), I find it more helpful to ask these questions about my listeners rather than about the text.
19. See Keller, *Preaching*, 110–14.

4. Relevant

As the old saying goes, a good sermon afflicts the comfortable and comforts the afflicted. It is both comforting and challenging. I suggest that preachers devote as much time to wrestling with the implications of a text for their church family as they spend on exegesis. An expository sermon is not a data dump. To be sure, it should be exegetically solid and possess depth. Yet it must relate to the lives of the listeners—corporately as well as individually. For this reason, it is helpful to identify a sermon's purpose. The discipline of writing out a purpose statement helps preachers identify what they expect to happen in their listeners' lives as a result of listening to the sermon. God's Spirit may well do more than we ask or imagine. Yet identifying our purpose will help us preach with greater urgency.[20]

5. Collaborative

We might think of preaching as individual effort, but it takes a village to produce a good sermon. Even if an individual can produce a good sermon, a village will produce a better one. To be sure, preachers need to spend hours alone in study, thought, and prayer. Yet a sermon will be better for the blend of biblical insights, life experiences, socioeconomic perspectives, and relational connections brought by a team of voices within a congregation.[21] Such a team can meet weekly or monthly to speak into a preacher's sermon preparation. The team members can be a cross-section of members or ministry staff members or a combination of the two. When I served as a pastor in Montana, I experimented with the use of a focus group that met weekly to help me think through the three developmental questions discussed above. This group consisted of six to eight people from various demographics (life stage, gender, occupation, etc.) within the congregation. I asked for a one-month commitment in order to involve more people and lessen the time investment. Later, in a larger church in Illinois, I utilized members of our ministry staff as a "preaching preparation team." We worked through the same three developmental questions. In both instances, I did not ask for advance preparation other than reading through the preaching text a couple of

---

20. For more help on a sermon's purpose, see Robinson, *Biblical Preaching*, 71–75.
21. For a helpful guide to implementing a collaborative approach to sermon preparation in your ministry setting, see J. Peterson, "Sermon Preparation."

times. Of course, additional training and requirements may make such a team even more effective.

Collaboration also means sharing the preaching with other qualified, trained preachers. Even though a church may have a primary preaching pastor—either a lead pastor or a teaching pastor—sharing the preaching ministry with others allows a church to hear other voices and gives the primary preaching pastor opportunities to sit under the ministry of the Word and affords time for other pastoral duties. Another benefit of this approach is that it helps prevent pastors from developing a fiefdom or a cult-like following. For the past decade, I have averaged about thirty-seven Sundays a year in the pulpit, meaning that I scheduled others to preach on the remaining fifteen Sundays.

6. Spirit-Empowered

Recently, as I read Acts 4, I was struck again by our need for the Spirit when we preach the Word of God or speak it in any situation. First, we need the Spirit to proclaim the Word with boldness. When the religious leaders in Jerusalem seized Peter and John and questioned them as to "what power or what name" by which they proclaimed in Jesus the resurrection of the dead, Peter responded with clarity and courage (see Acts 4:8–13). Luke, the author, prefaces Peter's response with these words: "Then Peter, filled with the Holy Spirit, said to them." Later in the chapter, after the release of Peter and John, the believers responded to their report by praying together. Acts 4:31 describes the aftermath of this prayer meeting: "After they prayed, the place where they were meeting was shaken. And they were all filled with the Holy Spirit and spoke the word of God boldly." Second, we need the Spirit to work in the lives of those to whom we speak the Word. Between the two accounts of bold proclamation in the power of the Holy Spirit (4:8, 31), Luke describes the religious leaders' deliberation about what to do with these men who were so insistent on proclaiming the word about Jesus. Their response is rather ironic: "Everyone living in Jerusalem knows they have performed a notable sign, and we cannot deny it. But to stop this thing from spreading any further among the people, we must warn them to speak no longer to anyone in this name" (4:16–17). They acknowledged the sign, yet they rejected Peter's message. Patrick Schreiner comments, "Signs even with preaching are not necessarily effective. The Spirit of God must work in their hearts."[22] Yes! No sign or sermon—or the combination of the two—has the power to change human hearts without the powerful work of the Holy Spirit.

So how do we become Spirit-empowered preachers? The answer is prayer. Like D. Martyn Lloyd-Jones, I approach this matter with "much hesitation" and "a sense of unworthiness." He says that we all fail at prayer more than anywhere else. I know that I do. Yet, "Prayer is vital to the life of the preacher."[23] So, his advice for preachers is, "Always respond to every impulse to pray." This call to prayer comes from the Holy Spirit and "must never be regarded as a distraction."[24] Pray when poring over the text and struggling with an exegetical issue. Pray when wrestling with how the text relates to the life of your listeners. Pray when crafting your outline or manuscript. Pray throughout the sermon preparation process. Pray for spiritual insight. Pray for clarity and boldness in your delivery. Pray for your listeners to be receptive. Spirit-empowered preaching comes only through prayer.

7. Revelatory

Ultimately, preaching is the re-revelation of God. D. A. Carson says that whenever the word of the Lord is re-announced, "there is a sense in which God, who revealed himself by that Word in the past, is re-revealing himself by that same Word once again. Preachers must bear this in mind. Their aim is more than to explain the Bible."[25] This means that our goal when we preach Proverbs, for example, is more than just to help listeners build solid friendships, manage their emotions, and handle their wealth. It is to re-reveal the living God. This means that faithful preachers will care about faithfully representing "the Master and his message."[26]

8. Redemptive

The final characteristic of an effective expository sermon that I wish to highlight is its location of the text in the larger story of redemption. This brings us to the debate over Christ-centered preaching.[27] On one

---

22. Schreiner, *Acts*, 178.
23. Lloyd-Jones, *Preaching and Preachers*, 169.
24. Lloyd-Jones, *Preaching and Preachers*, 171.
25. Carson, "Twenty-First-Century Pulpit," 176.
26. Carson, "Twenty-First-Century Pulpit," 177.
27. For a more detailed summary of this debate, see Mathewson, *Old Testament Narrative*, 15–26.

side is a theocentric approach, preaching only what is in the text—that is, the theology of a text of Scripture based on a grammatical-cultural-historical-literary study of it—without any reference to biblical theology or the larger metanarrative of the Bible. The other side is a Christocentric approach to reading that finds an image or reference to Jesus in almost every detail in the text and that shies away from preaching the ethical exhortations in the text for fear of moralizing and failing to "preach Christ."

In my view, the theocentric and Christocentric approaches to interpretation and preaching are friends, not enemies. We must engage in a careful grammatical-cultural-historical-literary study in order to discern a text's theological message and ethical thrust—whether the "imperative" comes through grammatical exhortations or more subtle implications. But we must also consider the larger context of a biblical text—the metanarrative of Scripture. This is often referred to as the story of redemption. Its hero is the Lord Jesus Christ. Through his death and resurrection, he redeemed us from sin to experience life in the presence of God.[28] Thus, a theocentric approach should lead to a Christocentric approach, and a Christocentric approach should build upon a theocentric approach.

Those who lean more toward a theocentric view must remember that when we preach the divine demands in Old Testament poetic texts, we must ground these demands in the gospel—what God has done for us in Christ. Those who lean more toward a Christocentric view must remember Timothy Keller's warning that "it is possible to 'get to Christ' so quickly in preaching a text that we fail to be sensitive to the particularities of the text's message. We leapfrog over the historical realities to Jesus

---

28. When I preach, I tell my listeners that the Bible is the story of God reestablishing the gift of his presence. He redeems us from sin to experience life in his presence. Other biblical scholars concur. For example, L. Michael Morales says, "Indeed, all of the drama of Scripture is found in relation to this singular point of focus: *YHWH's opening up the way for humanity to dwell in his Presence once more*" (*Who Shall Ascend?*, 55). J. Scott Duvall and J. Daniel Hays claim that "the presence of God" is the "megatheme" that drives the biblical story, "uniting and providing interconnecting cohesion across the canon for all of the other major themes" (*God's Relational Presence*, 1). They note that what lies at the heart of the Bible's overall message is that "the Triune God desires a personal relationship with his people and so makes his presence known to establish and cultivate this relationship" (325). After surveying the entire sweep of Scripture from Genesis to Revelation on the theme of temple, G. K. Beale understands that "our task as the covenant community, the church, is to be God's temple, so filled with his glorious presence that we expand and fill the earth with that presence until God finally accomplishes the goal completely at the end of time" (*The Temple*, 402).

as though the Old Testament Scriptures had little significance to their original readers."[29]

With these thoughts about preaching in hand and heart, we are ready to think about the specific task of preaching Old Testament poetic texts. The place to begin is with how Old Testament poetry works.

How Old Testament Poetry Works

What makes a poem a poem? In the Old Testament, a poem consists of lines with an artistic, elevated style of expression.[30] This style is the result of three elements: terseness, parallelism, and imagery.[31] As previously noted, modern English versions format poetry in lines rather than in paragraphs as they do with prose—whether discourse (instruction) or narrative. These lines are terse, parallel, and full of metaphor and imagery. Let us take a look at these features in more detail.

Terseness

Skillful poets say more with less. For example, Amanda Gorman—a contemporary poet who is currently the youngest presidential inaugural poet in US history—begins one of her poems with this concise two-line stanza:

> It is easy to harp,
> Harder to hope.[32]

29. Keller, *Preaching*, 66.

30. Some literary scholars refer to a line of poetry as a "verse." However, I will not use that term, since it can easily be confused with a "Bible verse" such as Psalm 23:1. That Bible "verse" contains two poetic "verses": (1) "He makes me lie down in green pastures," (2) "he leads me beside quiet waters."

31. Adele Berlin views the elevated style of poetry as the product of two elements: terseness and parallelism (*Biblical Parallelism*, 5). Bruce Waltke identifies three features of poetry: parallelism, brevity and terseness, and imagery and figures of speech (Waltke and Zaspel, *Psalms*, 133–36). Similarly, Tremper Longman says that Old Testament poetry "has three major characteristics: terseness, parallelism, and intense use of imagery" (*Proverbs*, 33). For Jan Fokkelman, a poem is the result of (1) an artistic handling of language, style, and structure, and (2) applying prescribed proportions to all levels of the text. By "prescribed proportions," he refers to the accepted length of the lines, stanzas, and sections of a poem (*Biblical Poetry*, 34–35). Fokkelman also says that the "poet's main strategy for shaping his verses" is parallelism (60). Dominick Hernández suggests that poetic texts have two shared characteristics: rhythm and rhetoric. Specifically, in the Old Testament, this turns out to be parallelism (rhythm) and the proliferation of metaphors (rhetoric) (*Old Testament*, 183–85).

32. Gorman, "& So."

This is an essay, even a book, distilled into eight words spread over two lines. The lines are compact, even terse. The verb "harp" in line one has no complement such as a prepositional phrase. Then, in line two, the words "it is" are elided.

This is precisely what Old Testament poetry does. Adele Berlin says, "A poem distills and condenses its message, removing 'unnecessary' words and leaving only the nucleus of the thought."[33] Bruce Waltke notes that Old Testament poetry "often omits verbal particles, leaves gaps, and it often states its point in briefest fashion."[34] Jan Fokkelman refers to this as "density," describing Old Testament poetry as compact and concentrated speech. A prime example is the well-known opening verse of Psalm 23:

> The LORD is my shepherd,
> I lack nothing.

The two-line verse is even more compact in Hebrew, consisting of four words rather than the eight words utilized by most English translations. Here is my rather literal translation of the four Hebrew words in Psalm 23:1:

> Yahweh / my-shepherd
> Not / I-lack

The terseness of this verse enhances rather than diminishes its power. Admittedly, Psalm 23 goes on to unpack this idea in some depth. Yet the opening four words have the rhetorical effect of a bold declaration.

We can see compactness or terseness at work when we compare narrative and poetic descriptions of the same event in the book of Judges: the way Jael shows hospitality to Sisera, the commander of the Canaanite army, before she kills him. Here is a comparison of the narrative account in Judges 4 with the poetic account in Judges 5:

> And he said to her, "Please give me a little water to drink, for I am thirsty." So she opened a skin of milk and gave him a drink and covered him. (4:19 ESV)

---

33. Berlin, *Biblical Parallelism*, 6.
34. Waltke and Zaspel, *Psalms*, 134. Similarly, Robert Alter refers to "the very common maneuver of ellipsis in which a word in the first verset, usually a verb, governs the parallel clause in the second verset as well" (*Biblical Poetry*, 23). That is, the verb in the first line, or verset, is omitted—but understood or assumed—in the second line.

> He asked for water and she gave him milk;
>   she brought him curds in a noble's bowl. (5:25 ESV)

In the Hebrew text, the narrative account consists of fourteen words, while the poetic account needs only eight words—two lines, each with four words.[35]

Although the lines of Old Testament poetry are succinct, they are also interrelated. The lines correspond with each other.[36] This brings us to our next element, or feature, of Old Testament poetry.

Parallelism

A significant discovery in biblical studies took place in 1753. Robert Lowth, a bishop of the Church of England and professor of poetry at Oxford, published a treatise on poetry in the Hebrew Bible. In this treatise, he highlighted a feature he eventually described as "parallelism."[37] While he was "not the first to recognize parallelism," Lowth "promoted it to a place of prominence in biblical studies."[38] He defined *parallelism* as the correspondence of one line of poetry to another. Usually, two lines, or versets (the expression some biblical scholars prefer), work together. Occasionally, though, three lines (versets) correspond.[39]

Lowth identified three main types of parallelism. Waltke says that while they oversimplify the matter, they "remain somewhat helpful."[40] In *synonymous* parallelism, the two lines say nearly the same thing. The second line simply echoes the first line using different words. Here are three examples.

> Therefore the wicked will not stand in the judgment,
>   nor sinners in the assembly of the righteous. (Ps. 1:5)

> Why do the nations conspire
>   and the peoples plot in vain? (Ps. 2:1)

35. Berlin provides a fuller discussion of these two accounts and how the poetic account heightens the contrast between what Sisera requested and what Jael provided (*Biblical Parallelism*, 12–13).
36. Hernández, *Old Testament*, 185.
37. See Berlin, *Biblical Parallelism*, 1–3; Waltke and Zaspel, *Psalms*, 136–38; Alter, *Biblical Poetry*, 3, 204; Fokkelman, *Biblical Poetry*, 25–27.
38. Berlin, *Biblical Parallelism*, 1.
39. To add to the confusion, some scholars or commentators refer to a line of poetry, or verset, as a colon. A bicolon is a set of two cola (the plural of colon). That is, it consists of two lines, or versets. A tricolon has three cola.
40. Waltke and Zaspel, *Psalms*, 137.

Out in the open wisdom calls aloud,
    she raises her voice in the public square. (Prov. 1:20)

Another type of parallelism is *antithetical*. This kind of parallelism involves a contrast between two lines. In some instances, both lines make the same point, with the second affirming the truth in the first by looking at it from an opposite perspective.[41] Antithetical parallelism is easy to spot because our English translations typically translate the Hebrew connector at the beginning of the second line as "but" instead of "and."[42]

For the Lord watches over the way of the righteous,
    but the way of the wicked leads to destruction. (Ps. 1:6)

A gentle answer turns away wrath,
    but a harsh word stirs up anger. (Prov. 15:1)

In other instances of antithetical parallelism, the two lines describe contrasting realities. Both opposite realities are true at the same time.

You evildoers frustrate the plans of the poor,
    but the Lord is their refuge. (Ps. 14:6)[43]

The third type of parallelism identified by Lowth is *synthetic*. Here the second line further develops the thought of the first line rather than simply restating it. That is, the second line expands the first line by adding further details or dimension to it. Here are a couple examples.

But his delight is in the law of the Lord,
    and on his law he meditates day and night. (Ps. 1:2 ESV)

Come, let us bow down in worship,
    let us kneel before the Lord our Maker. (Ps. 95:6)

41. Longman, *Proverbs*, 35.
42. What I refer to here as "the simple Hebrew connector" is the coordinating conjunction וְ (*we*), usually translated as "and," though translated as "but" when it precedes a clause or phrase with a contrasting idea.
43. In Ps. 14:6, the second line begins with the conjunction כִּי (*ki*). In this instances it introduces a counterstatement and is thus translated as "but" in most English versions.

There are, however, many verses in the poetic sections of the Old Testament that do not fit neatly into one of these three categories. In some verses, there is no clear relationship between the lines. Ronald Allen says, "In another context these verses might be prose; in a poem they help to add variety and an unexpectedness to the lines of frequent parallelism."[44] Scholars refer to this as *formal* parallelism or "formal relationship."[45] Here are a couple examples.

> My God, whom I praise,
>   do not remain silent. (Ps. 109:1)

> Then you will win favor and a good name
>   in the sight of God and man. (Prov. 3:4)

Another category is *climactic* parallelism, in which the second line takes some words from the first line and then completes the idea left unfulfilled in the first line.[46] Here is an example.

> Ascribe to the LORD, all you families of nations,
>   ascribe to the LORD glory and strength. (Ps. 96:7)

Still another kind of parallelism is *emblematic*. "In this type of parallelism, the first line may have a figure of speech that is explained in the second line."[47] Here are a couple of examples.

> As the deer pants for streams of water,
>   so my soul pants for you, my God. (Ps. 42:1)

> Like cold water to a weary soul
>   is good news from a distant land. (Prov. 25:25)

Unfortunately, these categories still do not account for all the ways that parallel lines of poetry interact with each other. These labels fit some

44. R. Allen, *Praise!*, 53–54.
45. Waltke and Zaspel, *Psalms*, 138; R. Allen, *Praise!*, 54. My seminary Hebrew professor Ronald Allen used to quip that we use expressions like "formal relationship" or "formal parallelism" to justify the cost of tuition!
46. R. Allen, *Praise!*, 52.
47. R. Allen, *Praise!*, 53.

bicola about as well as socks on a rooster. Trying to impose one of these labels on a particular bicolon can lead to missing the idea it intends to convey. Is there, perhaps, a more excellent way to go about assessing parallelism?

Jan Fokkelman is certainly right when he says, "Where poetry is concerned, literary sensitivity and an open mind are more valuable than constructing definitions."[48] So, we want to prioritize literary sensitivity over labels. Of course, labels can help us if they teach us to be literarily sensitive. But too often we are content to label something and move on. Some verses might even defy a label. That's okay. Just describe how the lines work together—what Robert Alter designates as "the shifting semantic relations between the versets." In the case of apparent repetitions, this might mean a focusing, a heightening, a concretization, a development of meaning. Or the lines might create a contrast, an intensification or crescendo development, or even "brief sequences of explicit narrative development."[49] I have found Robert Alter's system of typographic symbols helpful when wrestling with the relationship between lines of poetry (see table 1.1). Alter places these symbols between lines of poetry to signify the type of relationship they have. He feels free to use more than one symbol if the semantic relationship is "partly one thing and partly another." And he will use question marks if the relations between the versets (lines) do not seem "decidable."[50]

Table 1.1

Alter's System for Identifying How Parallelism Functions

=	Synonymity
(=)	Synonymity with verbatim repetition
{ }	Complementarity
>	Focusing, heightening, intensification, specification
→	Consequentiality

Below is my analysis, using Alter's system, of Psalm 23. I have used the NIV's division of this poem into lines, as well as its translation, and then removed punctuation. Also, I have occasionally used a symbol at the *end*

---

48. Fokkelman, *Biblical Poetry*, 35.
49. Alter, *Biblical Poetry*, 29.
50. Alter, *Biblical Poetry*, 30. For his analysis of 2 Sam. 22 // Ps. 18, see pp. 30–32.

of a bicolon—in addition to the symbol between the cola or lines—to signify my understanding of how one verse or bicolon relates to the one that follows it.

> [1] The LORD is my shepherd → I lack nothing
> [2] He makes me lie down in green pastures {=} he leads me beside quiet
>   waters > [3] he refreshes my soul
> He guides me along the right paths > for his name's sake
>   [4] Even though I walk > through the darkest valley →
> I will fear no evil > for you are with me
> your rod and your staff > they comfort me
> [5] You prepare a table before me > in the presence of my enemies
> You anoint my head with oil { } my cup overflows >
> [6] Surely your goodness and love will follow me > all the days of my life →
> and I will dwell in the house of the LORD > forever

A few explanatory comments are in order. I understand the second line of verse 1 ("I lack nothing") to be the consequence of having the Lord as my shepherd. Verses 2–3a consist of a tricolon. In my estimation, the second line shows both complementarity and synonymity with the first line— hence the combination of two symbols. The ideas are complementary, while the grammatical structure—in both English and Hebrew—is synonymous. In the English text, lines one and two both have a subject pronoun followed by a verb followed by the same indirect object ("me") followed by a prepositional phrase. Then, the third line of the tricolon provides focusing. What the two previous lines describe is refreshment of the psalmist's life. The second line of the bicolon of verse 3b specifies the purpose ("for his name's sake") of the Lord's guidance. Then, the first bicolon in verse 4 has specification as well with the second line specifying where the psalmist walks. At the end of this bicolon, the arrow symbol indicates consequentiality with the second bicolon in verse 4. Perhaps it is more accurate to describe the first bicolon in verse 4 as concessional, but the arrow symbol indicates the consequence or outcome of walking through the darkest valley: a lack of fear. Then, in the second bicolon, there is specification as the second line explains why the psalmist does not fear evil ("for you are with me"). The third bicolon in verse 4 is another instance of specification with the second line indicating the function of the rod and staff in the first line.

In the second and final movement of Psalm 23, the first bicolon in verse 5 is another case of specification with the second line indicating where the Lord prepares the table ("in the presence of my enemies"). By now, it should be apparent that some of the instances of "specification" in this psalm might be classified as *formal* parallelism because the second line simply completes the thought in the first line. The second bicolon in verse 5 seems to be an instance of complementarity. These lines are hardly synonymous, yet they are complementary in the sense that they describe blessings provided by God. Then, the symbol I have placed at the end of this second bicolon in verse 5 signals that the next bicolon in verse 6 is a heightening or intensification of both bicola in verse 5. Verse 6 is a kind of summary exclamation. In the first bicolon, the second line specifies the duration of the pursuit of the Lord's goodness and love ("all the days of my life"). The arrow symbol at the end of this bicolon indicates that the second bicolon provides the consequence: "I will dwell in the house of the Lord forever." The symbol before the one-word second line, "forever," specifies the duration.

This is an example, then, of how to use Alter's system. Admittedly, there is subjectivity involved in determining what symbols are appropriate. But that's okay. The point of the exercise is to wrestle with how the lines work together. In short, the goal is to make us think. If this particular system seems too cumbersome, then by all means, use or devise something simpler. You can use the categories I described earlier, although they will not account for every instance. Perhaps the easiest way would be simply to describe the relationship of the lines in each bicolon or tricolon, as well as the relationship between the various verses—that is, poetic verses, not necessarily the verses in our English Bibles. For each bicolon, simply make statements like the following (based on Ps. 23 as our example):

- Verse 1: The second line describes the consequence of the first line.
- Verses 2–3a: The second line describes a complementary blessing that the Lord provides, while the third line provides focus, describing both blessings as refreshment.
- Verse 3b: The second line establishes the purpose for the first line.
- Verse 4a: The second line specifies where the psalmist is walking.

- Verse 4b: The second line provides the reason for the first line. Also, 4b is the consequence of 4a.
- Verse 4c: There is no clear relationship. Line two supplies the action for the subjects in line one.
- Verse 5a: Line two specifies where the action in line one takes place.
- Verse 5b: Line two lists an additional blessing along with the one in line one.
- Verse 6a: Line two describes the duration of the action ("all the days of my life"). Also, 6a heightens or intensifies the affirmations of 5a and 5b by providing a summary exclamation ("Surely your goodness . . .").
- Verse 6b: Line two describes the duration of the action ("forever"). Also, 6b is the consequence of 6a.

A final step in wrestling with parallelism is thinking about the relationship verses have with one another and about the relationship between larger textual units. Biblical scholars refer to these as strophes and stanzas. The stanza is a larger unit of thought that consists of smaller units of thought called strophes.[51] For these larger units of thought, the white space between groups of lines in our English versions is a good place to start. For example, the NIV places a space between verses 4 and 5 in Psalm 23, indicating that verses 1–4 and 5–6 are the two main sections in the psalm, probably best identified as stanzas.[52] Often, it is challenging to determine the appropriate labels for sections, let alone the appropriate divisions of text. Waltke makes an interesting observation: "In a poem two closely connected verses are called a *quatrain*, a smaller collection, a *strophe*, and a larger division, a *stanza*. The division between these, however, sometimes becomes attenuated."[53] Exactly. Thus,

---

51. Fokkelman, *Biblical Poetry*, 6–7, 30; Waltke and Zaspel, *Psalms*, 452; Waltke, *Proverbs: Chapters 1–15*, 45–46.

52. Waltke says there are three scenes in Psalm 23: verses 1–4, verse 5, and verse 6. Presumably, these three scenes are the three strophes of the poem that make up the two stanzas: verses 1–4 and verses 5–6 (Waltke and Zaspel, *Psalms*, 157). However, while the white space in the NIV layout of Ps. 110 divides it into five units (vv. 1a, 1b, 2–3, 4, 5–6), Waltke divides Ps. 110 into two stanzas: verses 1–3 and 4–7 (Waltke and Zaspel, *Psalms*, 125). Thus, the NIV's layout in Ps. 110 reflects strophes, while its layout of Ps. 23 reflects stanzas. Once again, we must remember that the goal is literary sensitivity, not precise division of a poem into sections and applying the "right" label to these sections.

53. Waltke, *Proverbs: Chapters 1–15*, 46.

we should not stress out over labeling sections precisely.[54] The key is to be as sensitive as possible to how Old Testament poets are structuring their poems. Now we must consider a final feature, or element, of Old Testament poetry.

Metaphor and Imagery

Metaphors and other figures of speech are not unique to Old Testament poetry. For example, the apostle Paul was fond of athletic metaphors in his New Testament letters,[55] and he also used warfare images involving a Roman triumph,[56] a Roman soldier and his armor,[57] and fighting in battle.[58] Furthermore, Paul and other apostles used imagery from the world of agriculture and shepherding,[59] marriage,[60] the human body,[61] and the family.[62]

What makes Old Testament poetry unique is its high concentration of metaphors and imagery. Tremper Longman describes this as "the intense use of imagery."[63] A good place to begin is to notice the proliferation of metaphor in Psalms, Proverbs, and the other Old Testament poetic books and texts. Dominick Hernández says that "metaphor is ubiquitous in poetry" and that metaphors are "at the heart of biblical poetry"—to use a metaphor.[64] Since the time of Aristotle, a metaphor has been defined as an implicit comparison of two categories, using the perceived resemblance between the two to explain one of them.[65] Often, a metaphor is stated as a direct, though implicit, comparison, as in "A is B." Elizabeth Hayes points out that "one entity is being understood in terms of another entity."[66] Here are some metaphors from Old Testament poetic texts.

---

54. Even Waltke opts for labeling the various sections of Prov. 4 as "lectures" rather than using the terminology of stanzas or strophes (*Proverbs: Chapters 1–15*, 274–301).

55. See especially 1 Cor. 9:24–26, which employs the image of runners competing in a race for a prize as well as a boxer beating the air. See also Gal. 2:2; 5:7; Phil. 2:16; 2 Tim. 4:7. The writer of Hebrews also uses the image of running a race (12:1).

56. 2 Cor. 2:14–17; Col. 2:15.

57. Eph. 6:13–18; 2 Tim. 2:3–4.

58. 1 Tim. 1:18.

59. Rom. 1:13; 1 Cor. 3:6–9; 9:7–11; Gal. 6:7–9; Heb. 13:20; 1 Pet. 2:25.

60. 2 Cor. 11:2; Eph. 5:22–31.

61. Rom. 12:4–5; 1 Cor. 12:12–25.

62. 1 Cor. 4:14–15; 1 Thess. 2:7, 11; 1 Pet. 2:2; 4:17.

63. Longman, *Proverbs*, 33.

64. Hernández, *Old Testament*, 193.

65. Evans, *Cognitive Linguistics*, 306.

66. Vermeulen and Hayes, *How We Read the Bible*, 106.

But you, LORD, are a shield around me. (Ps. 3:3)

The LORD is my shepherd. . . .
    He makes me lie down in green pastures. (Ps. 23:1–2)

Cleanse me with hyssop, and I will be clean;
    wash me, and I will be whiter than snow. (Ps. 51:7)

Gracious words are a honeycomb,
    sweet to the soul and healing to the bones. (Prov. 16:24)

I am a rose of Sharon,
    a lily of the valleys. (Song 2:1)

Metaphors like these require us to understand the *source* (the entity used to explain) in order to understand the *target* (the entity being explained).[67] This insight comes from Conceptual Metaphor Theory (CMT).[68] The idea is that a metaphor should be understood as "a mapping between two domains."[69] The purpose for mapping from one domain to another is to use concepts grounded in common human experience (source domain) to explain concepts that are more difficult to understand.[70] Consider the above examples. In Psalm 3:3, God's protection is explained by using an item from the domain of warfare: a shield used by a warrior to fend off enemy arrows and spears. In Psalm 23:1–2, God's provision and refreshment are explained by the domain of a shepherd. In Psalm 51:7, God's spiritual restoration of sinners is explained by the domain of herbs and cleansing rituals. In Proverbs 16:24, beneficial speech is explained by the domain of natural substances. Then, in Song of Songs 2:1, the fruitfulness and beauty of the woman speaking are explained by the domain of plant life.

---

67. Vermeulen and Hayes, *How We Read the Bible*, 106.

68. Conceptual Metaphor Theory (CMT) is the brainchild of George Lakoff and others working from an approach now known as cognitive linguistics. For more in-depth discussion of CMT, see Geeraerts, *Lexical Semantics*, 204–10; Evans, *Cognitive Linguistics*, 300–319. For the application of CMT to biblical studies in general, see Vermeulen and Hayes, *How We Read the Bible*, 106–18. For the application of CMT to Old Testament poetry, see Hernández, *Old Testament*, 192–207.

69. Geeraerts, *Lexical Semantics*, 204.

70. Evans, *Cognitive Linguistics*, 311.

This understanding of how metaphors work should convince us to ponder what the source is implying about the target. We need to ask, What does this mean? Sometimes, the answer will come almost instantaneously, given the information stored in our long-term memory that comes from our past experiences and our "general encyclopedic background knowledge of the world."[71] In other instances, we will have to reflect a bit on the material culture of the biblical poet. For example, when the woman in Song of Songs 2:1 claims to be a "rose of Sharon" and "a lily of the valleys," we are confident that these are beautiful flowers. A bit more investigation reveals that the first flower is an asphodel (חֲבַצֶּלֶת, habatselet), a Hebrew word whose only other appearance in the Old Testament is in Isaiah 35:1. There it describes "the blossoming of the desert as fertility returns to a wilderness" and is connected to the splendor of Carmel and Sharon (Isa. 35:2).[72] Then, the lily (שׁוּשַׁן, shushan)—a lotus or crocus—is used elsewhere to describe the decorations of the temple (1 Kings 7:19, 22, 26; 2 Chron. 4:5), suggesting its association with beauty.[73] Furthermore, the lotus appears in Egyptian love songs and is associated with love, freshness, and radiance.[74] Thus, Richard Hess concludes that metaphors in Song of Songs 2:1 portray the woman as fruitful, beautiful, and loving.[75]

We have spent time on metaphor because it is so foundational to the imagery in the poetic books of the Old Testament. Yet there are some additional figures of speech or imagery we should be able to identify as well.

Simile. This is an explicit comparison using "like" or "as." For example, Psalm 42:1 says, "As the deer pants for streams of water, so my soul pants for you, my God." Proverbs 25:25 says, "Like cold water to a weary soul is good news from a distant land." Similes require us to contemplate how the target resembles the source, just as we did for metaphors. Like a deer, we pant out of thirst, perhaps a thirst exacerbated by exhaustion or heat. Like the refreshing taste of cold water when we are worn out, good news from a distant land refreshes and enlivens us.

---

71. Vermeulen and Hayes, *How We Read the Bible,* 107.
72. Hess, *Song of Songs,* 75.
73. Hess, *Song of Songs,* 75.
74. Keel, *Song of Songs,* 80.
75. Hess, *Song of Songs,* 75. For a slightly different understanding, see Longman, *Song of Songs,* 110–11. He suggests that the metaphors convey joy and humility as well as "a modest expression of her beauty."

Metonymy. This is a reference to something by using an associated item.[76] Karolien Vermeulen says that metonymy expresses a "stands-for" relationship.[77] For example, the "crown" that is not secure for all generations in Proverbs 27:24 stands for kingship. Proverbs 10:21 says, "The lips of the righteous nourish many." There are actually two metonymies in this line. First, "the lips" stand for the speech or words of a righteous person. Second, the verb "nourish" stands for sustaining or meeting the needs of people. A subcategory of metonymy is *synecdoche*, the usage of a part to represent the whole. For example, when the psalmist says, "All my bones shall say . . ." (Ps. 35:10 ESV), he means that his whole being will speak. Likewise, Proverbs 1:16 says about violent people, "Their feet run to evil" (ESV). In this case, "feet" represent the whole person, and "run" represents how quick they are to do evil.[78]

Merism. This is another figure of speech in which a part refers to the whole. A merism "uses two opposite statements to signify the whole."[79] Some of my favorite examples of merism appear in Psalm 121. Verse 6 declares, "The sun will not harm you by day, nor the moon by night." This is a way of saying, "Absolutely nothing will harm you." It includes all other sources of danger—asteroids, animals, trees, rocks, and so on. Then, verse 8 says, "The Lord will watch over your coming and going both now and forevermore." This is not simply a reference to the times when you are on the move—when you leave your house and when you return. The "coming and going" pair can refer to sitting, resting, sleeping, and every other activity in your day.

Personification. This literary device describes something nonhuman (inanimate) as if it were human. For example, righteousness and peace kiss each other in Psalm 85:10. In the book of Proverbs, wisdom is frequently personified as a woman who speaks in the public square, cries out at the city gate, and invites the simple to a banquet (see Prov. 1:20–21; 8:2–3; 9:1–6). Closely related to personification is an *apostrophe*. This literary term refers to addressing directly a nonhuman object as if it were a human being. For example, Psalm 98:8 is a call for rivers to "clap their hands" and

76. Waltke, *Proverbs: Chapters 1–15*, 40.
77. Vermeulen and Hayes, *How We Read the Bible*, 119.
78. These examples, from Ps. 35:10 and Prov. 1:16, are cited and discussed in L. Ryken, *Sweeter Than Honey*, 58–59.
79. Waltke, *Proverbs: Chapters 1–15*, 40.

for the mountains to "sing together for joy." Similarly, Psalm 24:7 says, "Lift up your heads, you gates."

Hyperbole. This figure of speech employs overstatement or exaggeration for effect. In Psalm 6:6, the psalmist says, "All night long I flood my bed with weeping and drench my couch with tears." In Psalm 22:6, David claims that he is a worm and not a man. In Proverbs 30:2, Agur even claims that he is too stupid or brutish to be considered a human being. None of these statements are to be taken literally. They simply convey how strongly the poet feels about something, and they grab our attention.[80]

Allusion. This is simply a brief reference to past events. For example, Psalm 103:7 alludes to God giving the law to Moses at Sinai when it says, "He made known his ways to Moses, his deeds to the people of Israel." Likewise, Psalm 33:6 alludes to the creation account in Genesis 1 when it says, "By the word of the LORD the heavens were made, their starry host by the breath of his mouth."[81]

Anthropomorphism. This literary term refers to the portrayal of God in human terms. For example, Psalm 34:15 says that "the eyes of the LORD are on the righteous, and his ears are attentive to their cry." Psalm 37:24 affirms that the one who delights in the Lord will not fall, because "the LORD upholds him with his hand." Obviously, God does not have literal eyes, ears, and hands. But it is helpful for us to picture him with these body parts to describe his attention to us, his care for us, and the way he helps and sustains us. A related concept is described by biblical scholars as *anthropopathism.* Personally, I don't find the term helpful, but the concept is. Bruce Waltke defines it as "ascribing human feelings, motives, or behaviors to God."[82] For example, Psalm 106:45 says that God, out of his great love, "relented." Proverbs 24:18 says that "the LORD will see and disapprove."

Repetition. Sometimes, a repeated word or expression will drive a poem. For example, the Hebrew word שָׁמַר (*shamar*), translated as "guard, watch over, keep," occurs six times in Psalm 121. The message of the psalm revolves around this word. In Psalm 136, the refrain "his love endures forever" is the second line of every verse. The psalm's thirty-six verses provide a chronological list of "God's actions during creation and the exodus and

---

80. L. Ryken, *Sweeter Than Honey*, 50–51.
81. These two examples from Ps. 103:7 and Ps. 33:6 come from L. Ryken, *Sweeter Than Honey*, 62–63.
82. Waltke, *Proverbs: Chapters 1–15*, 40.

settlement"; the repeated refrain after each action declares that they result from "God's eternal loyalty."[83]

Inclusio. This is another form of repetition in which an element, usually a word or phrase, occurs at the beginning and end of a literary unit. Thus, it acts like a frame or brackets. Sometimes, I refer to it as "sandwich" or "Oreo cookie" structure because the element at the beginning and end acts like slices of bread or wafers that holds the insides of a sandwich or an Oreo cookie together. A classic example is the line that appears at the beginning and end of Psalm 8: "LORD, our Lord, how majestic is your name in all the earth!" (vv. 1, 9). Often, though, inclusion is a bit more subtle, simply utilizing a single key word. An example is the word אַשְׁרֵי ('ashre), "blessed," which appears at the beginning of Psalm 1 (v. 1) and at the end of Psalm 2 (v. 12)—psalms that introduce the entire collection in the book of Psalms and are intended to be read together.

Janus or hinge. I first came across this expression and concept in Bruce Waltke's magisterial commentaries on the book of Proverbs. Elsewhere, he explains that it "is a device that unites two units by looking both back and forward."[84] The term "janus" has its background in ancient Roman mythology. Janus was a god with two faces on his head, one on the front and one on the back. So, he was able to look forward and back at the same time. "Our month January is named after this god—a month that marks a new beginning as it closes the old year and introduces the new."[85] Waltke offers Psalm 92:8 as an example: "But you, LORD, are forever exalted." This statement "pivots the psalm by climaxing one statement and introducing the next."[86] I suggest that the great turning point in Psalm 73:16–17 is an example of a janus. After fifteen verses expressing frustration over the prosperity of the wicked and the seeming emptiness of keeping his own heart pure, the psalmist says,

> When I tried to understand all this,
>> it troubled me deeply
> till I entered the sanctuary of God;
>> then I understood their final destiny.

83. Berlin, *Biblical Parallelism*, 139.
84. Waltke and Zaspel, *Psalms*, 458.
85. Waltke and Zaspel, *Psalms*, 458.
86. Waltke and Zaspel, *Psalms*, 458.

This statement looks back to verses 1–15, summarizing them with the words "all this" and recounting the way this "troubled me deeply." But the turning point was entering the sanctuary of God, which enabled the psalmist to understand the final destiny of the wicked. He takes up this topic in the remainder of the psalm, in verses 18–28.

There is no doubt that we could come up with more categories. But time would fail me to tell of litotes, irony, paradox, and other figures of speech. And at this point, I do not think that additional labels and categories will help. After all, applying labels to the various figures of speech in a psalm or proverb is not the endgame. Rather, we need to stop and think about the meaning being conveyed by the particular figure of speech—whether a metaphor, a metonym, a simile, or whatever. If you learn to work with the categories listed above, you will learn a way of reading that will open your eyes to other figures of speech, regardless of how they might be labeled.

What Gets Lost in Translation

There is good news and bad news when it comes to our English translations of the poetic texts of the Old Testament. First, the bad news. Some elements of verbal artistry are lost when translated into another language.[87] Take words of a well-known English lullaby: "Twinkle, twinkle, little star / how I wonder what you are / Up above the world so high / like a diamond in the sky." I have not tried it, but I bet that the rhymes "star/are" and "high/sky" would get lost in translating the lines into Hebrew—or German or French or Spanish, for that matter. Likewise, there are some plays on sound (phonology), literary arrangement (syntax), and the form of words (morphology) that simply vanish when we translate from Hebrew to English. I remember, for example, the mesmerizing sound of the suffix pronoun "you" at the end of three lines in Proverbs 3:3 the first time I read it in Hebrew. Below is a crude phonetic transliteration of the Hebrew text that might help you hear what I heard when I read it. Read the "e" vowels as "short e" sounds and notice the accent marks. The syllables *ráme* in line two and *váme* in line three rhyme with "name." Finally, the *a* in the syllable *ka* (the suffix pronoun) at the end of each line should be pronounced like the word "awe." All right, give it a try!

---

87. For a helpful discussion of what gets lost in translation from Hebrew to English, see Hernández, *Old Testament*, 188–90.

Ḥésed ve-émet all yaz-vú-ka
Kōsh-ráme all gar-gi-row-té-ka
Kōt-váme all rúe-ach lĭ-bé-ka

When it comes to literary arrangement (syntax) and the form of words (morphology), Dominick Hernández provides a translation of Psalm 103:10 that captures what the Hebrew text does with both:

Not according to our sins does he deal with us,
    and not according to iniquities does he repay us.[88]

Note that both lines begin with negation ("not"). Then, there is a prepositional phrase ("according to our sins/iniquities"). Finally, the lines close with a verb ("does deal / does repay" and an object ("us"). Similarly, while reading Psalm 46 in Hebrew the other day, I noticed the interesting word order in the middle of verse 9.[89] The Hebrew reads, "The bow he breaks, and he shatters the spear." This word order is object-verb-verb-object. This inversion, or chiasm, highlights God's actions. Our English translations simply use a verb-object-verb-object arrangement, since that is how English works. For example, the NIV translates it as "He breaks the bow and shatters the spear." That is what you are missing when you read most English translations.

Occasionally, our English versions reflect—or come close to reflecting—the word order of the Hebrew text. But the priority on readable, flowing English means that the word order is obscured. I have no problem with this. In fact, I believe that it is the best approach to translation. An overly literal translation is clunky. Still, there is no way around the reality that we lose something in translation. The old saying has some truth to it: translation is treason.

That's the bad news. But there is good news! The good news is that the most important literary strategies for conveying meaning survive translation. This includes terseness (although English requires a few more words than Hebrew), parallelism, metaphor, and all the other literary features we examined. So you are not at a loss if you do not read Hebrew. Now, I

---

88. Hernández, *Old Testament*, 189.
89. This is actually verse 10 in the Hebrew Bible because the superscription at the beginning of the psalm is identified as verse 1.

love Hebrew and encourage preachers to learn it and use it. But in God's providence, the literary features that matter most for understanding the text are left standing when Old Testament poetry is translated into English.

Reading Slowly

Finally, there is an important implication of the need to pay attention to the terseness, parallelism, and metaphors and other figures of speech in Old Testament poetry. We must read slowly. As Tremper Longman says, "Poetry is to be read reflectively and not quickly."[90] This is good advice in any section of Scripture. Yet it is even more critical in Old Testament poetry, given the density of its metaphorical, figurative language. Bruce Waltke recognizes that we are not accustomed to reading thoughtfully. He remarks, "We usually want to read linearly and quickly get to the point. But poetry just does not work that way."[91] If we are to understand Psalms and the other poetic books of the Old Testament, we must "pause and meditate" and "take our time."[92]

The Path Forward

Now that we have some leads on how to read Old Testament poetry, we will spend the remaining chapters thinking about how to preach the various poetic books in the Old Testament: Psalms (chap. 2), Proverbs (chap. 3), Job (chap. 4), Ecclesiastes (chap. 5), and Song of Songs (chap. 6). The "Helpful Resources for Studying and Preaching" sections offer both online materials and books (publishing details are found in the bibliography), and the appendices provide some sample sermons on various poetic texts.

Remember, the more you read and preach these books, the more you will love them. So take the plunge. Let's learn how to preach these amazing books of poetry in a way that showcases the glory of God and contributes to making disciples of the people God brings our way.

---

90. Longman, *Proverbs*, 33.
91. Waltke and Zaspel, *Psalms*, 143.
92. Waltke and Zaspel, *Psalms*, 143.

2

Preaching Psalms

'

Powell's Books is a legendary independent bookstore in downtown Portland, Oregon. It occupies a city block, has three levels, and houses about one million books. One of its entrances features a sandstone carving of a stack of eight of the world's great books. The titles on the spines of these books include *Hamlet*, *The Odyssey*, and *The Whale* (*Moby-Dick*). The first time I saw this "pillar of books," though, one particular title caught my eye:

תהלים

Do you recognize it? It is the Hebrew word for "praises," the Hebrew title of the book of Psalms. I'm not sure who chose the titles for this pillar, but they were spot-on with their choice of Psalms as one of the eight. Psalms has been the soundtrack for the lives of many believers over the centuries, including our Lord and Savior, Jesus.

In this chapter, we will explore how to preach the book of Psalms—a stunning collection of 150 songs and prayers. However, the psalms are often neglected by preachers who find them intimidating and are perplexed as to what some of them mean and how they relate to God's people. To understand how to preach the book of Psalms effectively, we will begin by studying the text—sermon exegesis. Then, we will think about preaching the text—sermon crafting.

Studying Psalms

When we study the psalms, we must pay attention to the poetic elements discussed in the previous chapter. Yet, there are some additional features that we need to consider, and we will do well to help our listeners understand them as well. Specifically, we need to consider the stance a psalm takes, a psalm's emotional plot development, the various types of psalms, and the structure of the book of Psalms.

The Stance a Psalm Takes

This first feature is as profound as it is obvious. Each psalm, given its status as Scripture, is a word from God to his people. However, a psalm presents itself as a word from people to their God. This can be confusing. We must remember and remind our listeners that even though the psalms are songs and prayers directed *to* God, they are a word *from* God to us. This is a good place to note as well that the psalms call all people to worship and praise God. "In this sense the Psalter is a missionary hymnbook."[1]

Emotional Plot Development

The psalms are highly emotive. The psalmists shout for joy—and call others to do the same—and shed tears. They express confidence in God, and they complain about their circumstances. They long for Zion and loathe evildoers. Walter Brueggemann says that they move back and forth between the "polar moods" of "deep anguish and misery" and "profound joy and celebration."[2] In short, the psalms are filled with emotion. However, we must temper this observation with a couple clarifications. First, emotion is not unique to the book of Psalms. Who can fail to detect the apostle Paul's anger when he writes, "You foolish Galatians! Who has bewitched you?" (Gal. 3:1)? Or who can miss his ecstasy and wonder when he writes, "Oh, the depth of the riches of the wisdom and knowledge of God!" (Rom. 11:33)? Once again, it is the prevalence of emotion, not simply its presence, that makes it noticeable. Michelle Knight offers a second clarification. She rightly argues that Old Testament poetry "is an appeal to *reason* just as much as it is an appeal

1. Waltke and Zaspel, *Psalms*, 207.
2. Brueggemann, *Psalms*, 67.

to emotion."[3] We dare not pit emotion and reason against each other. For all the emotion in the book of Psalms, it makes theological points and arguments.

One of the most important strategies for reading is to pay attention to the emotional flow or plot development of a psalm. For example, we have already observed a mood swing in Psalm 73, so let us consider the entire psalm. Verse 1 begins with a statement of confidence:

> Surely God is good to Israel,
>   to those who are pure in heart.

Notice the parallel relationship between the two lines. The second line further develops the object in line one. But immediately after this confident declaration, Asaph the psalmist describes his "unsettling doubt" due to the prosperity of the wicked.[4] This runs all the way from verse 2 to verse 15. In this section the psalmist even surmises that his inward purity and outward integrity have been "in vain" and have only brought him affliction and "new punishments" (vv. 13–14). Then the mood shifts suddenly in verses 16–17, which I described above as a janus.

> When I tried to understand all this,
>   it troubled me deeply
> till I entered the sanctuary of God;
>   then I understood their final destiny.

The remainder of the psalm, verses 18–28, expresses a mood of confidence. In fact, verse 18 begins with the same particle of certainty with which the psalm begins in verse 1, the word "surely" (אַךְ, 'ak).[5] Thus, we can outline the emotional plot of Psalm 73 like this:

  I. Confidence (v. 1)

  II. Unsettling doubt (vv. 2–15)

  III. *Janus* (vv. 16–17)

  IV. Confidence (vv. 18–28)

3. Knight, "The Rational Poet."
4. Kidner, *Psalms 73–150*, 260.
5. See *HALOT*; van der Merwe, Naudé, and Kroeze, *Hebrew Reference Grammar*, 388–89.

Obviously, the word "janus" does not express an emotion. But the hinge between doubt and confidence is prominent enough that I have chosen to reflect it in my outline.

Psalm 3 is another example. The superscription identifies it as "A psalm of David. When he fled from his son Absalom." The NIV divides Psalm 3 into four stanzas. We can detect a different mood in each one.

> [1] LORD, how many are my foes!
>   How many rise up against me!
> [2] Many are saying of me,
>   "God will not deliver him."
>
> [3] But you, LORD, are a shield around me,
>   my glory, the One who lifts my head high.
> [4] I call out to the LORD,
>   and he answers me from his holy mountain.
> [5] I lie down and sleep;
>   I wake again, because the LORD sustains me.
> [6] I will not fear though tens of thousands
>   assail me on every side.
>
> [7] Arise, LORD!
>   Deliver me, my God!
> Strike all my enemies on the jaw;
>   break the teeth of the wicked.
>
> [8] From the LORD comes deliverance.
>   May your blessing be on your people.

The psalm begins in verses 1–2 with a lament or complaint. We can characterize the emotion here as frustration. Then, there is a shift in mood when we come to verse 3. Verses 3–6 express confidence in the Lord, resulting in sleep and the absence of fear. Verse 7 offers a plea to the Lord, a prayer that expresses urgency. Finally, verse 8 is a closing statement of confidence. Thus, we can outline the emotional development of Psalm 3 as follows.

I. Frustration (vv. 1–2)

II. Confidence (vv. 3–6)

III. Urgency (v. 7)

IV. Confidence (v. 8)

Psalm 89 has a kind of reverse mood swing. It begins in praise for the Lord's great love and faithfulness and continues to recount evidence of this in the exodus, in creation, and in the anointing of David as king (vv. 1–29). We might describe the mood as one of exuberance or joy. Then, verses 30–37 introduce a subtle yet clear mood shift to apprehension. These verses constitute a warning about how the Lord will respond if David's sons disobey him. In verse 38 there is a "radical shift" as the psalmist "accuses God of breaking the covenant by allowing Israel's enemies to defeat them and to shame the Davidic king."[6] It is not an overstatement to describe this emotion as anger. This continues through verse 45. Then, verses 46–51 offer an appeal or plea to the Lord to show his love and faithfulness to his people. The emotion here is urgency. Finally, the psalm ends abruptly with a cry of joy in verse 52: "Praise be to the Lord forever! Amen and Amen."[7] Thus, we can outline the emotional plot of Psalm 89 as follows:

  I. Joy (vv.1–29)
 II. Apprehension (vv. 30–37)
III. Anger (vv. 38–45)
IV. Urgency (vv. 46–51)
 V. Joy (v. 52)

Of course, there is not a wild mood swing or shift in many psalms. For example, Psalm 121 begins with a note of anxiety: "I lift my eyes to the mountains—where does my help come from?" Although the KJV translated the second line of Psalm 121 as a statement of confidence ("from whence cometh my help"), almost all modern English versions understand it to be a question prompted by the dangers of travel to Jerusalem. The trip through the hill country up to the holy city threatened travelers with bad weather or heat, slips and falls, and even robbers. The remainder of Psalm 121, verses 2–8, expresses confidence. So there is no great mood swing in Psalm 121. Furthermore, the urgency of Psalm 88:1–2 leads to a mood of despair in the remainder of the psalm (vv. 3–18). This never

6. Longman, *Psalms*, 322.
7. This cry of praise is an ending to Book 3 of the Psalter as much as it is an ending to Ps. 89. For a discussion of how the five books in the Psalter conclude, see below under "The Structure of the Book of Psalms."

resolves into confidence. If anything, it intensifies with the chilling words in the final line: "Darkness is my closest friend" (v. 18b).[8] On the other hand, Psalm 100 begins with a call for exuberant praise, and this mood is sustained throughout the remainder of this brief psalm.

Paying attention to the emotional development of a psalm, if there is one, can help readers and preachers understand its meaning and message. Often, these mood swings go hand in hand with certain types of psalms. That is the next feature to which we must devote some attention.

Psalm Types

There are various types of psalms, reflecting the "real experiences of life" faced by God's people.[9] These psalm types or forms are categorized based on their structure and/or content. There is basic agreement, with some slight variation, about the major categories of psalms (see table 2.1).

Table 2.1

Some Approaches to Categorizing the Psalms

Futato[a]	Waltke[b]	Brueggemann[c]
Hymns	Praise psalms (Hymns)	Songs of orientation (descriptive hymns)
Laments	Petition-lament psalms	
		Songs of disorientation (laments)
Songs of thanksgiving	Individual songs of grateful praise	
		Songs of reorientation (declarative hymns)
Divine kingship songs	Messianic psalms	
Wisdom songs	Didactic psalms	

a. Futato, *Psalms*, 145–73.
b. Waltke and Zaspel, *Psalms*, 173–450.
c. Brueggemann, *Psalms*, 10–15, 24.

8. For an outstanding study of Ps. 88, see Held, "'Fists Flailing at the Gates of Heaven.'"
9. Though Walter Brueggemann discusses lament psalms as giving "authentic expression" to the "real experiences of life" (*Psalms*, 67), this observation could apply to any psalm type or form.

Perhaps the most helpful way to categorize the psalms for our listeners is to refer to five main types. Two of the most common categories are *psalms of praise* and *psalms of lament*. Within each category, there are two further subcategories: the praise psalms include "hymns" (what some refer to as "psalms of descriptive praise") and "songs of thanksgiving" (what some refer to as "psalms of declarative praise"). Then, the lament psalms subdivide into "individual laments" and "community laments." A third main category is *psalms of confidence*. Two additional categories include *royal psalms*, which include "divine kingship" or "messianic" psalms, and *wisdom* (or *didactic*) *psalms*. We will look at each one of these categories along with a couple of additional subtypes: "penitential psalms" and "imprecatory psalms."

1. *Psalms of praise*. Praise in the psalms is excited boasting. The catalog of words in praise psalms includes shouts of triumph, expressions of joy, and ringing cries that are directed to God. As noted above, there are two main types of praise psalms. One is "hymns" or "psalms of descriptive praise." These psalms praise God for who he is and focus on his attributes or characteristics. They have a definite structure: (a) an introductory call to praise; (b) the cause for praise; (c) a renewed call to praise. Some psalms add a renewed cause to praise. Table 2.2 shows how several hymns in the Psalter follow this pattern.

Table 2.2

The Structure of Hymns of Praise

	Psalm 98	Psalm 100	Psalm 103	Psalm 117
Call to praise	1a	1–2	1–2	1
Cause for praise	1b–3	3	3–19	2a–b
Renewed call	4–9a	4	20–22	2c
Renewed cause	9b–d	5	—	—

Psalm 117 is the shortest psalm in the Psalter and reflects the basic pattern.

> [1] Praise the LORD, all you nations;
>   extol him, all you peoples.
> [2] For great is his love toward us,
>   and the faithfulness of the LORD endures forever.
> Praise the LORD.

Verse 1 serves as the call to praise. Its two lines call for the same action in different words. Then, lines *a* and *b* of verse 2 provide the cause for praise. This is easy to spot because the second line begins with the conjunction כִּי (*ki*, "for"). In this instance, it introduces the cause or reason for the command.[10] Sometimes, there is no discourse marker like the conjunction כִּי (*ki*), which signifies causation. For example, Psalm 100:3 begins with an imperative ("Know that the Lord is God") and then makes two declarations: the Lord created us for himself, and we are the sheep of his pasture. This verse functions as the reason for calling all the earth to praise the Lord.[11] In Psalm 117:2a–b, the cause or reason for praise is the Lord's great love for us (his people) and his enduring faithfulness. Throughout the book of Psalms, "love" (חֶסֶד, *hesed*) and "faithfulness" (אֱמֶת, *'emet*) are often paired together in an echo of Exodus 34:6, where the Lord proclaims his name, describing himself as "abounding in love and faithfulness." Finally, Psalm 117:2c issues a final, renewed call to praise. Of course, some hymns of praise might vary slightly from the pattern or add an additional element or two, but the basic pattern is well established.

A second type of praise psalm is a "song of thanksgiving" or "psalm of declarative praise." Whereas hymns, or songs of descriptive praise, offer praise to God for who he is, songs of thanksgiving, or psalms of declarative praise, offer praise to God for what he has done. Often, they express joy for God's deliverance.[12] Rather than calling other people or all creation to praise God, these psalms take a more individual stance. They typically begin with "I" statements.

- "I will give thanks to you, Lord, with all my heart . . ." (Ps. 9:1)
- "I love you, Lord, my strength . . ." (Ps. 18:1)
- "I will exalt you, Lord, for you lifted me out of the depths . . ." (Ps. 30:1)
- "I will extol the Lord at all times . . ." (Ps. 34:1)
- "I love the Lord, for he heard my voice . . ." (Ps. 116:1)

10. See van der Merwe, Naudé, and Kroeze, *Hebrew Reference Grammar*, 432, 434.
11. Waltke considers Ps. 100:3 to be an intercalation that "interrupts the call to praise to state an implied condition for praise" and "functions also as the pivot of the psalm" (Waltke and Zaspel, *Psalms*, 208). While this is true, this intercalation also functions as the reason for the praise commanded in verses 1–2 of the psalm.
12. Futato, *Psalms*, 158.

Songs of thanksgiving, or of declarative praise, follow a common pattern. Waltke says that these psalms include the following components:

- Proclamation—a statement of praise or declaration of an intention to praise
- Introductory summary—a statement of what God has done
- Reflection—a consideration of the psalmist's past need and God's deliverance
- Praise—an appeal to join the psalmist in praise

One of the key words that shows up in both kinds of praise psalms is "thanksgiving" or "give thanks." To quote Inigo Montoya in *The Princess Bride*, "You keep using that word. I do not think it means what you think it means." A few years ago, a couple people in our church family spent hours helping us paint the interior of the house we purchased. (Here I'll call them Russ and Debbie.) They even stayed late into the night so we could finish painting some rooms before a crew showed up to install new flooring. In North American culture, the appropriate way to express gratitude is to go to Russ and Debbie personally and say, "Thank you for helping us paint our house." However, the Hebrew word ידה (*yadah*), translated as "give thanks," refers to confession or acknowledgment.[13] Furthermore, as Waltke observes, "This confession is never merely private. It is a public acknowledgment—praising God by confessing his goodness to others."[14] So if my intent is to "give thanks" to Russ and Debbie in the Old Testament way, I have not done so simply by going to them and saying, "Thank you." Rather, I must express my gratitude to them in a public setting, telling the community of faith what Russ and Debbie have done for me. So it is with God. It is not enough to say, "Thank you, Lord," in a private prayer. We have not given thanks until we have shared with other believers what God has done for us.

We should note here that the "songs of Zion" are a subcategory of praise psalms. Some examples are Psalms 48, 76, 84, 87, and 122. These are psalms that extol Jerusalem, the holy city, and often express praise and joy at the thought of standing and remaining in the temple in the presence

---

13. *HALOT*; L. Allen, "ידה," 406.
14. Waltke and Zaspel, *Psalms*, 319.

of the Lord.[15] Psalms 46 and 121 are songs of Zion as well, although typically they are classified as "songs of confidence" (see below). Now we are ready to move to a second major category of psalms.

2. *Psalms of lament.* Imagine this experience. The orange glow of the evening sky is fading as you gaze from the second-story window of your house. Night is softly falling. You hear the occasional bark of a dog or the distant bleating of a sheep. Otherwise, all is calm and still. But your mouth is dry, and a shiver goes up your spine. The men are still there. From your vantage point, you can see three or four, maybe even five. The king has sent them to kill you. This is as frustrating as it is frightening. You think, "I have done no wrong, yet they are ready to attack me. God, help me! Can't you see what's going on?"[16] This is the situation that David, the king-elect, faced shortly after his defeat of Goliath.[17] Out of this experience he wrote Psalm 59, a lament psalm.

The psalms of lament express the fear, doubt, frustration, anger, grief, resentment, and despair of God's people. As already noted, Brueggemann refers to them as "psalms of disorientation."[18] These psalms are for those who feel as though God has smashed them underfoot like a cigarette.[19] Whereas praise psalms affirm that God is good, lament psalms exclaim that life is tough. Yet, most lament psalms eventually lead to praise. The movement is from "Life is tough" to "yet God is good."[20] These psalms give us permission to vent our outrage and sorrow to God, as well as the words to do so, even though we eventually affirm that he is loving and faithful—no matter what our circumstances seem to scream. Mark Vroegop observes, "Lament is how you live between a hard life and trusting in God's sovereignty."[21]

There are two subtypes of lament psalms, although both follow the same basic form. Community laments reflect times when the entire nation

15. Waltke and Zaspel, *Psalms*, 192.
16. The first line comes from Ps. 59:4, and the second line is a paraphrase of that same verse.
17. See the account in 1 Sam. 19:11–18.
18. Brueggemann, *Psalms*, 11.
19. This image comes from Joni Eareckson Tada in her foreword to Vroegop, *Dark Clouds*, 11.
20. R. Allen, *Praise!*, 34. One psalm that does not appear to resolve itself from a minor key back into a major key is Ps. 88. As previously noted, it ends with the line "darkness is my closest friend." Still, I believe that this psalm is not entirely negative. The ending is for rhetorical effect. Even in such despair, the confident claim with which the psalm begins is still true: "Lord, you are the God who saves me" (v. 1).
21. Vroegop, *Dark Clouds*, 21.

of Israel is experiencing trouble, while individual laments express the pain of a person dealing with sickness, injustice, or some other difficulty.[22] There are five basic components of these psalms.[23]

- Introductory petition—a direct address to God followed by an appeal to hear the psalmist's petition
- Lament—a complaint in which the psalmist describes his difficult situation
- Confidence—a confession of trust in God despite the difficult situation
- Petition—a request for God to act in a certain way, along with the reasons why this is appropriate
- Praise—a shout or vow of praise in anticipation of God's response

David's lament in Psalm 59 follows this basic pattern. Verses 1–2 form the introductory petition, in which David asks the Lord for deliverance. Verses 3–7 express his lament over the fierce men who lie in wait for him, like snarling dogs, even though he has done nothing wrong. Next, the mood shifts to confidence in verses 8–10, where David notes that the Lord laughs at them and that he is "my strength" and "my fortress." Then, in verses 11–13, David makes his petition. Surprisingly, he does not ask God to kill them. Instead, he asks God to bring them down and catch them in their pride in a way that will make God's rule known to the ends of the earth. Verses 14–16 provide a transition into the shout of praise in verse 17. Specifically, verse 14 repeats verse 6, describing the fierce men as snarling dogs that, as verse 15 adds, "wander about for food and howl if not satisfied." Then, verse 16 reaffirms David's confidence. This leads into David's praise of God as his strength, fortress, and one on whom he can rely (v. 17).

There are a couple of subcategories of lament psalms to consider. First, "penitential psalms" focus on confession of sin and repentance of it. Seven psalms are traditionally given this label: Psalms 6, 32, 38, 51, 102, 130, and 143.[24] A second, and more controversial, category is

---

22. Waltke and Zaspel, *Psalms*, 233–34.
23. I have adapted this list from Waltke and Zaspel, *Psalms*, 237–38; and R. Allen, *Praise!*, 34–35.
24. R. Allen, *Praise!*, 35.

"imprecatory psalms." These are lament psalms that include, of course, "imprecation." As Tremper Longman notes, "There are no psalms that are only imprecatory."[25] Rather, there are some lament psalms with imprecatory elements. The more prominent examples of "imprecatory psalms" include Psalms 35, 59, 69, 83, 109, and 137. These psalms are controversial because they seem to call down a curse on an enemy. Strictly speaking, that is what an imprecation is. However, these psalms pray instead for God to avenge the psalmist and punish the wrongdoer.[26] Still, the harsh language has led some to conclude that these psalms are "sinful expressions of angry human beings" that should not be repeated by believers today "in the light of Christ's redeeming love." Yet, Longman says that such an approach would be "a grave mistake" because these "prayers do not ask God for the resources and opportunity to take vengeance on our enemies; they ask God to do so and acknowledge his freedom to act or not act as he sees fit."[27] This conforms with the instructions given in Romans 12:19: "Do not take revenge, my dear friends, but leave room for God's wrath, for it is written 'It is mine to avenge; I will repay,' says the Lord."

Still, it is hard to stomach the language of Psalm 137:9, which says, "Happy is the one who seizes your infants and dashes them against the rocks." To be sure, this is strong, even repulsive language to our ears. Yet, as Waltke notes, "The exiles are asking for strict justice."[28] Their statement reflects the horrible realities of ancient warfare, in which warriors spared neither women nor children. Yes, the language is shocking and troubling, but it reflects the realities of war (for a sermon manuscript on Ps. 137, see appendix B).

3. *Psalms of confidence.* These psalms express "a settled confidence in the Lord for his goodness and continuing care."[29] Although these psalms do not express lament, they seem to be "a derivative of the lament psalm in that they typically reflect a context of trouble or concern."[30] Furthermore, while they express trust, they do not offer praise per se. These psalms of confidence do not follow a particular form, but they

25. Longman, *Psalms*, 51.
26. Waltke and Zaspel, *Psalms*, 306.
27. Longman, *Psalms*, 52.
28. Waltke and Zaspel, *Psalms*, 307.
29. Waltke and Zaspel, *Psalms*, 347.
30. Waltke and Zaspel, *Psalms*, 347.

"often communicate their confident attitude through the use of striking metaphor."[31] For example, they portray God as a shepherd (Ps. 23), as a refuge and fortress (Pss. 46; 91), as a rock (Ps. 62), as a mother hen (Ps. 91), as one who watches and guards (Ps. 121), and as a mother with a young child (Ps. 131).

4. *Royal psalms.* This classification is based on content, not form. These psalms focus either on God as king (some refer to these as "divine kingship psalms") or on the human king. In the latter instance, a royal psalm might be written *by* the human king (Ps. 21) or *about* the human king (Ps. 20). In a sense, all royal psalms are messianic because they focus on the Lord's "anointed"—the translation of the Hebrew term מָשִׁיחַ (*mashiah*), from which we get the word "messiah."[32] However, some are more explicit in their reference to the promised Davidic Messiah of 2 Samuel 7:8–16. This includes Psalm 2 and Psalm 110—psalms often quoted in the New Testament. Jill Firth has argued convincingly that "the concept of 'servant' is consistent across the Psalter, connoting status, dependence or loyalty, and that a righteous, royal, suffering servant is depicted in the portrayal of David."[33]

5. *Wisdom psalms.* Once again, this designation is based on content, not form. The wisdom psalms echo the themes of the wisdom books (Proverbs, Job, Ecclesiastes), providing instruction in living before God in obedience and devotion (Ps. 15) or reflecting on life when it does not work (Ps. 73) or seems fleeting (Ps. 49). Some wisdom psalms focus on the Torah (Pss. 1; 19; 119), while others consider Israel's history (Pss. 78; 136).[34]

Finally, we should readily admit that some psalms are harder to categorize than others and that there is definitely overlap between categories. For example, Psalm 32 could be classified as a praise psalm (declarative), or a penitential psalm, or a wisdom psalm.[35] Furthermore, some psalms seem to be a hybrid between types. Waltke calls them "combination psalms." For

---

31. Longman, *Psalms*, 40.

32. See Ps. 20:6 (v. 7 in the Hebrew Bible), which says, "The Lord gives victory to his anointed [מָשִׁיחַ, *mashiah*]." Psalm 20 is a prayer on behalf of the king.

33. Firth, "The Suffering Servant," 112.

34. Waltke prefers the overall designation "didactic Psalms" and then recognizes three subtypes: Torah psalms, historical psalms, and wisdom psalms (Waltke and Zaspel, *Psalms*, 414–18). However, I am going to stick with "wisdom psalms" as the category label because it is so widespread among Psalms scholars. I view Torah psalms and historical psalms as subsets.

35. Waltke and Zaspel, *Psalms*, 328–29.

example, Psalm 40 is a combination of declarative praise or thanksgiving (vv. 1–12) and lament (vv. 13–18).[36] Psalm 150 is regarded as a "prophetic psalm" because it takes the form of speech-*from*-God rather than the usual speech-*to*-God.

In appendix G, I have provided "A Categorization of the Psalms," offering a category label for each of the 150 psalms. You might disagree with the way I categorize certain psalms, and so might I, for that matter, upon further reflection! But this will provide a starting point for discussion. The end goal is not to label each psalm precisely but to gain a better understanding of any given psalm—how it functions and what it means.

The Structure of the Book of Psalms

Another issue that preachers need to consider is the way the book of Psalms is put together. The Psalter is arranged in five books. This arrangement reflects the five books of Torah—not in a one-to-one correspondence (as in Book 1 with Genesis, Book 2 with Exodus, etc.), but rather that the Psalter is a response to Torah and has the same authority as the word of God.[37] Each of the first four books closes with a doxology (word of praise), and the final book closes with five praise psalms, Psalms 146–50 (see table 2.3). Again, this seems to be a tip of the cap to the five books of Torah. Furthermore, Psalms 1–2 provide an entry point into the book of Psalms.[38] As we noted previously, the word אַשְׁרֵי ('ashre, "blessed") appears at the beginning of Psalm 1 (v. 1) and at the end of Psalm 2 (v. 12). The message of these psalms, when read together, is "Blessed are those who delight in the Lord's law (Ps. 1) and take refuge in his Messiah (Ps. 2)."

Bible scholars have long pondered the significance of the five-book arrangement. In recent times, Gerald Wilson argued that the canonical arrangement of the 150 psalms is not "an accidental product of an extended

36. Waltke and Zaspel, *Psalms*, 331.
37. See Longman, *Psalms*, 36.
38. Franz Delitzsch says that the collection of 150 psalms "bears the impress of one ordering mind. For its opening is formed by a didactic-prophetic couplet of psalms (Ps. i, ii) . . . and its close is formed by four psalms (Ps. cxlvi–cxlix [146–149]) which begin and end with הללו־יה [*hallelu-yah*]. We do not include Ps. cl [150] for this psalm takes the place of the *beracha* [blessing] of the Fifth book" (*Psalms*, 1:19–20).

Table 2.3

The Doxologies at the End of the Five Books of the Psalter

Book	Doxology
1 Psalms 1–41	"Praise be to the LORD, the God of Israel, from everlasting to everlasting. Amen and Amen." (41:13)
2 Psalms 42–72	"Praise be to the LORD God, the God of Israel, who alone does marvelous deeds. Praise be to his glorious name forever; may the whole earth be filled with his glory. Amen and Amen. This concludes the prayers of David son of Jesse." (72:18–20)
3 Psalms 73–89	"Praise be to the LORD forever! Amen and Amen." (89:52)
4 Psalms 90–106	"Praise be to the LORD, the God of Israel, from everlasting to everlasting. Let all the people say, 'Amen!' Praise the LORD." (106:48)
5 Psalms 107–50	Psalms 146–50: each begins and ends with "Praise the LORD."

collection process."[39] Instead, he contended that there is evidence of an effort "to bind the whole together" in a way that "speaks the message intended by the final editor(s)."[40] While I tend to agree with Tremper Longman that the specifics of Wilson's analysis do not hold up,[41] there are some general insights we might make from the overall structure. These are represented in table 2.4.[42] Although the two approaches differ in places (especially in their analysis of Book 4), they share a lot of similarities. The difficulty comes when scholars (or pastors) try to identify more precise

39. G. Wilson, *Hebrew Psalter*, 2.
40. G. Wilson, *Hebrew Psalter*, 4, 11. To see how Wilson applied his conclusions to the relationships between the various individual psalms, see his volume in the NIV Application Commentary series (*Psalms*). Sadly, Wilson passed away before he could complete his commentary on the remainder of the Psalter.
41. Longman, *Psalms*, 34.
42. The "Historical Approach" column is an adaptation of the discussion in Waltke and Zaspel, *Psalms*, 5–6, 482–94. The "Biblical-Theological Approach" is a summary of the Bible Project's analysis of the book of Psalms (https://bibleproject.com/guides/book-of-psalms/).

functions of the various psalms in these books. While it is good to note the overall movement of the five books in the Psalter, it is best to read each psalm on its own terms.

Table 2.4

The Contents of the Five Books of the Psalter

Book	General Comments	Historical Approach	Biblical-Theological Approach
Book 1 Psalms 1–41	Written almost exclusively by David; high concentration of individual laments	King David's suffering at the hand of his enemies	David as a model of covenant faithfulness in suffering
Book 2 Psalms 42–72	Written primarily by the Sons of Korah and David; high concentration of individual laments	King David's reign: a time of crisis and hope	Hope for the Messiah's kingdom
Book 3 Psalms 73–89	A "dark book" containing a lot of communal laments; written primarily by Asaph and the Sons of Korah	The fall of the house of David	Hope for the Messiah's kingdom after the exile
Book 4 Psalms 90–106	High concentration of praise and royal psalms; initial psalm written by Moses, then mostly anonymous, though two by David	Israel in exile, with hope still alive	The God of Israel as the king of all creation
Book 5 Psalms 107–150	A mixture of praise, lament, and confidence psalms; mostly anonymous or written by David	Israel's return from exile and restoration	Songs of ascent and poems of praise for the future king's defeat of evil and benevolent reign

One further collection within the Psalter deserves mention. The superscriptions of Psalms 120–34 identify each one as "A Song of Ascents." Most scholars agree that the "ascent" refers to the journey people made through the hill country to Jerusalem to worship at one of the three annual feasts.[43] Thus, these are pilgrim songs that were sung by travelers en route to Jerusalem. The fact that the Mishnah tractate (treatise) Middot links these fifteen psalms with the fifteen steps leading up to the temple, where the Levites were said to sing them, does not mitigate against this understanding.[44] Both can be true.

Preaching Strategies

Now we can turn our attention to preaching the psalms. First, we will consider how to engage our listeners. Second, we will explore ideas for sermons and for sermon series from the book of Psalms. Finally, we will think about how to preach Christ in the psalms.

Engaging Your Listeners

Whenever we preach a psalm, we must work hard at engaging our listeners. After all, some have heard few sermons from the book of Psalms. Others may simply prefer other parts of Scripture, particularly the New Testament letters.

Poetic Flair

If we are going to preach in a way that reflects the kind of literature we have selected for our sermon, then the book of Psalms requires us to preach with what I call "poetic flair." This is simply sensitivity to the aesthetics of poetry—its beauty and the emotion it evokes. Obviously, we cannot deliver our sermons in parallel lines of verse like the psalmists do. But there are a couple ways we can preach with poetic flair.

First, invite your listeners to savor the imagery and rhetorical effects of the psalm you are preaching. Paint a picture with your words. Let's look at Psalm 23:2.

> He makes me lie down in green pastures,
> he leads me beside quiet waters.

43. See Longman, *Psalms*, 409–10; Waltke and Zaspel, *Psalms*, 103–7; VanGemeren, *Psalms*, 890; Ross, *Psalms*, 3:599; Goldingay, *Psalms*, 3:752; Alter, *Hebrew Bible*, 3:291.

44. The statement in Middot 2:5 is "And fifteen steps go up from it to the Israelite courtyard, one each for the fifteen Songs of Ascents in Psalms [Ps. 120–134], on which the Levites say their song" (Neusner, *Mishnah*, 877).

Now, rather than pointing out what type of parallelism this is, say something like, "Imagine you are a sheep. The place where you want to feed and then bed down is not a brown, overgrazed hillside. Rather, you want a lush hillside, with plenty of green grass for food. And when it comes to quenching your thirst, you do not want a rushing stream that is swollen from rain and comes roaring through the wadi, or riverbed. It can sweep you away. What you want is a canal that flows gently, where you can slurp water without fear of being swept away. This is the kind of care a good shepherd provides for sheep. This is the kind of care the Lord, our shepherd, provides for his people."

Here's another example. In Psalm 121:5–6, the psalmist writes,

> ⁵ The LORD watches over you—
>   the LORD is your shade at your right hand;
> ⁶ The sun will not harm you by day,
>   nor the moon by night.

It is not advisable to tell your listeners, "Verse 6 has a figure of speech called a 'merism.'" Rather, you might describe it something like I do when I preach Psalm 121. This is what I say about verse 6: "Notice how the psalmist refers to opposites in verse 6. The first line makes sense. You get it if you've ever spent a summer day out working or hiking in the hot sun. You can get sunburned, or you can even get sunstroke. My wife got sunstroke during a high school tennis match, and ever since, she can't spend much time in the direct sun on a hot day without finding shade. That's the point of the second line in verse 5, that the Lord is our shade. He is our protector. He is the reason the sun will not harm us by day. The second line of verse 6 doesn't make as much sense, though, does it? There's no evidence that the Israelites worried about being harmed by the moon. But this is poetry, and the psalmist is doing more here than speaking literally. By referring to these opposites, he's saying that we do not need to fear the dangers of the day or the dangers of the night. He's referring to any danger we might face by day or by night. The Lord's protection is constant. He works the day shift and the night shift."

Sometimes a word or concept needs a bit of elaboration. We must be careful not to sound like a Bible dictionary or a reference book, which simply gives explanation. Previously, we noted that the Hebrew word שָׁמַר

(*shamar*), translated as "guard, watch over, keep," occurs six times in Psalm 121. The best way to explain it is to ask our listeners to imagine the effect this word would have had on them.[45] You might say, "The word 'watch' or 'keep' would have caused some images to flash in the minds of those who first heard this psalm. It was used in the Old Testament of a shepherd caring for sheep. Think about the effort that goes into caring for sheep, during the day and during the night. It was used of a watchman guarding a city. These guards kept watch in guard towers on the top of city walls. They scanned the horizon for the first sight of the enemy. When dawn began to break, they strained to look for any movement, anything that looked out of place. Sometimes the word referred to a group of guards who stood around a field, ready to confront and drive away anyone who tried to steal grain or grapes. That's what God does for his people. He watches over us like a shepherd watches sheep, a guard protects a city, or a group of guards surround a field." Spending a bit of time painting the pictures the psalmist has provided will help your listeners experience them and thus understand them better.

A second way we can preach with poetic flair is to read a psalm with feeling. This means reading with vocal variety—that is, variation in your tone or pitch (higher, lower), your volume (louder, softer), and your rate (faster, slower). Expressions of praise, such as Psalm 145:1–2, should be read with joy, excitement, and enthusiasm. Expressions of lament, like the "How long?" questions in Psalm 13:1–2, must reflect exasperation and weariness. Once we learn to read with more expression, we can learn to preach with more expression, reflecting the emotion of the psalm we are preaching. Recently, one of my grandsons chose a "word for the year" as part of a grade school assignment. His word was "weight." He likes football, and he wants to gain more weight. I was tempted to choose the same word for the new year, although for the opposite reason. My suggestion is

---

45. We must always be cautious when we comment on words. It is easy to overanalyze them and find meanings that the psalmist did not intend, or to try to import every possible meaning a word can have (its semantic range) into a particular instance. Words get their meaning from the context, beginning with the phrases or clauses in which they appear. However, those working with cognitive linguistics remind us that a word (and groups of words) can evoke "our stored, encyclopedic knowledge of the world" (Vermeulen and Hayes, *How We Read the Bible*, 9). Ellen van Wolde says, "Cognitive Grammar cannot accept a dictionary view of meaning but takes an essentially encyclopedic view of meaning in which even the meaning of everyday terms is seen as being supported by a vast network of interrelated knowledge" (*Biblical Studies*, 55). This is why it is important to understand the historical-cultural context in which Scripture was written.

that preachers who are committed to the exposition of Scripture commit to a key word when preaching the book of Psalms: "expression." Don't settle for explanation. Of course, we must provide insight into words, customs, and concepts if our listeners are going to understand and obey the book of Psalms. But we will have a better chance of communicating all of this when we express ourselves with a bit of poetic flair.

Track the Flow of Thought

One of the best ways to engage our listeners is to help them track the flow of thought. As noted earlier, psalms tend to have an emotional plot development rather than a tight, linear argument where A leads to B which leads to C. Often, A, B, and C return to the same ideas and express them from a different angle. Psalm 46 is a good example. Here is an outline a preacher shared with me and requested feedback.

> I. God is our protector in any circumstance (vv. 1–3).
>
> II. God is present in all circumstances (vv. 4–7).
>
> III. (*Big Idea*) God is our promise in every circumstance (vv. 8–11).

What do you think? First, this outline is right about the structure of the psalm. There are three movements: verses 1–3, 4–7, 8–11. Also, I appreciate the clarity of this outline. This is due in large part to complete sentences. It is also concise. The outline uses alliteration ("p" words)—something that you may view as an advantage or disadvantage. The outline also abstracts from the specifics in the psalm something more general to which listeners can relate (any/all/every circumstance[s]). This is something preachers need to do.

Ultimately, however, I think that this outline does more harm than good. The attempt to alliterate ends up skewing the emphasis of the psalm. I suppose "protector" is acceptable, but verse 1 describes God as a "help"— a highly significant term in the Old Testament. I would far rather see the word "help" in point I, even though it wrecks the alliteration. While the first part of point II is spot-on when it says, "God is present," the opening words of point III fail to capture the emphasis of the third movement as well as the entire psalm, given that the third point intends to serve as the big idea for the sermon. Exactly how is God our promise according to verses 8–11? It's apparent that the preacher needed another word starting with "pr." This resulted in the choice of "promise." Of course, this idea is not heretical. God is our promise. But that is not what the third movement of this psalm is saying. The repeated refrain in verse 11, which already appeared in verse 7, emphasizes God's presence and that he is a place of refuge. Moreover, while the preacher's instincts to abstract the particulars of this psalm to "any/all/every circumstance[s]" are correct, I believe that the abstraction has become too vague. Finally, the outline gives the impression that Psalm 46 is making three different points about what God does for us in every circumstance we face.

Here is a better way to outline Psalm 46. This outline captures the particulars of the psalm, as well as its flow, more effectively.

> I. God's help gives us a reason not to fear in times of chaos (vv. 1–3).
>
> II. God's presence provides calm in the midst of the chaos (vv. 4–7).
>
> III. God's presence assures ultimate victory over evil (vv. 8–11).
>
> IV. (*Big Idea*) God is present to help you when your world falls apart.

The first point is as profound as it is simple. I chose to use the word "help" from the text. I thought about "strong help," but as soon as I choose one qualifier, I minimize the other two. God is a protective ("refuge"), strong, and ever-present help. I will develop these ideas when I preach, but I do not need to squeeze them into the main point. They would show up in my outline, though, as subpoints. The remainder of point I is an abstraction of verses 2–3. I have heard preachers say something like, "Since God is our help, we do not need to fear when we face natural disasters." Yet I am convinced that the language in verses 2–3 is describing something bigger than an earthquake or flood. It refers to the very undoing of creation! I chose to abstract this to "times of chaos." I could have said, "God is our help when all hell breaks loose," or "God is our help when our world falls apart." But for now, I am sticking with chaos.

Verses 4–7 do not make an additional point as much as they flesh out the point made in verses 1–3. One way I can make sure to bring out that notion is to add a transition statement between the two points. I could simply say, "The second movement of this psalm, verses 4–7, fleshes out the reason we do not need to fear." Notice that points II and III both speak of God's presence because that is the emphasis in the refrain that ends both sections (vv. 7, 11). In point II, I chose the word "calm" because it captures the mood with which verse 4 begins. In contrast to the chaos of creation falling apart in verses 2–3, verse 4 is a picture of calmness, even joy. Rather than waters roaring and foaming, there is a manageable source of water—a river with streams or canals—in the city of God. If you have ever visited Jerusalem or done a bit of geographic study, you know that no river runs through it. This is imagery that takes us back to the garden of Eden, where a river was separated into four canals (literally, "four heads") as an expression of God's life-giving presence (Gen. 2:10–14). This calm is important because it turns out that the city in which God dwells is under siege (v. 5). Yet God is more powerful than the nations, causing them to melt when he lifts his voice (v. 6).

I believe that the last movement in verses 8–11 zeroes in on another blessing of God's presence for people who are facing chaos. Here, God's presence provides the assurance of God's ultimate victory over evil. Again, I would use a transition statement between points II and III. I might say, "But will the chaos we face ever come to an end? Is it always going to be this way, or will everything sad one day come untrue?" The promise in verse 9 is similar to the promise in Isaiah 9:5. God will one day end war by destroying the very implements of warfare—breaking the bow, shattering the spear, and burning the shields in a bonfire. Thus, he commands the nations, "Be still, and know that I am God" (v. 10). Yes, I believe that these words are directed to the nations rather than to God's people, even though that spoils the good piece of artwork hanging in your living room with the first line of verse 10 on it.

In my outline, I am adding an additional point to communicate the big idea of Psalm 46. I believe that the three movements in the psalm work together to convey this idea. Hopefully, my example shows the need for a clear, concise outline that reflects the flow of the text and does not obscure it by trying to be memorable. My goal is not for people to remember my outline. It is for them to think through the flow of the text. I want them to see that the second movement defines God's help in terms of his presence. Then, the third movement assures us that God's presence guarantees not only help (or calm) in our present difficulties and tragedies, but also the eventual defeat of evil itself.

When preaching Psalm 121, a psalm of confidence, we need to help our listeners feel the emotional movement from concern in verse 1 to confidence in verses 3–8. This is a real mood shift, even though it is more subtle than in other psalms. Here is a possible preaching outline for Psalm 121:

I. The Lord helps his people when they face danger (vv. 1–2).
II. (*Big Idea*) When you face danger, you can be sure that God is watching over you (vv. 3–6).
III. This "watch-care" guarantees eternal safety, not the absence of physical harm (vv. 7–8).

Once again, the outline intends to track the flow of thought rather than pressing into a neat list of "three encouragements when you face danger" or some such scheme. The first point seems rather obvious, yet I have been intentional about using the word "help" (עֵזֶר, *'ezer*), which occurs twice, once in verse 1 and once in verse 2. My subpoints under point I would highlight the contrast between concern (v. 1) and confidence in the face of that concern (v. 2).

I believe that the main idea of Psalm 121 surfaces in verses 3–6. Here we need a transition statement between points I and II that talks about how the psalmist shifts the imagery. While verses 1–2 speak of the Lord as "my help," the remainder of the psalm switches to the imagery of watching or guarding—as we previously noted. Verses 3–6 provide some vivid images of the Lord's watch-care over his people. Verses 7–8 may appear to do the same, but I see a real, though subtle, change in what this psalm affirms. The Lord's watch-care extends to all harmful situations, to your whole life, to your coming and going (a merism that implies everything else in between), and to now and forevermore. It appears that the psalmist is anticipating an objection. The reality is that the feet of believers sometimes slip, and sometimes believers are harmed during the day and during the night. So what does this psalm promise? My third point answers this question, clarifying that the Lord's watch-care guarantees eternal safety, not necessarily the absence of physical harm.

Preach Lament Psalms

Another piece of advice for preachers who want to engage their listeners is, perhaps, a bit counterintuitive. We might think that people want upbeat, happy messages. Yet we dare not avoid lament psalms, or we will fail to provide them with the kind of perspective and resources they need when they face difficulty. Mark Vroegop is right on target: "Lament is how we bring our sorrow to God. Without lament we won't know how to process pain. Silence, bitterness, and even anger can dominate our spiritual lives instead. Without lament we won't know how to help people walk through sorrow. Instead, we'll offer trite solutions, unhelpful comments, or impatient responses."[46] This is why I have always resisted attempts to call a worship service a "celebration service." The psalms help us see that worship involves praise and lament. Our preaching should reflect this too. Our listeners will appreciate the raw honesty of the psalms and learn how to voice complaints to God in a way that still affirms his goodness.

Ideas for Sermons and Series

When it comes to preaching the book of Psalms, there are a myriad of options. If you have not preached the psalms before, it would be wise to preach Psalms 1 and 2 (by themselves or together) and then choose a handful of other psalms that touch on the needs of the church you serve or that reflect the content of the Psalter. Choose a praise psalm, a lament psalm, a song of confidence, a royal psalm, and a wisdom psalm. An eight-week series will provide your listeners with sufficient exposure to the psalms without overwhelming them.

Once your church acquires a taste for the psalms, you can either preach favorites from various places in the Psalter or preach eight to twelve consecutive psalms. The Psalms of Ascent (Pss. 120–34) are always a good choice. So are Psalms 113–18, the "Hallel" (praise) psalms. I suggest keeping a master list of psalms that you and others have preached in your church so that you eventually cover all 150 psalms over the years. Of course, some psalms deserve to be preached again and again. But some of the psalms you neglect might turn out to be the most powerful ones you preach. If you preach a sermon series from the books of Samuel, consider taking a break occasionally to preach one of the psalms that matches an incident in the life of David. As already mentioned, Psalm 59 emerged from the time Saul sent men to watch David's house in order to kill him (1 Sam. 19:11–18). Psalm 57 grew out of the time David fled from Saul into a cave (1 Sam. 22:1), while Psalm 51 was written when the prophet Nathan came to David after David committed adultery with Bathsheba (2 Sam. 12:1–14).

46. Vroegop, Dark Clouds, 21.

Certain seasons of the year lend themselves to preaching psalms. Summer is a great time, given that people usually come and go more than during the school year. Understanding Psalm 13 does not require hearing sermons on Psalms 11 and 12 in the same way that the argument of Hebrews 4:1–13 builds on the paragraphs and chapters that precede it. I have frequently done "Psalms for Summer" series. However, if this is the only time you preach Psalms, it might diminish their value in the eyes of your listeners. They might think of them as filler until you can get to the fall and start a series on Romans or Genesis. The solution is simply to preach them at other times during the year as well.

Advent/Christmas and Lent/Easter are also opportune seasons for preaching Psalms. Whether you focus more on Advent or the Christmas season, a series on Christ's rule as king in the royal psalms would be appropriate for either. The lament songs are a good choice during the Lenten season and its focus on the suffering of Christ. The lament in Psalm 22:1–21 is highly appropriate for Good Friday because it contains words that Jesus spoke on the cross and words that the Gospel writers used in their accounts of the crucifixion. Then, the declaration of praise in Psalm 22:22–31 is a fitting text for Resurrection Day (Easter Sunday) as we can imagine its words on the lips of our risen Lord.

Make the book of Psalms a staple in your preaching. You will teach your people how to pray, how to praise, how to lament, how to express confidence. We need the psalms to be the soundtrack for our lives.

Preaching Christ in the Psalms

There are ample opportunities for focusing on Jesus in our preaching of the book of Psalms. We will always do well to run the theological message of a psalm through the lens of Jesus's teaching and the apostles' teaching. We will also do well to pay attention to how Jesus and the apostles quoted these psalms. We will also want to read the book of Psalms in light of what Jesus said to his disciples in two conversations on the day of his resurrection recorded in the Gospel of Luke. The first was with two of his disciples on the road to Emmaus.

He said to them, "How foolish you are, and how slow to believe all that the prophets have spoken! Did not the Messiah have to suffer these things and then enter his glory?" And beginning with Moses and all the Prophets, he explained to them what was said in all the Scriptures concerning himself. (Luke 24:25–27)

The reference to "Moses and all the Prophets" was one of the ways of referring to the Hebrew Bible—what we call the Old Testament. The verb "explained" refers to a more extensive and formal explanation of something difficult to understand, or even obscure.[47] It is clear, then, that all the Scriptures, including the psalms, speak of the Messiah.[48]

Later, after the two met up with the other disciples, Jesus appeared to the entire group. In response to their joy and amazement, he brought up the issue again, making the same point with a slightly different emphasis.

> He said to them, "This is what I told you while I was still with you: Everything must be fulfilled that is written about me in the Law of Moses, the Prophets and the Psalms." Then he opened their minds so they could understand the Scriptures. He told them, "This is what is written: The Messiah will suffer and rise from the dead on the third day, and repentance for the forgiveness of sins will be preached in his name to all nations, beginning at Jerusalem." (Luke 24:44–47)

In this conversation, Jesus uses the threefold designation for the Hebrew Bible, or Old Testament. This is no different than what people do today when talking about the city of Chicago. Sometimes, they refer to it with a two-part breakdown: the north side and the south side. At other times, they speak of it in a three-part breakdown: the north side, the south side, and the Loop (the main section of downtown). Interestingly, Jesus refers to the third section of the Hebrew Bible, known as "the Writings," as "the Psalms." Although the reference is to the Writings, it shows us that "the Psalms" were prominent enough to be used as shorthand for the entire third section of the Scriptures. Once again, Jesus affirms the truth that the Old Testament speaks of him. This means, then, that it is appropriate to read the psalms in anticipation of Christ. Tremper Longman offers wise counsel here. He suggests three practices for discerning how the psalms anticipate Christ.[49] First, we can read a psalm as a prayer *to* Christ in similar

47. Culy, Parsons, and Stigall, *Luke*, 749.
48. For the way Psalms consistently conflates "the human and divine identities of the Messiah," see Postell, "Does the Book of Psalms Present a Divine Messiah?"
49. Longman, *Psalms*, 48–50.

fashion to Hebrews 1:10–12, in which the writer prays Psalm 102:25–27 to Jesus. Second, we can read a psalm as a prayer *of* Jesus, recognizing that Jesus himself used language from the psalms in his prayers.[50] Third, we can reflect on how Jesus fulfills descriptions of God in the psalms. For instance, he is a shepherd (Ps. 23:1; John 10:11; Heb. 13:20), a helper in trouble (Ps. 46:1; Heb. 4:14–16), and the king of glory and mighty warrior (Ps. 24:7–10; Rev. 19:11–16). In our study and preaching of the book of Psalms, we do not need to choose between a historical-cultural-literary reading and a christological reading. The two go hand in hand.

Helpful Resources for Studying and Preaching

Thankfully, we have an endless stream of resources for the book of Psalms at our disposal. For commentaries, I still treasure Derek Kidner's two volumes that were originally part of the Tyndale Old Testament Commentaries. Now they are published as Kidner Classic Commentaries, testifying to their enduring value. The new Psalms volume in the Tyndale Old Testament Commentaries is by Tremper Longman. Personally, I love using Kidner and Longman together. A couple years ago, I read through the psalms—at the rate of one per day, with an extra day(s) for longer psalms—and read the commentary by both Kidner and Longman along with my reading of the biblical text. Willem VanGemeren's commentary on Psalms in the Expositor's Bible Commentary is excellent. So are the three volumes by Allen Ross in the Kregel Exegetical Library. While Ross's commentary has a lot of depth and substance, he wrote it with preachers in mind. John Goldingay's three volumes in the Baker Commentary on the Old Testament Wisdom and Psalms are insightful as well. I still love using Peter Craigie's Word Biblical Commentary volume on Psalms 1–50. The format of the Word Biblical Commentary series drives me crazy, but Craigie's material in the comment and explanation sections for each psalm is worth the price of the volume. Unfortunately, Craigie's life was cut short by a car accident before he could finish his work on the remaining psalms. I still like Franz Delitzsch's commentary on Psalms in the Keil and Delitzsch series. Although some of the exegetical details

50. For example, Jesus's prayers incorporated Ps. 6:3 (John 12:27), Ps. 22:1 (Matt. 27:46), Ps. 31:5 (Luke 23:46), Ps. 41:9 (John 13:18), and Ps. 42:5 (Matt. 26:38). I retrieved these from a list in Waltke and Zaspel, *Psalms*, 370.

are out of date, he had a knack (similar to Derek Kidner) for brilliant theological insights. Gerald Wilson's volume covering Psalms 1–72 in the NIV Application Commentary is helpful. Finally, I have profited from *The Psalms as Christian Worship: A Historical Commentary*, by Bruce K. Waltke and James H. Houston. There are other good volumes as well in the standard commentary series (Word Biblical Commentary, the NIV Application Commentary, New International Commentary on the Old Testament, etc.), but I have highlighted the ones that I have found most helpful for preaching.

There are numerous volumes on understanding or interpreting the psalms, but I have found most of this material at the beginning of the better commentaries. However, the best of these books include Mark D. Futato's *Interpreting the Psalms: An Exegetical Handbook* and Tremper Longman's *How to Read the Psalms*. Also, the thick volume by Bruce K. Waltke and Fred G. Zaspel, *How to Read and Understand the Psalms*, pulls together a lot of material from Waltke's decade of Psalms scholarship and makes it accessible in one place. Walter Brueggemann's writings are always thought-provoking, and *The Psalms and the Life of Faith* is no exception. The chapters "The Psalms as Prayer" and "The Costly Loss of Lament" are worth the price of the book. Claus Westermann's little book *The Psalms: Structure, Content, and Message* is helpful too. If you can find Ronald Allen's books *Praise! A Matter of Life and Breath* (retitled as *And I Will Praise Him*) and *Lord of Song: The Messiah Revealed in the Psalms*, snatch them up. The former is an excellent overall study of the psalms, while the latter focuses on how the Messiah is revealed in the psalms.

Another helpful category of books includes multicontributor volumes with studies of various psalms. *Interpreting the Psalms for Teaching and Preaching*, edited by Herbert W. Bateman IV and D. Brent Sandy, has excellent studies of Psalms 1–2, 19, 46, 63, 73, 89, 99, 103–4, 110, 116, 130, 135, and 148. Lexham Academic has recently published two volumes with helpful essays on various psalms and theological issues in the Psalter: *A New Song: Biblical Hebrew Poetry as Jewish and Christian Scripture*, edited by Stephen D. Campbell, Richard G. Rohlfing Jr., and Richard S. Briggs; and *Reading the Psalms Theologically*, edited by David M. Howard Jr. and Andrew J. Schmutzer.

The Bible Project resources on the psalms are quite helpful for both preachers and their listeners. This includes the Book Overview video on the book of Psalms as well as the episode on Psalms in the How to Read the Bible series of videos.[51]

For help with preaching various psalms, it is worthwhile to consult Kenneth Langley's chapter on Psalms in *The Big Idea Companion for Preaching and Teaching*. It only covers one-third of the psalms, but Langley's brief comments and "big idea" suggestion for each of them are golden.

I have found some of the devotional, or popular level, books on Psalms helpful as well. Eugene Peterson's little volume on the Psalms of Ascent, *A Long Obedience in the Same Direction*, has become a classic. Matthew Jacoby's *Deeper Places: Experiencing God in the Psalms* has helps to deliver what its title promises. Mark Vroegop's *Dark Clouds, Deep Mercy: Discovering the Grace of Lament* is tremendously helpful on the usefulness of lament psalms in the lives of believers. I have also profited from *The Songs of Jesus: A Year of Daily Devotions in the Psalms*, by Timothy and Kathy Keller. Any of these devotional, or popular-level, books are excellent resources to make available to a church during a sermon series on Psalms.

Finally, for those who like to drink at old wells (and I am one of them), get a copy of *Praying the Psalms with Augustine and Friends*, by Carmen Joy Imes. She has provided a brief devotional entry for each psalm from men and women throughout church history who were passionate about the psalms. Another terrific resource is the two-volume *St. John Chrysostom Commentary on the Psalms*, by Robert Charles Hill. He has translated Chrysostom's commentary on fifty-eight psalms—all the ones we have available from the "golden-mouthed" preacher from the fourth century.

51. You can access these resources at https://bibleproject.com/.

3

Preaching Proverbs

Every culture has its proverbial sayings. These one- or two-liners condense wise observations about life into short, memorable statements. Several years ago, I made frequent trips to Haiti to visit the sister church with which our local church in Montana had partnered. On one occasion, I stopped at a bookstore in Port-au-Prince and purchased a little volume titled *999 Haitian Proverbs in Creole and English*. Here are a few of my favorites:

Pretty teeth are not the heart.[1]

Shaking the head doesn't break the neck.[2]

The face which sells (on credit) is not the one who collects the money.[3]

Their meanings surface easily with a bit of reflection. First, outward beauty does not guarantee inward beauty. Second, it is all right to say no. Declining a request will not hurt you. Third, beware of a compelling sales pitch that requires you to borrow for a particular product or service. The friendly sales representative will not be the one you deal with if you are unable to keep up with your payments.

During my years of pastoral ministry in Montana, I found a book of Western proverbs in the Country Bookshelf in the city of Bozeman. The

---

1. Jeanty and Brown, *999 Haitian Proverbs*, 34.
2. Jeanty and Brown, *999 Haitian Proverbs*, 35.
3. Jeanty and Brown, *999 Haitian Proverbs*, 34–35.

title is simply *Savvy Sayin's*. It contains the sayings that cowboys fashioned as they ate together and swapped stories in bunkhouses and around campfires. Here are a few of my favorites:

> Never approach a bull from the front, a horse from the rear, or a fool from any direction.[4]

> Saddle your horse before sassin' the boss.[5]

> Broke is what happens when you let your yearnin's get ahead of your earnin's.[6]

> Tryin' to brand with a cold iron don't save no time.[7]

Again, while these sayings require some pondering, their meaning is clear. First, don't have anything to do with fools. They are more dangerous than you realize. Second, if you are prepared to give your employer a piece of your mind, be prepared to find a new job. Lashing out in anger at your boss will likely get you fired. Third, people who can't control their impulses will not control their spending; and the result will be running out of money. Finally, taking shortcuts will take more time than taking time to make the right preparations for the task at hand.

Thanks to Benjamin Franklin, some of the sayings of eighteenth-century Western civilization have become timeless. Although he borrowed them from various sources, he filtered them through his wit and humor. Here is a sample of the proverbs he included in *Poor Richard's Almanack*:

> Fish and Visitors stink after three days.[8]

> The Things which hurt, instruct.[9]

> Three may keep a secret, if two of them are dead.[10]

It's not hard to recognize the ideas that these sayings convey. First, there is a limit of time in which guests are welcome. Staying too late in the evening

4. Alstad, *Savvy Sayin's*, 8.
5. Alstad, *Savvy Sayin's*, 63.
6. Alstad, *Savvy Sayin's*, 86.
7. Alstad, *Savvy Sayin's*, 106.
8. Franklin, *Poor Richard's Almanack*, 1.
9. Franklin, *Poor Richard's Almanack*, 26.
10. Franklin, *Poor Richard's Almanack*, 27.

after dinner at a friend's house is unpleasant for your friend. And if you stay for too many days at a friend's house while traveling through the area, you will wear out your welcome. Second, it's often the painful situations in life that teach us the greatest life lessons. Finally, the only way to guard a secret is not to share it with anyone else.

Traveling further back in time, we find proverbial sayings older than any proverbs in the Bible. Here are a few of my favorite proverbial sayings from Mesopotamia. They date back to the Early Old Babylonian period (ca. 1800–1700 BC).[11]

Upon my escaping from the wild-ox, the wild-cow confronted me![12]

Into an open mouth, a fly will enter![13]

Like a barren cow, you are looking for a calf of yours which does not exist![14]

Once again, the meanings of these proverbs surface readily with a little reflection. I have sometimes joked that the first one is my life story in a sentence! As soon as I escape one challenge or difficulty, another one stands in my way. Second, you will keep bad things from happening if you keep your mouth shut—certainly an oblique reference to controlling one's speech. Third, be realistic and beware of idealism and chasing fantasies.

Like all of these cultures, the people of Israel had a rich deposit of proverbial sayings. The key figure was King Solomon. According to 1 Kings 4:29–34, Solomon was the GOAT (Greatest of All Time) when it came to wisdom. He was to the pursuit of wisdom what Michael Jordan is to basketball or what Taylor Swift is to pop music. This passage claims that he was wiser than the people everyone considered to be the wisest. First Kings 4:31 even lists their names: Ethan the Ezrahite, Heman, Kalkol, and Darda. Although those names are lost to us, it must have been the ancient equivalent of saying that Taylor Swift is more popular than Ed Sheeran, Ariana Grande, or Rihanna. Among his accomplishments, Solomon "spoke three thousand proverbs" (1 Kings 4:32). And he is responsible for much of the book of Proverbs, where some of his proverbs ended up as Holy Scripture.

11. Pritchard, *Ancient Near East*, 244.
12. Pritchard, *Ancient Near East*, 245.
13. Pritchard, *Ancient Near East*, 245.
14. Pritchard, *Ancient Near East*, 245.

Yet the book of Proverbs is more than a collection of one-liners or aphorisms. As we will see, it is a carefully crafted book that has two tactics. First, it seeks to convince its readers that wisdom is a superior lifestyle to foolishness (chaps. 1–9). Then, once its readers are on board, it shows them how to live wisely (chaps. 10–31).

In this chapter, we will explore how to preach the book of Proverbs. We will follow the same approach as the previous chapter on preaching the book of Psalms. We will begin with studying the text—sermon exegesis. Then, we will think about preaching the text—sermon crafting.

Studying Proverbs

Like other kinds of biblical literature, the book of Proverbs communicates its meaning in a particular way. This requires us to adapt to the structure and strategies employed by the writers of Proverbs. The book of Proverbs is more than a book of sayings. To be sure, it includes the maxims or aphorisms—short, pithy sayings—that we dub "proverbs." Yet the book has an interesting design to it, one that must be understood if we are to interpret it correctly. As I've already said, there are two major chunks to the book. Chapters 1–9 argue that wisdom is superior to folly as an approach to life. Then, chapters 10–31 describe how to live according to wisdom. Within these large sections there are various other literary units or collections. As Jared Alcántara notes, the book of Proverbs "is a collection of collections."[15]

Table 3.1 provides an overview of the book's structure. Understanding this will help you interpret the individual sections and sayings more accurately, and it will provide you with leads for choosing sermon texts. Working through these sections in more detail, though briefly, will help us understand the key concepts and major interpretive issues in the book of Proverbs.

Prologue (1:1–7)

The prologue identifies the book's main author, its purpose, its audience, its literary strategy, and its theological foundation. Any sermon series on the book of Proverbs will benefit from a sermon devoted to unpacking this important text.

15. Alcántara, *Proverbs*, 4.

Table 3.1

An Overview of the Book of Proverbs

Argument: Wisdom is a superior lifestyle to Folly (chaps. 1–9)
Prologue (1:1–7)
Sermonettes (1:8–9:18)

Application: This is what it looks like to live according to wisdom (chaps. 10–31)
The proverbs of Solomon (10:1–22:16)
The sayings of the wise (22:17–24:22)
Further sayings of the wise (24:23–34)
More proverbs of Solomon compiled by Hezekiah's men (25:1–29:27)
The sayings of Agur (30:1–33)
The sayings King Lemuel's mother taught him (31:1–9)
The wife of noble character (31:10–31)

Verse 1 identifies the main author and the content of the book of Proverbs. The main author is Solomon. As noted above, 1 Kings 4:29–34 describes his prowess as a sage. His reputation grew to the level where Jesus could say that the Queen of the South "came from the ends of the earth to listen to Solomon's wisdom, and now something greater than Solomon is here" (Matt. 12:42).[16] Although Solomon is the main author, there are clearly other contributors to the book as noted in table 3.1, beginning in Proverbs 22:17. In regard to the content of the book, it is a book of "proverbs." This word, though, refers to more than one-liners or pithy sayings. The Hebrew word for "proverb" in verse 1 is מָשָׁל (*mashal*). According to Michael Fox, it can refer "to a great range of utterances, from one-line adages to extended poems."[17] For example, מָשָׁל (*mashal*) is used in the Old Testament for Balaam's message or oracle (Num. 23:7), for maxims or memorable sayings (Job 13:12), for a byword or parable (Deut. 28:37; Ps. 44:14), and for a taunt song (Mic. 2:4; Hab. 2:6).[18] Ryan O'Dowd says that the expression "is less concerned with a specific form of speech than with the fact that these sayings have a culturated history,

16. The account of the Queen of the South's visit, to which Jesus refers, is in 1 Kings 10:1–13.
17. Fox, *Proverbs 1–9*, 54.
18. *HALOT* summarizes the semantic (meaning) range of the term in five categories: 1. Saying, of different types and genres; 2. Proverb; 3. Wisdom saying; 4. Song of jest, mocking; 5. Title of a collection.

or a time-tested currency, among the folks."[19] Likewise, according to Fox, the expression simply claims that the sayings are "well-known and in widespread use."[20]

The purpose of the book is expressed in a series of infinitives ("to know," "to understand," etc.) in verses 2–6, although verse 5 breaks the pattern with verbs that offer an exhortation ("let the wise listen," etc.).[21] Tremper Longman offers a helpful breakdown of this section. Verses 2–3 provide a "general statement of intention" that applies to all readers of the book.[22] While there are a rich variety of words used to describe the general purpose of Proverbs, a couple of ideas stand out. First, the overall objective of the book is the acquisition of "wisdom"—the Hebrew term חָכְמָה (hokmah). I am astonished at how many sermons are unclear about the meaning of this word when the meaning of the Hebrew term is crystal clear. It simply means "skill." It (or its cognate adjective hakam) is used in the Old Testament of the skill of garment making (Exod. 28:3), artistic work with precious metals (Exod. 31:3–4; Jer. 10:9), woodworking (Exod. 31:5), mourning (Jer. 9:17), and sailing (Ps. 107:27). In Proverbs, "wisdom" is the skill of living in God's created world—adapting and adjusting to the economic, social, sexual, and emotional patterns that God has built into life. I will have more to say about this in a moment when we get to verse 7. A second key idea is the connection between living wisely and doing justice. The end of verse 2 reads, "to receive instruction in prudence—in righteousness, justice, and equity" (my translation). This theme serves as bookends to the entire book of Proverbs, as it surfaces in the final poem in 31:20, where the woman of strength "opens her arms to the poor and extends her hands to the needy."

In verses 4–5, we discover the audience for the book. Verse 4 addresses the simple and young, while verse 5 speaks to the wise and discerning.[23] Our first hint, though, as to the audience comes in verse 1. There we get a hint that the book of Proverbs is for everyone. The study of wisdom

---

19. O'Dowd, Proverbs, 55.

20. Fox, Proverbs 1–9, 55. He argues that attempts to find a single feature common to the uses of the term have failed, including the idea of "likening." Often, he observes, the term מָשָׁל (mashal) "refers to an utterance that has nothing to do with comparison" (Proverbs 1–9, 54). Thus, preachers and teachers will do well to avoid treating the word "proverbs" in Prov. 1:1 as anything more than well-known, well-used sayings.

21. The Hebrew text of Prov. 1:5 has three jussive verbs (which function as imperatives).

22. Longman, Proverbs, 95.

23. Longman, Proverbs, 95.

typically was the domain of the royal court. Kings passed on wisdom to their sons—princes who may one day assume the throne. According to Bruce Waltke, while ancient Near Eastern wisdom texts typically name "the son or apprentice to whom the sage directed his instruction," there is no addressee, such as Solomon's son Rehoboam, mentioned in verse 1. This "democratizes" the work, aiming it at all people and not simply princes.[24] The ending of the book confirms this too. I will say more about this later in the chapter, but it is stunning that the book ends with a woman rather than a prince as the exemplar of wisdom.

Now verses 4 and 5 break down this wide audience into two groups. The first is the "simple." This term refers to someone who is rather "open-minded" and could pursue a lifestyle of either wisdom or folly. This person is vulnerable to being misled, even gullible. Thus, the purpose of the book for these folks is to give them "prudence" and "discretion" (v. 4). These terms speak to the "dark side" of wisdom—that is, street sense.[25] The Hebrew term עָרְמָה ('ormah), translated as "prudence" or "shrewdness" by most English versions, refers to cleverness or cunning that can result in either good or evil.[26] However, it is used positively in its three occurrences in Proverbs (1:4; 8:5, 12). It is not difficult to think of present-day examples. For instance, we teach children how to refuse a stranger's offer to give them a ride home, and we teach adults how to deal with phishing attempts via email or text message. The second group in this wide audience consists of wise people. According to verse 5, the wise never stop learning.[27] They continue to add wisdom and to pursue guidance. Kathryn Dell rightly observes that the formation of character, an important theme in Proverbs, is not

---

24. Waltke, *Proverbs: Chapters 1–15*, 174.

25. My seminary Hebrew professor Ronald Allen used these descriptors years ago in a Hebrew exegesis course on Proverbs.

26. *HALOT*.

27. As previously noted, verse 5 has three jussive verbs (which function as imperatives), breaking the pattern of infinitives in verses 2–4 and 6. This variation may be understood in one of two ways. First, it might emphasize that the invitation to pursue wisdom is for the already-wise, not only the simple-minded, given that "people do not grow out of the teaching in Proverbs. Even if adults have acquired wisdom and become discerning (vv. 2–3), they can still *add to what they have received* and gain *expertise*" (Goldingay, *Proverbs*, 25). Second, it is possible that the variation might clarify the means to attaining the infinitives in verses 2–4 and 6. Thus, instead of reading the infinitives as the reason why the proverbs of Solomon were collected, the infinitives might be the result: what happens when wise people listen, increase in learning, and understand (see Johnson, "Proverbs 1:1–7," 428–30).

simply for the "very young." Rather, "it includes character formation throughout the life cycle."[28]

Verse 6 zeroes in on the literary strategy of the book. It requires an understanding of "proverbs and parables, the sayings and riddles of the wise." These expressions, and the shades of difference between them, are hard to pin down. What they have in common, notes Longman, is "indirect language, and therefore language difficult to understand at first glance."[29] This requires deep reflection, not surface reading. It is an approach to reading adopted by John Steinbeck's character Tom Hamilton—an approach I described in the preface. Tom was not content to ride lightly on the top of a book the way Samuel his father did. Instead, he tunneled like a mole among its thoughts and came up with it all over his hands and face. That is the kind of effort required to understand the catchy, memorable, and often enigmatic sayings in Proverbs.

Finally, verse 7 reveals the theological purpose of the book of Proverbs, as well as the theological grid through which its wise sayings have been sifted. This verse is the motto of the book and "its most foundational truth."[30] The "beginning" here is the first step in gaining knowledge and wisdom, but it is the foundation on which we build—not a starting point from which we move away. The fear of the Lord is a way of referring to our worship, reverence, and awe of the person of Yahweh. Exodus 20:20 is intriguing, using the verb and noun form of the same root—יְרָא (yrʾ) / יִרְאָה (yrʾh) "fear"—in two different ways: "Moses said to the people, 'Do not be afraid [יְרָא, yrʾ]. God has come to test you, so that the fear [יִרְאָה, yrʾh] of God will be with you to keep you from sinning.'" The interplay of "don't fear" and "do fear" invites reflection. The term obviously has different senses in each instance, yet there is a fine line between what Moses tells the people not to do and the purpose for God's testing. Moses does not want the people to be terrified of God, yet he does. This is the tension with which they must live. They must not run for cover in the presence of

28. Dell, *Proverbs*, 135–36.
29. Longman, *Proverbs*, 99.
30. Longman, *Proverbs*, 100. He notes that "it is repeated with some variation in a number of places in the book." See 1:29; 2:5; 3:7; 8:13; 9:10; 10:27; 14:2, 26, 27; 15:16, 33; 16:6; 19:23; 22:4; 23:17; 24:21; 28:14; 29:25; 31:30. I would add that 1:7 and the similar statement in 9:10 function as bookends to the first major section of the book, chapters 1–9. Likewise, 1:7 and 31:30 (the declaration that "a woman who fears the Lord is to be praised") provide bookends to the entire book.

God. Yet, there must be a healthy sense of awe and reverence in the presence of their Creator and Judge and King. It is this attitude of worship that governs the pursuit of wisdom. Thus, the pursuit of wisdom, when done properly, is an act of worship. As Longman says, "Wisdom begins with a relationship with God."[31]

Sermonettes (1:8–9:18)

This section is a series of sermonettes, or mini-lectures, designed to convince the reader that wisdom is a superior lifestyle to folly. These are the two ways to live. In Proverbs, the fool is a morally deficient person, not an intellectually deficient person.[32] Several years ago, my wife, Priscilla, volunteered to drop off our vehicle's flat tire at an auto shop for repair. I removed the flat tire, and then replaced it with the spare tire. Just as I finished hand-tightening the lug nuts to secure the wheel and tire assembly to the axle, I received a phone call. When I finished the call, I looked at the spare tire and assumed I had completed the task. However, I forgot that I had not tightened the lug nuts with a lug wrench. By the time my wife arrived at the auto shop, the wheel was wobbling and about to fall off. The mechanic took one look at it and said, "Someone forgot to tighten the lug nuts. What were they trying to do, kill you!?" It is tempting to describe my mistake as "foolish." That's how we sometimes use the term in English, to describe a stupid mistake. We consider an inept person a fool. Yet, according to Proverbs, my failure to tighten the lug nuts with a lug wrench was a mistake—even a stupid one. But it was not foolish, because it was unintentional. My act would have been foolish only if I had a malicious intent and wanted to cause harm to my wife. The burden of Proverbs 1:8–9:18 is to convince the simple-minded person to choose wisdom over folly as a way of living life.

As you work your way through this section of Proverbs, you will find the expression "my son" functioning frequently as a discourse marker, which stands at the head of a new section (see 1:8; 2:1; 3:1, 21; 4:1, 10, 20; 5:1;

31. Longman, *Proverbs*, 57.
32. Bruce Waltke observes that the "ethical terms" used for the fool in Proverbs imply "the fool's moral culpability, not his lack of intelligence. The wisdom terms for the unwise, however, are not correlatives but distinguish three or four classes of fools according to their educative capacities: the gullible, the fool, and the mocker. Worse than the fools is the sluggard (cf. 28:12, 16), but not as incorrigible or vile are the senseless" (*Proverbs: Chapters 1–15*, 111).

6:1, 20; 7:1).[33] There is general agreement among commentators as to the units themselves, although they differ in the way they label these as either lectures/admonitions or interludes. The culmination of the sermonettes or lectures is the invitation of Lady Wisdom and Madam Folly to rival banquets (9:1–18). Lady Wisdom promises life (9:6), while the chilling observation at the end of Madam Folly's invitation is that her house is a place of death and "that her guests are deep in the realm of the dead" (9:18).

The Proverbs of Solomon (10:1–22:16)

The section that runs from chapters 10–29 contains the individual sayings for which the book of Proverbs is known. The first collection, in 10:1–22:16, consists of 375 proverbial sayings, which is the numerical value of the Hebrew letters in Solomon's name.[34] The Hebrew language used letters to represent numbers (a system known as *gematria*). Here are the numerical values for the name שלמה (*shlmh*), which add up to 375:

$sh = 300$

$l = 30$

$m = 40$

$h = 5$

This literary device appears to highlight Solomon's role in collecting, revising, and, in some instances, creating these sayings.

Proverbs 10:1–22:16 further divides into two main parts: 10:1–15:33 (part A) and 16:1–22:16 (part B).[35] Part A has a "high density of antithetical sayings," or contrasts, particularly between the righteous and the wicked, while part B contains a wider variety of topics and "gives more prominence to kingship."[36]

Beginning in Proverbs 10:1, we encounter a huge interpretive issue that shapes the way we understand and preach the proverbial sayings in chapters

---

33. In some instances, "my son" does not stand at the head of a new section but introduces a new subsection or adds rhetorical flourish (1:10; 3:11; 5:20; 6:3; 7:24).

34. O'Dowd, *Proverbs*, 177.

35. Fox, *Proverbs 10–31*, 509. He notes that the exact boundary between the two parts is uncertain. It is possible that 15:20 ends the unit, although Fox's division takes 15:33 as a pivot verse between the two parts.

36. Fox, *Proverbs 10–31*, 509.

10–29. Do these one-verse sayings appear in random, scattered fashion, or have they been grouped together with a careful, intentional design?

Tremper Longman is one of the leading Proverbs scholars who argues that the proverbs in this part of the book are "arranged in a more or less random fashion, especially with regard to contents."[37] He observes that this is the case with most ancient Near Eastern wisdom collections and that a random collection reflects "the messiness of life." Furthermore, Michael Fox argues that there is "a sweet disorder" in chapters 10–29 with "no overall designs determining the placement of these sayings," even though there are pairs and clusters of proverbs around a shared topic.[38] Rather, he says, "A proverb is like a jewel, and the book of Proverbs is like a heap of jewels. Indeed, it is a heap of different *kinds* of jewels. Is it really such a loss if they are not all laid out in pretty, symmetric designs or divided into neat little piles?"[39]

This raises the question of why the writers of Proverbs did not group all the sayings about anger in one collection, all the proverbs about work in another collection, and so on. Imagine how easy it would be if all the proverbs on material wealth occurred in chapter 10, all the proverbs about speech and words were located in chapter 11, and all the proverbs about friendship resided in chapter 12. Why did the writers avoid this approach? I believe that it tests the reader's resolve to pursue and acquire wisdom. Proverbs 2:4–5 likens the pursuit of wisdom to the pursuit of silver or hidden treasure:

> And if you look for it [wisdom] as for silver
> and search for it as for hidden treasure,
> then you will understand the fear of the LORD
> and find the knowledge of God.

The search for silver in 2:4a may refer to the pursuit of a sulphide ore of lead from which silver is extracted.[40] Or, given its parallelism with the search for hidden treasure in 2:4b, it more likely refers to silver articles such as amulets, jewelry, ornament, or even fine tableware. These kinds of items were constantly recycled.[41] The silver articles might even include

37. Longman, *Proverbs*, 40.
38. Fox, *Proverbs 10–31*, 477.
39. Fox, *Proverbs 10–31*, 481.
40. King and Stager, *Life in Biblical Israel*, 173.
41. King and Stager, *Life in Biblical Israel*, 172.

pieces of wire or small sheets of silver that people carried to pay for goods and services.[42] Any of these silver articles might be the "hidden treasure" in 2:4b. The Hebrew term מַטְמוֹן (*matmon*) is related to the verb טָמַן (*taman*), "hide," which occurs in the Old Testament to describe Jacob hiding earrings under an oak tree (Gen. 35:4), Achan hiding silver under a tent (Josh. 7:21), and lepers hiding items, including silver, that they had pillaged from a military camp (2 Kings 7:8).

Searches for hidden treasure, whether ancient or modern, require an enormous investment of time and energy. In 2010, Forrest Fenn, an artifacts dealer, hid a treasure chest full of jewelry and gold coins, worth about two million dollars, in an undisclosed location in the Rocky Mountains. Then he published a memoir, *The Thrill of the Chase*, which included a 24-line poem with clues as to the whereabouts of the treasure. A decade later, a medical student found it after his two-year search, but not before an estimated 350,000 people searched for it. Some of them quit their jobs on a quest to find the hidden treasure, and five people lost their lives.[43] The arrangement of proverbial sayings in Proverbs 10–29, then, in what seems like a haphazard arrangement, forces us into a painstaking search to uncover what the book of Proverbs has to say about various life issues.

On the other hand, Bruce Waltke is a leading Proverbs scholar who believes that the individual proverbial sayings in chapters 10–29 have been grouped together in clusters with a careful literary design. It's true, he observes, that the sayings in these chapters lack the "normal syntactic links" (conjunctions, particles, pronouns, etc.) that appear in chapters 1–9. This creates the impression that the collection of sayings in this part of the book of Proverbs is "disparate, atomistic, and without coherence."[44] In other words, the sayings appear in random fashion. However, careful attention to the poetics of a text reveals an arrangement of these individual sayings into literary units. By "poetics," Waltke refers to "the author's use of key words, inclusion (i.e., marking off a literary unit by matching the end with the beginning), janus (i.e., linking sections together with a piece of literature that looks backward and forward), catch words that stitch the work together, paronasia (i.e., all sorts of sound plays often connected

---

42. Pehlke, "Metallurgy," 302.
43. See Barbarisi, "Forrest Fenn's Treasure"; Kuta, "Forrest Fenn's Treasure."
44. Waltke, "Proverbs 10:1–16," 161.

with sense), repetition of grammatical forms, chiasms (i.e., by reversing the structure), etc."[45] Thus, we may consider groupings like 10:1–16 and 26:1–12 as literary units, and thus as preaching units.[46]

Which approach should we follow? Perhaps we can have our cake and eat it too. I see merit in both approaches, so we may not need to treat them as exclusionary. In fact, I think that we need both approaches. There is value in grouping individual sayings together and studying what Proverbs 10–29 has to say about anger, friendship, laziness, speech, and so on. Yet, we need to consider how the authors of Proverbs have grouped individual sayings together around a common theme. As Ryan O'Dowd says, "Every saying, by virtue of its poetic nature, has a vagueness that can be taken in more than one way."[47] This means that we should look both at the meaning of a particular saying on its own and at its role in a larger cluster of proverbs. O'Dowd cautions, "There is a danger in pushing this vagueness to the point that we see structures everywhere, making Proverbs 10–29 look like a neat and tidy book. . . . In the end, proverbs are imaginative, poetic creations, full of beauty, wonder, and nuance."[48] So we read with imagination and a sense of wonder. We do not let our imagination run wild, but rather submit it to the poetics of the text. Our goal is to reflect on the beauty and nuance of each saying, and to see how (or if) it is connected to a larger cluster of sayings.

This is a good place to consider a feature of parallelism (see the previous chapter) that comes into play in the verses in the short sayings in the book of Proverbs. I ran into it while working through Bruce Waltke's two-volume commentary on the book of Proverbs. At several points in the commentary, Waltke refers to "imprecise parallelism." This is not another category describing how the lines in a verse, or proverb, work together. Rather, it is the recognition that the imprecise correspondence between elements means that an element in one verset (or line) of a proverb applies to the other verset (line) as well. Consider Proverbs 10:21:

> The lips of the righteous nourish many,
>   but fools die for a lack of sense.

45. Waltke, "Proverbs 10:1–16," 162–63.
46. For an exposition of Prov. 26:1–12, see Waltke, "Interpretation Issues."
47. O'Dowd, *Proverbs*, 31.
48. O'Dowd, *Proverbs*, 31.

Waltke comments, "The imprecision [between the lines] suggests that though the fool is surrounded by the life-preserving words of the righteous that nourish many, he starves to death because he lacks the good sense to feed on them. He can neither receive life nor give it."[49] Conversely, the righteous person will experience life due to their possession of good sense. Another example is Proverbs 15:20:

> A wise son brings joy to this father,
>   but a foolish man despises his mother.

In this proverb, the expressions "brings joy" and "despises" are not a precise match. Thus, they suggest "that a son who makes his parents rejoice does not despise them, and the one who despises them gives them grief"—the opposite of joy.[50]

The Sayings of the Wise (22:17–24:22)

The call to pay attention and listen to the "sayings of the wise" in 22:17 signals a new section. It runs through 24:22, given that 24:23 begins a new section with "These are also sayings of the wise." The proverbial sayings in 22:17–24:22 are full of commands (imperatives) to help the reader live and lead wisely. This section, especially 22:17–23:11, shares some parallels with the Egyptian text Instruction of Amenemope.[51] It is likely, though not certain, that the Egyptian text is older.[52] Whatever the case, the overlap between the contents of Proverbs and Amenemope does not pose a problem for the doctrine of inspiration. Since the book of Proverbs is a God-breathed text (2 Tim. 3:16), the Holy Spirit directed the human author of Proverbs 22:17–24:22 to incorporate wisdom sayings from various wisdom traditions, using the fear of the Lord as a filter or grid. Besides, a careful reading of both Proverbs and Amenemope shows parallels and adaptation, not wholesale borrowing.

---

49. Waltke, *Proverbs: Chapters 1–15*, 472.
50. Waltke, *Proverbs: Chapters 1–15*, 632. For further examples, see Prov. 10:21; 21:26.
51. Waltke, *Proverbs: Chapters 15–31*, 217.
52. Waltke dates this text between 1186 and 1066 BC (*Proverbs: Chapters 15–31*, 217). Goldingay comments, "Our oldest (fragmentary) copies of Amenemope come from a period that might be as late as Solomon's time, so it is logically possible that Amenemope incorporated lines from Proverbs, but it is a stretch, and it is easier to assume that Proverbs adapted phrases from Amenemope or that other examples of Egyptian works are in the background of both" (*Proverbs*, 296).

Further Sayings of the Wise (24:23–34)

This brief section opens with the line "These are also sayings of the wise" (24:23). There are no hints inside or outside this text as to the identity of these sages. The section begins with a call for justice in legal proceedings (24:23–29) and ends with "an extended satire on lazy people."[53] It is also possible to view the contents of this section as instructions on "behavior in court" and "behavior at work"—that is, justice and work as two spheres of life.[54]

More Proverbs of Solomon Compiled by Hezekiah's Men (25:1–29:27)

Proverbs 25–29 consists of "more proverbs of Solomon, compiled by the men of Hezekiah king of Judah" (25:1). Although Hezekiah (who reigned from 715 to 687 BC) had "lapses in good judgment," he was known for his devotion to God.[55] The Hebrew term עתק (*'tq*), translated as "compiled" (NIV) or "copied" (ESV, CSB), means "move" or "remove."[56] This pictures a team of sages in Hezekiah's court moving some of Solomon's three thousand proverbs (see 1 Kings 4:32) from one source to this collection. Although the book of Proverbs shows an "openness to learning from other peoples" outside of Israel, "the reference to work by Hezekiah's people points to ongoing work in Jerusalem by people collecting sayings."[57]

The Sayings of Agur (30:1–33)

According to Proverbs 30:1, the contents of this chapter come from "Agur son of Jakeh" and are directed to "Ithiel."[58] The identities of these people are unknown to us. What is striking about this chapter is how Agur's wisdom differs from the previous sections of Proverbs. It has an autobiographical flavor, a tone of humility, extended reflections on various aspects of nature, and an awareness of the disordered world in which we

---

53. Longman, *Proverbs*, 443.

54. Waltke, *Proverbs: Chapters 1–15*, 24–25. See also Goldingay, *Proverbs*, 321.

55. Longman, *Proverbs*, 449. See 2 Kings 18–20; 2 Chron. 29–32; Isa. 36–39.

56. This is its meaning when it appears in the Hiphil stem, as it does in Prov. 25:1. See *HALOT*.

57. Goldingay, *Proverbs*, 293.

58. There is a challenging issue with the text of Prov. 30:1. The words translated as verbs at the end of the verse, "I am weary, God, but I can prevail" (NIV), may also be understood as nouns, and thus translated as "to Ithiel and Ukal." The NASB, CSB, NJPS, NET, and KJV all follow this approach.

live.[59] Ryan O'Dowd suggests that Proverbs 30 reads more like Ecclesiastes than the rest of Proverbs.[60] He also observes that Proverbs 30–31, along with chapters 1–9, function as the outer frame of highly structured poems, enclosing the "free collection of sayings inside."[61]

The Sayings That King Lemuel's Mother Taught Him (31:1–9)

I often refer to this text as "the other Proverbs 31 woman." At first read, this text sounds like a rather crass appeal neither to chase women nor to drink beer. Yet it's a remarkable challenge from a mother to her son—who is or will become king—about using his privileges to serve the poor and destitute rather than to satisfy his desires. The three references to her son in verse 2 (literally, "what, my son; and what, son of my womb; and what, son of my vows") along with the three negative particles in verses 3–4 heighten the urgency, suggesting that "Lemuel has already done wrong and his mother is imploring him to cease."[62] We have no clue as to the identity of Lemuel.[63] Tremper Longman's observation is notable: "This is the only place where we actually hear the voice of the mother independently of that of the father."[64] I will have more to say later in this chapter about preaching this incredible text.

The Wife of Noble Character (31:10–31)

The final section of the book of Proverbs is an acrostic poem that presents a final picture of what wisdom looks like fleshed out in a person's life. As an acrostic, the first letter of the first word of each verse begins

59. O'Dowd, *Proverbs*, 396–97.
60. O'Dowd, *Proverbs*, 397.
61. O'Dowd, *Proverbs*, 29.
62. Fox, *Proverbs 10–31*, 885.
63. "Traditional commentators identified Lemuel with Solomon" (Fox, *Proverbs 10–31*, 884), although this is simply speculation. Waltke surmises that the name "Lemuel" is probably a long form of "Lael," which means "belonging to God." Then he says, "Since such a king is unattested in Israel's history, he is probably a proselyte to Israel's faith" (*Proverbs: Chapters 15–31*, 502–3). Waltke also suggests that Lemuel's mother is also the author of the poem in verses 10–31, since "it lacks a superscription ascribing its authorship"—something that is common to all previous sections in the book of Proverbs. Of course, the style of both poems is different. Yet, "diverse poems with unique forms do not prove different authorship" (502). However, Longman cautions against seeing too close a connection between the two poems and argues that it is best to "treat these two poems as separate rather than intentionally linked"; he particularly notes, "I do not think the noble woman [in 31:10–31] is intended to provide an alternate choice to the women to whom the king might inappropriately give his strength (v. 3)" (*Proverbs*, 537).
64. Longman, *Proverbs*, 538.

with the next letter of the Hebrew alphabet. In English, the approach would look like this, with the first word of each new line beginning with successive letters of the English alphabet:

> A wife of noble character who can find?
> Beauty flows from her inner being.
> Charm is deceitful, but she fears the LORD.
> Daily she opens her arms to the poor and cares for the needy. (etc.)

The surprising feature is that the grand finale to the book chooses a woman to be the exemplar of wisdom rather than a crown prince or a successful king. She is an אֵשֶׁת־חַיִל (*'eshet-hayil*), a "woman of might" (31:10).[65] She is an ideal wife, but also she is a model for both women and men to aspire to. She is wise in her actions and attitudes, industrious, and cares for the poor and afflicted as well as for her family.[66] To top it all off, she is one who fears the Lord (31:30). Thus, the book of Proverbs ends where it begins: the fear of the Lord as the foundation of wise living.

The above survey of the structure of Proverbs touched on most of the key issues that preachers need to understand for interpreting and proclaiming the book of Proverbs: the nature of wisdom, the book's target audience, the book's literary strategy, the book's theological purpose, the arrangement of the saying in chapters 10–29 (randomly scattered versus intentionally grouped), the relationship with the wisdom texts of the ancient Near East, and the role of the final poem in the book—the "Proverbs 31 woman" in 31:10–31. Now we can turn our attention to preaching strategies.

Preaching Strategies

In my experience, believers have heard fewer sermons on Proverbs than we might suspect. If they have heard any Proverbs text expounded, it's likely to have been in a Mother's Day sermon on Proverbs 31:10–31. So, we need to think strategically about how to preach this vibrant book. Before we think about a sermon series or how to outline a sermon on Proverbs, we

---

65. O'Dowd points out the contrast between the prohibition of giving *hayil* ("strength") to women in 31:3 with the woman of *hayil* ("strength") in 31:10, 29 (*Proverbs*, 420).
66. Longman, *Proverbs*, 540–41.

will do well to think about some of the key concepts or concerns that we
will need to address.

Key Concepts or Concerns

There are at least five key concepts or concerns that preachers will
wish to communicate—in addition to the features discussed above in the
survey of the book—when preaching from Proverbs: (1) the definition of
a proverbial saying; (2) the fact that proverbs are not promises; (3) the apparent contradiction in 26:4–5; (4) the challenge of proverbs advocating
physical discipline; (5) "the Proverbs 31 woman."

The Definition of a Proverbial Saying

We will do well to help our listeners understand the basics of a proverbial saying. Years ago, one of my seminary Hebrew professors, Ronald
Allen, defined a "proverbial saying" as "a *condensation* of a truth, stated
in *memorable* fashion, and *transferrable* to many situations in life." Let's
take those one at a time.

First, a proverbial saying is *condensed*. A quick glance at the pages in
my Hebrew Bible in Proverbs 11 and 14—the chapters to which I randomly
opened while writing this paragraph—shows that most proverbs have between six and eight words. Many of have them seven, a perfect number! It
takes a few more words to translate these proverbs into English, but most
proverbs in chapters 11 and 14 have eleven to fifteen words. You could write
a thousand-page essay on any of these proverbs. Yet they are distilled into
a few words. In fact, the English word "proverb" comes from a combination of two Latin words: *pro* ("for") and *verba* ("words"). The idea is that
the short saying is "for" or "in place of" words—perhaps many words.

Second, a proverbial saying is *memorable*. This is due, in part, to the
brevity or condensed nature of a proverb. As noted earlier, a string of
similar sounds (a technique known as assonance) or parallel syntax (word
order) gets lost in translation. But it's still easy to remember "A gentle
answer turns away wrath, but a harsh word stirs up anger" (Prov. 15:1)
because it is succinct. The parallelism helps us too.

Finally, a proverbial saying is *transferable* to many situations in life. We
are already familiar with this because of popular English proverbs. We
know that "A stitch in time saves nine" refers not just to sewing but to
other areas of life. If we don't take care of a small oil leak in our vehicle

or deal with a small disagreement with a friend, those problems can grow exponentially bigger and more difficult (or expensive) to fix. The same applies to the proverbial sayings in the book of Proverbs. For example, the admonition "Be sure you know the condition of your flocks, give careful attention to your herds" so that "the lambs will provide you with clothing, and the goats with the price of a field" (Prov. 27:23–27) applies beyond the world of animal husbandry. The idea is to care for the asset that enables you to make a living. That might be a fleet of vehicles, an up-to-date spreadsheet, or the relationships you have developed with potential clients.

Next we look at another concept or concern related to proverbial sayings, one that is more difficult for some listeners to accept.

Proverbs Are Not Promises

While preachers are not "shock jocks," I believe it is wise to make this provocative statement to our listeners when we preach the proverbial sayings in the book: proverbs are not promises. This in no way diminishes the fact that they are part of God's inspired Word. Rather, this is a literary observation. When we read the Bible, we must read it on its own terms. Proverbial sayings are observations about the way life works over and over again. Kathryn Dell's insights are helpful here: "The proverbs do not provide absolutes or universally valid generalizations; rather, they offer limited maxims or partial generalizations."[67] This means that a particular proverb is not an ironclad guarantee. For instance, I have friends who have trained up their children in the way they should go (Prov. 22:6), and those children have departed from it—at least until this point.[68] Similarly, there may be times when a gentle answer does *not* turn away wrath (per Prov. 15:1) or when a godly son or daughter who obeys their parents does not live a long life (per Prov. 3:1–2).

Years ago, I did the memorial service for a teen in our church family who was killed in a driver's education car accident. He was a young man who loved Christ and loved his family—an example of what we all hope our children will become. Yet his life was tragically cut short through no

---

67. Dell, *Proverbs*, 136.

68. I am aware of the various interpretations of "the way they should go" (דַּרְכּוֹ, literally, "his way"), but I still hold to the traditional interpretation that the reference here is to a moral way, not to a child's particular natural tendencies or "bent." See Waltke, *Proverbs: Chapters 15–31*, 203–6; Longman, *Proverbs*, 404; Fox, *Proverbs 10–31*, 698. See Prov. 21:19, where the same expression ("his/their way") appears with the same moral overtones.

fault of his own. Does this make Proverbs 3:1–2 untrue? No, that proverbial saying is an observation about how life works over and over again. This will be hard for some of our listeners—and perhaps for some of us preachers—to accept. We want a guarantee that if we live the right way, we will experience the right outcomes. But sometimes life does not work like that, and it is why we have wisdom books like Job. It is wise to live by the basic "rule," though, rather than fretting about the exceptions.

The Apparent Contradiction in Proverbs 26:4–5

Honestly, this probably will not be an issue with your listeners. But it was a problem in the Middle Ages when a few rabbis questioned whether Proverbs was canonical, given the obvious contradiction between the two back-to-back sayings in 26:4–5. Raising this concern and responding to it will help your listeners understand how proverbial sayings work—even though it is doubtful they will question the integrity of Proverbs. Anyway, the problem is not difficult to spot.

> Do not answer a fool according to his folly,
>   or you yourself will be just like him.
> Answer a fool according to his folly,
>   or he will be wise in his own eyes. (Prov. 26:4–5)

"Which is it?" asks Tremper Longman. "It depends on the circumstance. One must not only know the proverbs but also be able to read the people and the circumstance to know which applies."[69] Is this a situation in which engaging a fool in discussion or debate will make a fool out of you? Or is there a chance that this particular fool in this particular situation might listen? There is a need to "know your fool."[70] This proverb pair might be especially helpful when considering whether or not to jump into a debate on social media.

The Challenge of Proverbs Advocating Physical Discipline

A further minefield in Proverbs is the book's teaching on physical discipline. It does not mince words, claiming that the use of the rod on a

---

69. Longman, *Proverbs*, 31.
70. However, Waltke argues that "both proverbs are absolutes and applicable at the same time" rather than "relative to the situation" (*Proverbs: Chapters 15–31*, 349).

child is an act of love (13:24), that the rod will drive folly out of the heart of a child (22:15), that striking a child with the rod will not kill them but will save them from death (23:13), and that a rod gives wisdom (29:15). The question is whether the "rod of discipline" statements in Proverbs are "figurative, implying stern discipline indeed but not necessarily physical contact,"[71] or literal, meaning that we take them at face value and envision a wooden spoon or paddle—like the one that hung in the principal's office in the public grade school I attended. (Full disclosure: I saw this paddle on display, but the principal never used it on me.)

I believe we must resist any temptation to question the integrity of believers who take Scripture seriously and come down on different sides of this issue. Whatever view we take, we must be mindful of those who have been traumatized and harmed, either physically or emotionally, by physical discipline gone wild. One of my grandfathers walked with a stoop due to beatings he received from his alcoholic father.[72] This kind of behavior is inexcusable, and Proverbs does not condone it. Those who do not "spare the rod" must use it sparingly and never when angry. A child psychologist who is a committed believer told me years ago that spanking should be reserved only for willful disobedience.[73] Those who believe that the "rod" statements in Proverbs are figurative must not shy away from discipline in general.

Elaine Phillips is helpful here. She notes that while the statements about the use of the rod in Proverbs sound "harsh—even tyrannical and outdated," we must realize that "love is a major part of the disciplinary process. Not to discipline means, in effect, hating the child."[74] I want to highlight two further observations she makes. First, she says, "If our home life is shaped by loving and consistent boundaries, if expectations are clear, if we pray that we discipline in love and not in a burst of anger, if we pray for wisdom to discipline with the appropriate measure, if we confess to our children when *we* step over the boundaries that constrain us as well as them, and if we are quick to forgive and embrace repentant children, then we trust in the effectiveness of this process."[75] Second, she

71. Phillips, *Wisdom Texts*, 93.
72. I feel free to share this tragic, painful situation, since my grandfather and great-grandfather have been gone for many years.
73. I am not providing any documentation for this conversation for this psychologist's protection and for the fact that it took place several years ago.
74. Phillips, *Wisdom Texts*, 94.
75. Phillips, *Wisdom Texts*, 94.

warns against verbal abuse, noting that it can create "irreparable inner damage." She says, "Thoughtless and harsh words are not less destructive than ill-administered swats." Then, she notes that "these 'rod' verses do not condone uncontrolled and violent outbursts."[76]

"The Proverbs 31 Woman"

Perhaps no less controversial is the matter of preaching on "the Proverbs 31 woman." Actually, there are *two* women in Proverbs 31, unless you believe that the mother of King Lemuel stands behind both sections, verses 1–9 and 10–31. Both texts present their own unique challenges. Let me build on the observations I made about these texts earlier and talk about preaching them. Here are several suggestions and observations.

First, if you want to challenge and encourage your listeners on Mother's Day, consider preaching Proverbs 31:1–9 rather than Proverbs 31:10–31.[77] I suspect that the title of a book from four decades ago still resonates with a lot of women today: *The Proverbs 31 Lady and Other Impossible Dreams*.[78] I am not suggesting that we avoid Proverbs 31:10–31. I'll have more to say about it in a moment. But how about surprising your congregation with a sermon on "the other Proverbs 31 woman." Recently, I assigned Proverbs 31:1–9 to a seminary class on preaching the literature of the Old Testament, and I asked them to prepare a Mother's Day sermon on it. One of the students emailed to inform me of my "error," noting that the text should have been Proverbs 31:10–31. This reminded me how unfamiliar we are with Proverbs 31:1–9, a marvelous text in its own right. It can provide encouragement and a gentle challenge for mothers to teach their sons and daughters to use their privileges to serve those in need rather than to serve their own selfish desires.

Second, consider preaching Proverbs 31:10–31 on Father's Day. I'm serious, and I plan to do this the next time I have an opportunity to preach on Father's Day. The point is to show that the woman in Proverbs 31:10–31

---

76. Phillips, *Wisdom Texts*, 94.

77. I am not suggesting that you need to preach a Mother's Day sermon on Mother's Day. Over the years, there were women in every congregation I pastored who shared with me that they disliked gathering with the church for worship on Mother's Day. Some simply could not do so because of the pain of not having children, or the loss of their mother, or the difficulties they were facing in parenting their children.

78. The author was Marsha Drake, and the book was published in 1984 by Bethany House. I have not read it.

is a model of wisdom for women and men. Of course, I do not wish to diminish the woman's role as a wife and mother. Yet the final poem of the book does more than point out the kind of women that men should look to marry. Unfortunately, this lovely poem sometimes gets reduced to that and becomes an unwitting weapon. Many years ago, a young man in a class I taught on Proverbs proclaimed rather loudly that he was holding out for a "Proverbs 31 woman." I could tell that he was making women in the class uncomfortable, so one day I asked him if the woman he was hoping to marry was going to get a "Proverbs 1–30 man." Upon further reflection, I should have said a "Proverbs 1–31 man" because both poems in Proverbs 31 speak to men, directly (vv. 1–9) and indirectly (vv. 10–31).

Third, when you preach Proverbs 31:10–31, point out the possibilities and opportunities that wisdom provides rather than setting up the poem as a list of unrealistic expectations. I believe that the examples picture a woman who is resourceful in using her varied gifts. It's not that every woman needs to sew (see 31:13a, 19). My wife sewed our young children's clothes for a while, but neither of my adult daughters sew. Yet one of them spent several years teaching English to Chinese students online at 5:00 a.m. several times a week, and she is also an event planner. If there is mending to be done, her husband does it! Another daughter has served as a secretary for a local Christian ministry and now works in a health clinic. In her spare time she volunteers at the local grade school where her children are students. The point is, you don't have to sew to be a "Proverbs 31 woman." My daughters embody the kind of wisdom described in Proverbs 31:10–31, yet the details in their lives look different. Again, I believe that this poem is full of examples, not demands. My maternal grandmother and my paternal grandfather got up early and worked hard in their vegetable gardens. I have not planted a garden in three decades, but I do not berate myself for that. So be careful how you present the descriptions in this acrostic poem. Notice, too, that while the woman in Proverbs 31:10–31 centers her activities in her home (see 31:13–19, 21–22, 27), she works "outside" her home. She is involved in real estate (v. 16a), farming (v. 16b), and manufacturing and commerce (v. 24). It's wise to remind mothers—and fathers—that the way they care for their families changes with the seasons of life. Our churches need to hear Proverbs 31, but we need to preach it with sensitivity to the text and to our listeners.

Ideas for Sermons and Series

Prior to preaching a series on the book of Proverbs, I recommend reading and rereading the book several months in advance. One way to do this, often attributed to evangelist Billy Graham, is to read a chapter a day so that you can cover the book in roughly one month. It is worth doing this for a couple months in a row. Then, devote another month or series of months to a deeper dive into particular sections or themes in the book. A couple years ago, I put together a plan for reading Proverbs 10–31 in two years at the rate of one verse a day. You can read through chapters 10–20 in 328 days, and you can do the same for chapters 21–31 in 331 days. This gives you some margin if you take a day off per week or if you miss some days. Then, pair your reading of a daily proverb with a commentary. For two years, I read a verse (proverb) in my Hebrew Bible daily and then read the Proverbs commentary in Bruce Waltke's volumes in the New International Commentary on the Old Testament. It was an enriching experience. Some days, I wrote out the proverb on a three-by-five card and put it in a pocket to refer to it later (old school). Other days, I took a screen shot of the proverb in my Bible app on my smartphone to review later (new school). I also looked at the day's proverb in the translations by Robert Alter (*The Hebrew Bible: A Translation with Commentary*), Eugene Peterson (*The Message*), and John Goldingay (*The First Testament: A New Translation*). Another useful resource is *A Proverb a Day in Biblical Hebrew* by Jonathan Kline. He compiled and arranged a year's worth of proverbs (365) from Proverbs 10:1–22:16. Rather than presenting them in canonical order, Kline arranged them from the highest to the lowest number of frequently occurring words. This makes it easier to learn the vocabulary of the book of Proverbs as you read one proverb a day.

If you do not work with biblical Hebrew, read the day's verse in two or three English translations besides the one you usually use. The NET Bible should be one of them because its notes explain succinctly the various translation issues in a text.[79]

When it comes to planning a sermon series, shorter series seem to be the norm in the Western church these days. One approach is to cover the "entire" book in an eight-to-ten-week (two-month) series, devoting four messages to chapters 1–9 and then four to six messages on chapters 10–31.

79. You can access the NET Bible online at netbible.org.

For example, here is the outline of an eight-week series that we (myself and a couple other pastoral staff members) recently preached at our church.

- 1:1–7
- 3:1–12
- 5:1–23
- 8:1–22
- Emotional pain
- Decisions
- Words (speech)
- Conflict (handling/minimizing)

Obviously, I could have chosen different texts from chapters 1–9, although I strongly suggest preaching 1:1–7 as the first message. Further, I could have substituted texts like 10:1–16 or 26:1–12 in place of the topics. A good way of wrapping up this series (thus stretching it to nine or ten weeks) is to preach Proverbs 31—either the final poem in verses 10–31 or both poems (vv. 1–9 and 10–31) separately in two weeks or together in one week.[80]

Proverbs 30 is also fertile ground for a brief sermon series. One way is to preach the chapter in two sermons. The first, on verses 1–14, can focus on how to handle the massive gap between our understanding and God's understanding. To use Ryan O'Dowd's language, this section of the chapter describes "humble wisdom for a fallen world."[81] After verses 1–4 describe the problem—the massive gap described above—verses 5–6 present the solution: human beings need to take refuge in the words of God. This becomes the sermon's big idea. Agur cites both David (Ps. 18:30) and Moses (Deut. 4:2) to argue for the reliability and authority of God's words. Verses 7–9 follow this with a prayer, requesting that God spare us from the sin and circumstances that turn us away from his words. Finally, verses 10–14 function as a warning: those who reject God's words become part of a corrupt generation. I used to describe these verses as "snapshots." Now I describe them as "selfies." They are "selfies" of a corrupt generation. The second sermon, on verses 15–33, can focus on how

---

80. For a fine example of how to preach a single sermon on Prov. 31:1–31, see Ingrid Faro's sermon transcript in Alcántara, *Proverbs*, 191–202.

81. O'Dowd, *Proverbs*, 401.

to live for God's honor and our good. The various poems in this section recap some of the major themes of Proverbs.

- Avoid greed because getting more will never satisfy (vv. 15–17).
- Do not treat God's amazing gift of sex casually (vv. 18–20).
- Do not disrupt the stability of your home by creating misery (vv. 21–23).
- Learn how to overcome weakness and where to find strength (vv. 24–31).
- Do not be a troublemaker who makes trouble for yourself (vv. 32–33).

Of course, there is value in preaching the entire book of Proverbs. This will likely mean splitting it into multiple sermon series. You can preach chapters 1–9 in ten weeks, devoting a week to each chapter plus a week at the beginning to the prologue in 1:1–7. Then, you can break up chapters 10–29 into texts or topics—an issue I discussed previously. Personally, I have followed both approaches, and both were well received. The topics in chapters 10–29 are legion. Here are some of the topics on which I have preached over the years from these chapters (in alphabetical order with abbreviations).

- Anger (AR)
- Conflict (CF)
- Decision-making (DM)
- Friendship (FD)
- Generosity (GN)
- Grief/heartache (GR)
- Parenting (PR)
- Wealth (WE)
- Words/speech (SP)
- Work (WK)

The best way to find the scattered proverbs on these topics is to read through chapters 10–29 and label each one using the abbreviations in my list. Also, Tremper Longman has a terrific list of topics and the verses that go with them in the "Topical Studies" appendix at the end of his commentary.[82] It may be worth the price of the book. If you plan to preach through textual units, I propose following the breakdown in Bruce Waltke's commentary in chapters 10–29 and then taking one section of chapters at a time. My suggestion is to group the chapters into these units for the purpose of sermon series:

- 10–14
- 15:1–22:16
- 22:17–24:34
- 25–29

A few years ago, I preached chapters 25–29 in nine weeks, breaking it down into the following preaching units and topics:

- 25:1–15: Leadership/workplace lessons
- 25:16–27: Conflict (handling and understanding it)
- 26:1–12: The fool
- 26:13–28: Problem people
- 27:1–22: Friends and friendship
- 28:1–11: Contrasting lifestyles: discernment
- 28:12–28: Godliness as a means of gain (ruling, wealth)
- 29:1–15: Dealing with the poor and humble
- 29:16–27: Relationships

On occasion, it can be quite effective to preach a sermon on a single proverb. This models how to meditate and reflect deeply on a particular saying. It amounts to putting a proverb under a microscope. The well-known proverb about childrearing in 22:6 is a candidate. So is Proverbs 3:5–6. One of the most effective sermons I preached on a single proverb was on Proverbs 18:24.

> One who has unreliable friends soon comes to ruin,
>   but there is a friend who sticks closer than a brother.

82. Longman, *Proverbs*, 549–78.

My title for this sermon was simply "Why You Need Friendship." This proverb is built on a contrast between the two lines. The first line affirms that it is destructive to lack close friendships. Here, I pointed out that the NIV's "unreliable friends" are actually "many friends"—thus, a lot of acquaintances. It is like having over a thousand Facebook friends. You can have that many "friends" and find yourself ruined. The Hebrew verb (רעע, r‘) translated as "unreliable" or "comes to ruin" means "shattered." It has a similar sound to the Hebrew term for "friend, companion" (רֵעַ, re‘a), so that explains why some versions translate it as "shew himself friendly" (KJV) or "play at friendship" (NRSV). The contrast between the lines helps us understand why a person with many friends can be shattered. It's because casual friends or acquaintances will not come running when trouble hits. The second line affirms that a close friend—"one who loves" in the Hebrew—is more loyal to you than a sibling. Thus, this was the big idea of the sermon: "You need friendship because a close friend is more loyal than a sibling."

Preaching Christ in Proverbs

When we preach the instruction of Proverbs and its wise observations about how life works, we must not fail to point to Christ, the one "in whom are hidden all the treasures of wisdom and knowledge" (Col. 2:3). We can live the way the book of Proverbs calls us to live only as believers whose lives are hidden with Christ in God (Col. 3:3). Jesus himself provides a helpful link to Proverbs when he claims that the Queen of the South will condemn "this generation" because "she came from the ends of the earth to listen to Solomon's wisdom, and now something greater than Solomon is here" (Matt. 12:42). Below is an example of how to preach Christ in the book of Proverbs without obscuring the intent of the text. It is from my conclusion to the sermon I preached on Proverbs 18:24.

> Even a friend who sticks closer than a brother might betray you. And let's face it. We will all fail in some ways to be a Proverbs 18:24 kind of friend. However, there is one person who has called us "friend" who will never let us down, and that person is Jesus Christ.
> When Jesus explained his death to his disciples on the eve of that death, one of the images he used was friendship. In John 15:13, he said, "Greater love has no one than this: to lay down one's life for one's friends." In fact,

the gospel—the good news that Jesus died, rose, and reigns as king—has a wonderful effect on our friendships. The gospel teaches us how to be a friend. Do you struggle with forgiveness? Then forgive others as Christ forgave you (Eph. 4:32). Do you struggle with serving your friends? Then have the servant's attitude that Christ had (Phil. 2:6).

This is a good place to remember that we enter this friendship through faith. James 2:23 says, "Abraham believed God, and it was credited to him as righteousness." Furthermore, that verse says that "he was called God's friend." That is how you become a friend of God!

As important as it is to ask, "Do I have close friends?" or "Do I do what it takes to be a close friend?" the most important questions to ask are, "Am I a friend of God? Does he call me friend?"

A commitment to connecting Proverbs to the person of Jesus does not preclude us from instructing our listeners on how to live. Nor does our commitment to instructing our listeners on how to live preclude us from focusing on Jesus. The point is not to find Jesus in some detail in Proverbs or to make an obligatory tip of the cap to Jesus. Rather, it is to show how the wisdom of Proverbs culminates in Jesus and requires Jesus for living it out faithfully.

Helpful Resources for Studying and Preaching

Fortunately, there are great resources available for preaching Proverbs. For commentaries, the three I believe that every preacher should have are the volumes by Bruce Waltke (New International Commentary on the Old Testament), Tremper Longman (Baker Commentary on the Old Testament Wisdom and Psalms), and Michael Fox (Anchor Yale Bible). An alternative to Bruce Waltke's two volumes in the New International Commentary on the Old Testament is the abridgment he did with the assistance of his former student, Ivan De Silva. Their volume, *Proverbs: A Shorter Commentary*, is about half the size of Waltke's two-volume set. Thus, it might be more useful to preachers. One of the most helpful shorter commentaries for preachers is Lindsay Wilson's volume in the Tyndale Old Testament Commentaries. It has a list of topics and even suggestions for preachers. The shorter commentaries by Ryan O'Dowd (Story of God Bible Commentary), who is a pastor-scholar, and Derek Kidner (Tyndale Old Testament Commentaries; Kidner Classic Commentaries) are helpful too. Other useful commentaries on Proverbs include those by John Goldingay (Commentaries for Christian Formation), Allen Ross (Expositor's Bible Commentary), and Paul Koptak (NIV Application Commentary). Ray Ortlund's volume in the Preaching the Word series, *Proverbs: Wisdom That Works*, is a fine set of expositions on chapters 1–9 and then on various topics in the second half of the book. The chapters are essentially sermon manuscripts.

The Bible Project resources on Proverbs are excellent. This includes the Book Overview video on Proverbs as well as the video on Proverbs in the Wisdom Series videos in the Book Collections.[83]

As far as other helpful resources, I highly recommend Jared Alcántara's book *How to Preach Proverbs*. It delivers what its title promises. Also, Elaine Phillips provides some terrific chapters on Proverbs in her book *An Introduction to Reading Biblical Wisdom Texts*. For those with a scholarly bent, Katherine Dell's volume *The Theology of the Book of Proverbs* is an excellent resource. For a devotional journey through Proverbs, get a copy of *God's Wisdom for Navigating Life*, by Timothy and Kathy Keller.

---

83. You can access these resources at https://bibleproject.com/.

4

Preaching Job

Many years ago, a man watched his wife suffer with cancer and then die. Afterward, he wrote down the thoughts he had about her suffering and about God. His name was C. S. Lewis. In his little book of reflections, *A Grief Observed*, he wrote, "Not that I am (I think) in much danger of ceasing to believe in God. The real danger is of coming to believe such dreadful things about Him. The conclusion I dread is not 'So there's no God after all,' but 'So this is what God's really like. Deceive yourself no longer.'"[1]

Suffering disorients us. If we have tried to live according to the book of Proverbs, we are tempted to question God's goodness, justice, and love when we suffer. God promises to bless the righteous with prosperity and long life, right? When life does not turn out the way that Proverbs leads us to believe it will, we can end up cynical or in despair. The way we feel resembles the angst in Billy Joel's 1982 song "Allentown," which reflected on the decline of the steel industry in Pennsylvania's Lehigh Valley. One verse talks about waiting in Allentown for "the promises our teachers gave if we worked hard, if we behaved."

This is where the book of Job can provide us with tremendous help. It is a wonderful resource for believers who are suffering. Even though it never explains why the righteous suffer, it helps us understand God's character in a world where suffering abounds and afflicts even righteous, godly people.

---

1. Lewis, *A Grief Observed*, 6–7.

Yet, when we start reading the book of Job, we soon get bogged down in what seems like endless back-and-forth arguments between Job and his friends about his suffering. It is interesting at first, but soon gets tedious. However, I believe that this is part of the literary strategy of the book. I'll explain this shortly. Reading and preaching Job require patience. But it is well worth the effort. If Proverbs tells us how to live so that life goes smoothly, Job tells us how to live when life falls apart.

Studying Job

The best way to understand the book of Job and the challenging interpretive issues it presents is to work through the book to discern its structure and flow. Below is an overview of the book of Job. The outline I have provided in table 4.1 reflects my understanding of its structure.[2] While the book of Job is framed by a narrative epilogue and prologue, the core of the book, 3:1 through 42:6, is poetry. We will work through each section to understand the argument of the book of Job and to think through the interpretive challenges it presents.

Table 4.1

An Overview of the Book of Job

> Narrative prologue: The testing of Job (chaps. 1–2)
> Dialogues: Job and his friends (chaps. 3–27)
>> Job's lament (chap. 3)
>> Cycle 1: Admit you're wrong and deal with your sin (chaps. 4–14)
>> Cycle 2: Consider the fate of the wicked, for you are one of them (chaps. 15–21)
>> Cycle 3: God is rebuking you for your great wickedness (chaps. 22–27)
> Interlude: Wisdom hymn (chap. 28)
> Speeches: Job, Elihu, and the Lord (29:1–42:6)
>> Job's speech (chaps. 29–31)
>> Elihu's speech (chaps. 32–37)
>> The Lord's speeches (38:1–40:2; 40:6–41:34)
>> Job's responses (40:3–5; 42:1–6)
> Narrative epilogue: The blessing of Job (42:7–17)

2. My understanding has been influenced mainly by Andersen, *Job*, 17–19; Hartley, *Job*, ix; Walton, *Job*, 49. I have adapted my outline from theirs.

Narrative Prologue: The Testing of Job (Chaps. 1–2)

Narrative sections at the beginning and end of the book provide a frame. The initial narrative frame introduces us to a man whose name is Job. We know little about him except that he was extremely godly and wealthy (1:1–3). His customary offering of sacrifices on behalf of his children, after their feasting, reflects godliness but also some misunderstanding about God (1:4–5). John Walton explains, "Job's repeated rituals do not suggest that he considered his children to be closet apostates hurling drunken insults heavenward. Instead, he considered that anytime such revelry occurred, the possibility existed that unguarded statements could be made that deity would take offense at despite the innocent intentions of the speaker. . . . Job's behavior demonstrates an appeasement mentality toward an overly sensitive deity."[3] I believe that this foreshadows Job's understanding of God that surfaces in the dialogues with his friends.

In the next scene, Satan shows up, along with members of the divine council, and has a conversation with the Lord (1:6–12). There has been much discussion about the identity of "Satan" in the book of Job. The Hebrew word שָׂטָן (satan) means "adversary, opponent."[4] In the Old Testament, this term can be used in reference to human military or political opponents. For example, the Philistine commanders applied the word to David (1 Sam. 29:4), and Solomon used the term in reference to having no adversary due to the rest from enemy attacks provided by the Lord (1 Kings 5:4). Furthermore, even the angel of the Lord used the word of himself, describing himself as an adversary to Balaam (Num. 22:22, 32). Thus, there is a dispute as to whether הַשָּׂטָן (ha-satan), "the adversary," is simply a legitimate challenger whose role is to promote the general good or whether he is the "evil one" described in the New Testament.[5] Whatever the case, he plays a small but important role in the drama. After raising

---

3. Walton, *Job*, 62.

4. *HALOT*.

5. Walton concludes that although "interpreters commonly portray the Challenger as one who seeks out human failings, God's policies are the true focus of the challenge" (*Job*, 66). Walton believes that "we are not in a position to claim that the Challenger in Job should be identified with Satan as we know him in the New Testament. One cannot make the claim that they act the same way. In fact, there is little if any overlap between their two profiles. This does not prove that they are not the same individual; it merely reduces (if not eliminates) the basis for claiming that they must be equated" (67). On the other hand, Bill Kynes and Will Kynes view the accuser in Job as one who stands against God's people in some way and whose implicit hostility toward God "becomes explicit in the New Testament" (*Job*, 24, 32). For further

the question with which the book of Job is preoccupied and then, with the Lord's permission, afflicting the character Job, the adversary disappears from the stage.[6]

The question raised by Satan in 1:9 is what drives the drama and the dialogue in the book of Job: "Does Job fear God for nothing?" Satan goes on in 1:10–11 to argue that if God withheld his blessing and protection, Job would curse God to his face. So, then, Satan is questioning God's policy of allowing righteous people to prosper, suggesting that they serve God out of self-interest—only for what God gives them rather than for who God is. Bill Kynes and Will Kynes paraphrase the book of Job's central question like this: "In other words, is there really such a thing as a true believer? Aren't all those religious people just in it for the divine blessings? This raises an even more pressing question: Is there really a true God? Is there a God who is worthy of our worship, our love, our trust—regardless of the circumstances?"[7] This is the concern of the book of Job.

Two observations are worth noting here. First, we, the readers, know why Job is suffering, but Job does not. And God never tells him why. Job's suffering is a mystery to him. Second, this is a unique test—like God's test of Abraham (Gen. 22:1)—and is not a commonplace occurrence in the Old Testament.[8]

In the remainder of the narrative epilogue (1:13–2:10), Satan inflicts horrific emotional and physical pain on Job, though within the limits set by the Lord. After Job's first round of suffering, he worships, blesses Yahweh, and does not sin by charging God with wrong (1:20–22). Then, after Job's second round of suffering, he refuses to curse God and does not sin (2:10). So, in response to his crushing circumstances, Job demonstrates that God himself, and not his reward, is reason enough for people to trust God. This

---

discussion, see the chapter "Who Is 'Satan' in Job?" in Walton and Longman, *Job*, 50–56. I will adopt the practice of most English versions and simply refer to הַשָּׂטָן (*ha-satan*) as "Satan."

6. The last mention of הַשָּׂטָן (*ha-satan*), "the adversary," in the book is in Job 2:7. Walton and Longman conclude, "The challenger is only present in the first two chapters of Job and could therefore be considered a minor character were it not for the fact that he is the catalyst for the scenario that unfolds. He does not stand as an antagonist throughout the book, nor does he have a curtain call at the end. He plays his launching role and then disappears as the story plays out in his wake" (*Job*, 50).

7. Kynes and Kynes, *Job*, 20.

8. Of course, the New Testament tells us that Satan prowls about like a lion, looking for someone to devour (1 Pet. 5:8). Yet there is no indication that what happened to Job is a common experience.

means that God's policy of blessing the righteous is good. There is such a thing as disinterested righteousness—that is, worshiping God for who he is, not simply for what he gives us. Despite the resolution to Satan's question, there is much more to come.

Dialogues: Job and His Friends (Chaps. 3–27)

The book of Job switches from prose to poetry beginning in chapter 3. Here we begin the long, exhausting section of dialogues. At the end of chapter 2, three friends of Job come to comfort him. To their credit, they sat with him for seven days before saying anything (2:11–13). "After this, Job opened his mouth and cursed the day of his birth" (3:1). At this point, the switch to poetry takes place, and the remainder of chapter 3 records Job's lament. His message is, "I wish I had never been born. God has hedged me in, and peace and rest elude me" (see 3:2–3, 23, 26). Then, in chapter 4, the dialogue begins. We will consider the content in a moment, but we should consider the structure of this section (chaps. 4–27). As our overview in table 4.1 indicates, there are three cycles. In each cycle, the three friends speak, and Job responds after each speech. Later, we will consider the puzzling conclusion to the third section. The speeches in each cycle move like this: Eliphaz → Job → Bildad → Job → Zophar → Job (see table 4.2). The speeches get shorter in each successive cycle, and I will argue that the final cycle ends abruptly with no speech by Zophar and response by Job.

I have already said that this section of the book of Job gets tedious to read. Frankly, it is exhausting. It makes us want to say, "Just stop! What does God have to say?" I believe that this is part of the literary strategy of

Table 4.2

The Structure of the Cycles in Job 4–27

Speaker	Cycle One	Cycle Two	Cycle Three
Eliphaz	4–5	15	22
Job	6–7	16–17	23–24
Bildad	8	18	25
Job	9–10	19	26–27
Zophar	11	20	—
Job	12–14	21	—

the book. The seemingly endless cycle of back-and-forth verbal sparring makes us desperate to hear from the Lord.

The most profound observation we can make about the cycles of dialogue, in my opinion, is that both Job's friends and Job himself view his suffering in terms of retribution from God. John Walton helpfully refers to this as the "Retribution Principle." This "is the conviction that the righteous will prosper and the wicked will suffer, both in proportion to their respective righteousness and wickedness."[9] In short, then, God gives good to good people and bad to bad people. The righteous prosper and the wicked suffer. Of course, there is truth to the Retribution Principle. Deuteronomy 28–30 revealed that the Lord would bring his people blessings for obedience and curses for disobedience. Although believers today are not contractually bound to the Mosaic covenant, the Retribution Principle is still in play in the age of the new covenant. Galatians 6:7 puts it bluntly: "Do not be deceived: God cannot be mocked. A man reaps what he sows."[10] Both the friends and Job believed that suffering is always related to a specific sin. The friends concluded that Job had sinned. There could be no other explanation. Job argued that he had done nothing wrong to deserve the level of suffering he experienced, so God was treating him unfairly.

The problem is that the three friends and Job had an overly simplistic view of the Retribution Principle. It simply cannot explain every case of suffering. God is constant, but he is not predictable to human minds. Bill Kynes and Will Kynes explain this well:

> While it is true that God never acts unjustly, it is also true that God does not always exercise his retributive justice in an immediate and recognizable way. Additionally, God may have other reasons for his actions that are not explained by his justice. God cannot be put in some neat little moralistic box, such that his actions are entirely predictable based on our behavior. We like to think the world is that way. We assume there is some intelligible moral order that gives a clear-cut reason for everything that happens.[11]

Job's friends were wrong, then, to conclude that Job's suffering was a result of sin. As Webb observes, "Job himself never disagrees with their

---

9. Walton, *Job*, 39.

10. See also 1 Cor. 11:30, which reveals that some in the Corinthian church got sick and died because of their abuse of the Lord's Supper.

11. Kynes and Kynes, *Job*, 66.

generalization, just their inability or unwillingness to acknowledge that this particular case is an exception."[12] Yet Job was wrong to conclude that God was treating him unfairly since good deserves good. Job was right that he had done nothing wrong to deserve such suffering; he was wrong to insist that God should act out of a strict application of the Retribution Principle. Once again, God is on trial. While Satan questioned God's policy to bless the righteous (chaps. 1–2), Job questioned God's policy to let the righteous suffer. Still, although Job's responses are tainted by a misapplication of the Retribution Principle, they demonstrate that "disinterested righteousness" is possible. Job still worships God for who he is—even in great suffering.

Before we move forward, we need to consider a crucial interpretive issue. In Job's response to Bildad, he makes a strong statement that has become rather well known (Job 19:25–27):

> I know that my redeemer lives,
>   and that in the end he will stand on the earth.
> And after my skin has been destroyed,
>   yet in my flesh I will see God.
> I myself will see him
>   with my own eyes—I, and not another.
>   How my heart yearns within me!

Many believers today read this and immediately assume that it is a direct prophecy of Jesus the Messiah. They may be familiar with the stirring piece in Handel's *Messiah*, "I Know That My Redeemer Liveth." Or they might like Nicole C. Mullen's moving song "My Redeemer Lives." Another reason why believers read this as a direct prophecy of the Messiah is that several English versions capitalize the letter *r* at the beginning of "redeemer."[13] Regardless of the intention of the translators, it has been my experience that readers interpret "Redeemer" as a direct reference to Jesus, the one in whom we have redemption, the forgiveness of sins (Col. 1:14). As Kynes and Kynes observe, when people read or hear of the redeemer in Job 19:25, "they immediately conclude that this is the high point of

---

12. Webb, *Job*, 77.

13. Versions that capitalize the *r* ("Redeemer") include the ESV, NASB, NRSV, NET, and NLT. Even the NJPS, the Jewish Publication Society's translation, renders the word as "Vindicator." Although the HCSB used "Redeemer," the more recent CSB reverted to "redeemer."

Job's faith," that he "now understands that a Messiah is coming and that he will be raised with him to experience a full redemption."[14]

The question is, What did Job mean when he said these words? In short, I believe that Job was looking for someone to verify his innocence rather than to redeem him from his guilt and sin. He believed that this person was out there and would show up before he died. This reading understands "after my skin has been destroyed" (19:26) as hyperbole for his suffering, not as a reference to his death. The word "redeemer" translates the Hebrew word גֹּאֵל (go'el). This refers to "a protector of family rights"—that is, "one who enters a legal situation on behalf of another" to help them "recover losses" and salvage their dignity.[15] In the Old Testament, we see this redeemer getting someone released from slavery (Lev. 25:47–49), purchasing back family property (Lev. 25:25–34 [land or houses]), avenging a murder (Num. 35:19), and marrying a widowed relative (Ruth 3:12–13). (See fig. 4.1.) Job apparently envisions this vindicator or protector of family rights as the Lord himself.[16] Walton offers a helpful expanded paraphrase of Job 19:25–27: "I firmly believe that there is someone, somewhere, who will come and testify on my behalf right here on my dung heap at the end of all this. Despite my peeling skin, I expect to have enough left to come before God in my own flesh. I shall be restored to his favor and no longer be treated as a stranger. This is my deepest desire!"[17] We will return to this issue when we think about how to preach this great affirmation of faith and hope.

Interlude: Wisdom Hymn (Chap. 28)

In chapter 28, something remarkable happens. We expect a speech from Zophar, or at least for Job's reply to Bildad to continue. Instead, the tone changes completely, and we get a wonderful poem about wisdom. Some English versions provide headings suggesting that this is a continuation of

14. Kynes and Kynes, *Job*, 98.
15. Walton, *Job*, 218.
16. Francis Andersen says that "verses 25–27 are so tightly knit that there should be no doubt that the *Redeemer* is God" (*Job*, 209). Robert Hubbard says, "Job affirms Yahweh as the ultimate lawyer who will eventually intervene to protect Job's legal rights (Job 19:25)" ("גֹּאֵל," 793). Yahweh is frequently identified in the Old Testament as Israel's *go'el* (e.g., Exod. 6:6; 15:13; Ps. 19:14 [19:15 in the Hebrew Bible]; Prov. 23:11; Isa. 41:14; 43:14; 44:6, 24; 47:4; 48:17; 49:7, 26; 54:5, 8; 59:20; 60:16; 63:16). John Walton says that the redeemer or vindicator is perhaps "from the divine council, but unspecified" (*Job*, 221).
17. Walton, *Job*, 221.

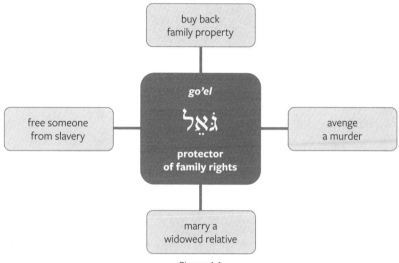

Figure 4.1

Job's speech,[18] but I contend that it is an interlude or hymn by the author of the book. When Job continues his discourse in chapter 29, he shows no hint of the convictions expressed in chapter 28. Furthermore, as John Walton observes, "Job's final speech in Job 27:7–23 shows a pessimistic, fatalistic despair that would be ill-matched and arguably irreconcilable with chapter 28."[19] Bill Kynes and Will Kynes eloquently capture the effect of chapter 28: "Job 28 comes as the eye of the storm, a calm reprieve from a tumultuous clash. In contrast both to the passionate and combative dialogue of the previous chapters and to Job's continuing protestation that follows, this chapter seems peaceful and untroubled. And it seems to have no clear connection with what comes before or after."[20]

Let me briefly sketch the argument of Job 28. It begins by observing that we know where to find hidden things such as precious metals (vv. 1–11). But where can wisdom be found? According to verses 12–19, it is elusive. It is not in the land of the living (v. 13), not in the deep (v. 14). It is too costly for purchase with precious metals (vv. 15–19). So where does wisdom come from? The answer, revealed in verses 20–28, is God. Wisdom

18. English versions identifying this as Job's speech include the ESV, NASB, KJV, LEB, NLT, and NKJV.
19. Walton, *Job*, 30.
20. Kynes and Kynes, *Job*, 110.

is the exclusive domain of God and calls for the fear of God. Webb says that "chapter 28 comes as an explanation of why Job and his friends have all, to varying degrees, strayed from the path of wisdom. They have been searching for it in the wrong way—by argument and protest rather than submission to God."[21] The friends have "relied too much on their own insight (Prov 3:5)," while Job has "tried to make God answerable to him" instead of deferring to God.[22]

This chapter, I believe, foreshadows God's speeches near the end of the book of Job.[23] It provides us with a hint that the way to respond to innocent suffering is to trust in the wisdom of God. For now, though, we do not have a resolution to the drama in progress. But chapter 28 points us in the right direction. Yet, whatever relief chapter 28 provides, chapter 29 throws us back into the ongoing dispute.

Speeches: Job, Elihu, and the Lord (29:1–42:6)

Beginning in 29:1, Job continues his discourse. The Hebrew text is specific here: "And Job continued again to take up his discourse, and he said . . ." (my translation). This suggests a new section or phase of his argumentation. It is Job's final speech and, according to Francis Andersen, "the final assertion of his innocence," not a soliloquy.[24] John Walton says that in chapter 29, "Job wallows in nostalgia, pining for his lost prosperity, honor, and dignity. This melancholy focus contrasts with his indignant posture in the book's dialogue section, where he expounded on his righteousness rather than his lost prosperity."[25] In general, Job describes his former state in chapter 29 and his present state in chapter 30.[26] Then, in chapter 31, Job vows that he is innocent of any offenses, including lust (v. 1), deceit (v. 5), turning away from the right path (v. 7), sexual impurity (v. 9), injustice to his servants (v. 13), failing to care for the poor and needy (vv. 16–21), trust in wealth (vv. 24–25), false worship (vv. 26–27), rejoicing

---

21. Webb, *Job*, 317.

22. Webb, *Job*, 317.

23. Similarly, Kynes and Kynes make this comment about Job 28: "The biblical author takes a moment to reframe the book's central struggle without resolving it, while pointing us in the direction from which the resolution must come" (*Job*, 111).

24. Andersen, *Job*, 248. A soliloquy is a monologue addressed to oneself rather than a speech addressed to others. Job's words in chapters 29–31 may sound reflective, but clearly he is defending himself to others rather than speaking to himself.

25. Walton, *Job*, 312.

26. Andersen, *Job*, 249; Walton, *Job*, 312.

at an enemy's misfortune (v. 29), neglect of strangers (v. 32), concealing sin (v. 33), and misuse of the land (vv. 38–39). Toward the end of the chapter, Job calls for the Almighty to answer him (vv. 35–37).

At the beginning of chapter 32, we learn that the three friends stopped answering Job "because he was righteous in his own eyes" (32:1). Then a new character appears: Elihu. He waited to speak because the three others are older than he is. Yet, when he saw that they had nothing more to say, he spoke up in anger against both Job and his three friends. Essentially, the friends said to Job, "You are suffering because you sinned," while Elihu said, "You are suffering because you think too highly of yourself. Your suffering was necessary to reveal this problem." John Walton and Tremper Longman point out that "Elihu does not advise Job to confess to sins of the past." Rather, he has a more specific accusation: "Elihu accuses Job of self-righteousness so extreme that even God's character is impugned before it."[27] Elihu concludes with a magnificent description of God's power in 36:22–37:24.

Suddenly, the Lord God enters the conversation and speaks, beginning in chapter 38. This is a stunning, magnificent speech! Yet it is not what Job has requested. Andersen says that Job has asked for "either a bill of indictment, with specific charges which he is prepared to answer, or else a verdict from his Judge which he confidently expects to be a declaration of his innocence."[28] Instead, the Lord bombards Job with an avalanche of questions and demands an answer. The rhetorical effect is to remind Job of all he cannot do that only the Lord can do.

There are three main parts to the Lord's words to Job. First, in 38:4–38, he describes his control of creation on a grand scale, in both creating and sustaining it.[29] Here are a few of the questions that the Lord asks:

- "Where were you when I laid the earth's foundation?" (38:4)
- "Have you ever given orders to the morning, or shown the dawn its place?" (38:12)
- "Have the gates of death been shown to you?" (38:17)
- "What is the way to the abode of light? And where does darkness reside?" (38:19)

27. Walton and Longman, *Job*, 70–71.
28. Andersen, *Job*, 289.
29. Walton and Longman, *Job*, 128–29.

- "Have you entered the storehouses of the snow, or seen the storehouses of the hail?" (38:22)
- "Can you bring forth the constellations in their seasons or lead out the Bear with its cubs?" (38:32)
- "Who can tip over the water jars of the heavens?" (38:37)

At one point, the Lord takes a gentle jab at Job. In 38:21, using playful sarcasm, he follows up his question about the way to the abode of light, the way to the residence of darkness, and Job's ability to take them to their places: "Surely you know, for you were already born! You have lived so many years!"

The Lord's point to Job is this: "You lack the wisdom, understanding, and power to question me." Job does not know enough about how the created world works, nor is he able to care for it, in a way that gives him the right to correct the Lord for not operating appropriately in respect to the Retribution Principle.

The second part of the Lord's speech, in 38:39–39:40, describes his control of creation on a more intimate scale. Specifically, he focuses on the animal kingdom. Here are a few of the questions he asks:

- "Do you hunt the prey for the lioness and satisfy the hunger of the lions?" (38:39)
- "Do you know when the mountain goats give birth?" (39:1)
- "Will the wild ox consent to serve you? Will it stay by your manger at night?" (39:9)
- "Do you give the horse its strength or clothe its neck with a flowing mane?" (39:19)
- "Does the hawk take flight by your wisdom?" (39:26)
- "Does the eagle soar at your command?" (39:27)

The Lord then confronts Job with another question in 40:2: "Will the one who contends with the Almighty correct him? Let him who accuses God answer him!" Job answers humbly in 40:3–5. My paraphrase of his answer is, "I am unworthy to reply to you. I am going to shut up now."

The Lord has made his point, and Job gets it. But the Lord is still not done. He tells Job to brace himself like a man and says, "I will question you, and you shall answer me" (40:7). The third part of the Lord's speech, in 40:7–41:34, begins by asking Job whether he has an arm like God's, whether his voice can thunder like God's, whether he can adorn himself with glory and splendor, and whether he can clothe himself in honor and majesty (40:9–10). If so, the Lord will admit to Job that his "own right hand" can save him. Then, in the rest of the third part of the Lord's speech, he turns Job's attention to two mighty creatures: Behemoth and Leviathan.

There are two challenges here. First, what exactly are these creatures? It is likely that they are not actual animals—like the hippopotamus and the crocodile, or dinosaurs, which are now extinct. Instead, they are mythological "chaos creatures."[30] Regardless of their precise identity, the second challenge is to understand the message that the Lord has for Job in describing these creatures. One approach is represented by Francis Andersen, who suggests that if no one can stand against the "fiercest land animal" and "the most terrifying sea creature," then "how could anyone be so foolhardy as to *stand* up against God, as Job has done?"[31] The solution is to trust God. Bill Kynes and Will Kynes take a similar approach, suggesting that the Lord is saying to Job, "If I can control these terrifying creatures, can't you trust me to manage the affairs of your life?"[32] John Walton and Tremper Longman suggest a different approach. They argue that "Yahweh presents Behemoth as an illustration for Job to emulate and Leviathan as an illustration of how Job should think about Yahweh."[33] Essentially, "Humans should respond to raging rivers with security and trust (as Behemoth does) and should not think they can domesticate or challenge God (since they cannot challenge or domesticate Leviathan, who is inferior to God)."[34]

The speeches end with Job withdrawing his case, admitting he has no right to question God and demand answers (42:1–6). Job has learned that he must trust in the wisdom of God when he suffers because God's ways are beyond our understanding and our control.

---

30. Walton and Longman, *Job*, 79–81. For a cogent presentation of the view that these creatures are actual animals, the hippopotamus and a crocodile, see Andersen, *Job*, 310–12.

31. Andersen, *Job*, 310, 312–13.

32. Kynes and Kynes, *Job*, 185.

33. Walton and Longman, *Job*, 83.

34. Walton and Longman, *Job*, 83.

Narrative Epilogue: The Blessing of Job (42:7–17)

The book of Job concludes with a brief narrative epilogue in 42:7–17, which creates a narrative frame along with chapters 1–2. This epilogue consists of two sections. First, in verses 7–9, the Lord reprimands Job's friends, and they respond in repentance by doing what the Lord tells them to do. He tells them to go to Job, to sacrifice a burnt offering for themselves, and to let Job pray for them. As a result, says the Lord, "I will accept his prayer and not deal with you according to your folly" (v. 8). Francis Andersen calls this a "delightful irony" because they are now required to enlist godly help from the one to whom they tried to offer godly counsel.[35]

The most challenging statement in this section is the Lord's explanation as to why he was angry with the three friends. Twice he says, "You have not spoken the truth about me, as my servant Job has" (vv. 7–8). Casual readers might put Job on a pedestal, reading 42:7–8 as a full exoneration of Job. Yet, we know that Job said some outrageous things about God and received harsh indictment for doing so (see 40:1–2, 7–14). The best solution is to translate the Hebrew expression דבר (*dbr*) + אל (*'l*) in a straightforward way. John Walton says that this combination "consistently throughout the Old Testament means to 'speak to' someone who is generally present."[36] Most English versions translate this as "spoken about me" (NIV, CSB) or "spoken of me" (ESV, NASB, KJV). However, the best translation of this expression in Job 42:7–8 is "spoken to me." The point is that Job's friends did not speak to God in an appropriate, truthful way as Job did. I believe that Walton is right when he says that the reference is "to what Job has spoken to God in his previous speech (Job 42:1–6). It would not describe everything Job has said throughout the book."[37] Job had repented, but they had not. At last, though, the three friends "did what the Lord told them," and "the Lord accepted Job's prayer" on their behalf (v. 9).

The second section in Job 42:10–17 concerns the Lord's restoration of Job. This happy ending may seem a bit troubling, though. Is the Lord's abundant blessing of Job a return to the Retribution Principle? Does the Lord expect that the gift of additional children will make up for the loss of the previous ones? First, the Lord is not returning to the Retribution Principle. He does not say, "All right, Job was good, so I'm going to bless

---

35. Andersen, *Job*, 316.
36. Walton and Longman, *Job*, 63.
37. Walton and Longman, *Job*, 63.

him." Rather, the Lord has been vindicated. He won Satan's challenge. So now he can go back to his policy of blessing the righteous for no other reason than his grace. Second, there is nothing in the text to suggest that by restoring Job's prosperity, the Lord is making up for what Job lost. Again, Job's restoration is a gift of God's grace, not a reward for righteousness.

Webb describes the "takeaway message" of the book of Job like this: "Be wise. Don't let undeserved suffering turn you against God as Satan hopes it will. There are good reasons to believe God is sovereign, merciful, and just, and the outcome, if you endure, will be vindication and blessing."[38]

Preaching Strategies

Preaching Christ in Job

It may be helpful to consider how to preach Christ in the book of Job before we think about formulating a sermon series and preaching specific texts. I will explore some of the connections we can make to Christ in the plan for a sermon series that I sketch below. Yet I believe there is one connection that towers above all the others. God's ultimate answer to our suffering is Jesus.[39] Job 28:12 asks, "Where can wisdom be found?" Craig Bartholomew is right that the "New Testament unequivocally answers, 'In Christ.'"[40] So we need to remind our listeners again and again that for those in whom Christ dwells, "our present sufferings are not worth comparing with the glory that will be revealed in us" (Rom. 8:18). Furthermore, no trouble or hardship or persecution or famine or nakedness or danger or sword can ever separate us from the love of Christ (Rom. 8:35–39). We need this promise more than we need explanations as to why God allows us to suffer in a particular way at a particular time.

An Ideal Sermon Series

The length of the book of Job (forty-two chapters) might suggest the need for a longer sermon series; yet a shorter sermon series makes more sense, given the nature of the book. If you devoted a sermon to each chapter, you would end up with a stretch of twenty-five sermons (almost

38. Webb, *Job*, 78.
39. Walton and Longman, *Job*, 160.
40. Bartholomew, *When You Want to Yell at God*, 50. For a helpful reflection on "Jesus, the Wisdom of God," see Bartholomew and O'Dowd, *Old Testament Wisdom Literature*, 231–60.

half a year!) in which there is no relief from the futile dialogue between Job and his friends. I'm thinking of chapters 3–27. To provide any kind of hope or gospel encouragement, you would have to fast-forward weekly to chapter 28 or chapters 38–42. The situation is similar in chapters 29–37. If you devote nine weeks to these chapters, you will need to find some kind of resolution each week at the end of the book or in the New Testament. Given that Job has its own resolution, I believe that it is better to preach these long stretches in a single sermon, including the resolution to which they lead. One way to preach the book of Job is in a five-sermon series. Here are the sermon texts and the way to develop them.

Job 1–2

My sermon title for Job 1–2 is "God on Trial." I introduced it with the quote from C. S. Lewis and the backstory that I used at the beginning of this chapter. Since I was introducing the sermon series as well as chapters 1–2, I raised the following question: "How do we think about God when we're suffering?" I told my listeners that the book of Job will provide insight into that question. Then I shared four keys to reading and understanding the book of Job.[41]

1. The book of Job is more about God than Job (Job's grief is the occasion for a look at God).
2. Job is not on trial (he *has* trials); God's policies are on trial (questioned by both Satan and Job).
3. The way to handle suffering is not to imitate Job but to understand God.
4. The book is more about trusting God's wisdom than about making sense of God's justice.

These points prepare listeners for the sermon series, addressing and clarifying some common misconceptions about the book of Job. Throughout my sermon series, I emphasized that the book of Job does not answer the question "Why do the righteous suffer?" Yet it provides encourage-

---

41. These "four keys" grew out of a weeklong study of the book of Job with John Walton and thirty-five other pastors in 2014. They are based on observations made by Walton in that setting.

ment for those who suffer by giving them insight into the wisdom of God.

For this particular sermon, I raised the question that will show up in Job 1:9: "Is it possible to worship God for who he is, or is he worthy of our worship only when he makes life go smoothly?" Here are the main points of my preaching outline.

I. Satan challenges God's policy of blessing righteous people, suggesting that Job worships God for what he gets from God (1:1–12).

II. Job's response to his crushing circumstances proves that (*Big Idea*) God himself, and not his reward, is reason enough to trust him (1:13–2:10).

III. Application: Suffering is an opportunity for us to demonstrate that we love and worship God for who he is, not just for what he gives us.

I developed my first two points just as I did in my summary of the narrative prologue (see above). As I previously explained, I do not make my outline points prominent. That is, I do not put them on a screen in a fill-in-the-blank outline point. You can choose whether or not to do that. But the content of points I and II indicates the ideas that I want to form in my listeners' minds. Point II is the big idea. I stated and restated it several times at the end of my unpacking of 1:13–2:10 and throughout the application section. That idea is that God *himself, and not his reward, is reason enough to trust him.* At twelve words, the idea is concise and somewhat memorable. People may express this in their own words, and that is even better. But this, I believe, is the thrust of the first two chapters.

As far as my application is concerned, I do not always make it a main point. But I did here because it reflects the amount of time I devoted to it in this particular sermon. To make my point that suffering is an opportunity to love and worship God, I encouraged listeners not to waste their sorrow. When we suffer, it is appropriate to pray for the alleviation of and even the removal of our suffering. But we should also pray that God will allow us to glorify him through our suffering. The truth is, God is worthy of worship even when we are in the furnace and wonder, "God, how much suffering are you going to let me face? I can't take any more!"

I recalled how I heard my dad, a pastor, say the following over the years of his ministry: "When we suffer, we often ask, 'Why?' when we really ought to ask, 'Why not?'" My dad not only said this; he lived it out. He got sick with cancer in his early sixties, and the last words I heard him say a few days before his death were, "No matter what happens to me, God is good and he is in control." The reality is, we live in a fallen world. Furthermore, it is the lot of Christians to suffer. And it might be the best way for people around us to see the glory of God.

I pointed out that this is possible through the power of Christ, who suffered and died for us (1 Pet. 2:21–24). Because of what Jesus did for us, we can entrust ourselves—as he did—to him who judges justly. Then I closed my sermon by quoting the words of "My Eternal King," a seventeenth-century Latin hymn.

> My God, I love Thee;
> Not because I hope for heav'n thereby,
> Nor yet because who love Thee not
> Must die eternally.
>
> Thou, O my Jesus, Thou didst me
> Upon the cross embrace:
> For me didst bear the nails and spear,
> And manifold disgrace.
>
> Why, then, why, O blessed Jesus Christ,
> Should I not love Thee well?
> Not for the hope of winning heav'n,
> Or of escaping hell.
>
> Not with the hope of gaining aught,
> Not seeking a reward;
> But as Thyself has loved me,
> O ever-loving Lord!
>
> E'en so I love Thee, and will love,
> And in Thy praise will sing;
> Solely because Thou art my God,
> And my Eternal King.

I told my listeners that I have a long way to go, but this is what I aspire to. By the grace and power of God, might that be our cry. No matter how much we suffer, may we sing the praise of God—solely because he is our God and our Eternal King!

Job 3–28

For my second sermon, I chose to cover the entire sweep of chapters 3–28. This includes Job's initial speech and the three cycles of dialogue in chapters 3–27, as well as the great interlude or hymn on wisdom in chapter 28. Although an entire sermon could be devoted to chapter 28, I included it with chapters 3–27 because it provides some resolution. Without it, chapters 3–27 simply leave the reader in despair. My title for the sermon is "Coping with Undeserved Suffering." Here is an outline of the body of the sermon.

I. Job shares his great grief over his suffering when his friends come to comfort him (2:11–13; 3:1–26).

II. The three friends and Job himself view his suffering in terms of retribution from God (chaps. 4–27).

   A. Cycle 1: Admit you're wrong and deal with your sin (chaps. 4–14).

   B. Cycle 2: Consider the fate of the wicked, for you are one of them (chaps. 15–21).

   C. Cycle 3: God is rebuking you for your great wickedness (chaps. 22–27).

III. (*Big Idea*) The way to respond to undeserved suffering is to trust in the wisdom of God (chap. 28).

   A. We know where to find hidden things like precious metals (vv. 1–11).

   B. However, wisdom is elusive (vv. 12–19).

   C. Wisdom is the exclusive domain of God and calls for the fear of God (vv. 20–28).

The big challenge is how to cover so many chapters in one sermon. The answer is simple. Select particular statements from each speaker to provide a window into their message. The dialogue gets intense. The words are pointed, and some drip with sarcasm. Job describes his friends as being as "undependable as intermittent streams" (6:15), as "worthless physicians" who would show wisdom by shutting up (13:4–5), as "miserable comforters" with "long-winded speeches" (16:2–3), and as those who console him with "nonsense" (21:34). At one point, he even says, "Bear with me while I speak, and after I have spoken, mock on" (21:3). Job's friends do not hold back either. Eliphaz eventually blasts Job with rhetorical questions, claiming that it is not for Job's piety that God rebukes him (22:4). He says, "Is not your wickedness great? Are not your sins endless?" (22:5). Bildad calls Job's words a "blustering wind" and urges him to "seek God earnestly" (8:2, 5). Zophar accused Job of "idle talk" and implies that Job is so sinful that "God has even forgotten some of your sin" (11:3–6). It takes only a few minutes to read enough statements to give your listeners a flavor for the nature of the dispute in this dialogue. Then, you can spend ample time in Job 28.

I should point out that I preached the third point of my sermon inductively.[42] The sermon is already inductive in its form since the big idea shows up in the final point. But when I arrive at chapter 28, I do not reveal my big idea at the outset. Rather, I wait until I have worked through the entire chapter. That is, the big idea comes *after* my subpoints, not before them.

Appendix D contains a sample sermon on Job 28. It demonstrates how to preach a sermon on this hidden gem of a chapter in a way that helps listeners see it in the flow of the book's argument. Although it is possible to preach the book of Job in a single sermon, another way to provide an overview of the book is to preach chapter 28 and connect it—through brief summaries—to the chapters that precede and follow it. The sermon's introduction and conclusion provide an example of how to introduce a sermon on Job 3–28, as well as a sermon that focuses only on chapter 28.

Job 19:25–27

For my third sermon, I opted to preach on Job 19:25–27, the text containing Job's affirmation, "I know that my redeemer lives." My title for

---

42. There are two major ways to present ideas. In a *deductive* approach, you reveal the answer or conclusion at the outset and then look at the details or component parts. In an *inductive* approach, you look at the parts or the details, and then you reveal the answer or conclusion. A sermon is deductive if you reveal its big idea at the beginning and inductive if you save its big idea for the end. What is true for the entire sermon also applies to its main movements, which are reflected in your outline as main points. You have the option of preaching each movement, represented by your main point, in either a deductive or an inductive fashion. See Mathewson, *Old Testament Narrative*, 128–33.

this sermon is "The Need for a Redeemer." I devoted an entire sermon to this brief text for two reasons. First, I felt that it needed more time than I could give to it in my sermon on Job 3–28. Given the way this text is often misunderstood, I wanted to help my listeners understand it. Second, there is value in slowing down to focus on a smaller detail or text when your approach to a book is to cover several chapters at a time. In my introduction, I raised the concern that I shared above, that our minds often jump so quickly to Christ's work of redemption on our behalf that we assume that Job was referring to this when he declared, "I know that my redeemer lives." I also took time to remind my listeners what the book of Job is about: God's policies are on trial. While Satan questions the wisdom of God's policy to bless the righteous, Job questions the wisdom of God's policy to let the righteous suffer. I reminded my listeners too that both Job and his friends are operating out of a rather strict, mechanical view of the Retribution Principle, which says that God gives people exactly what they deserve. Then, my outline for the body of the sermon looked like this.

I. Job expressed his need for a redeemer to verify his innocence.
II. (*Big Idea*) Job's need for a redeemer to verity his innocence reminds us of our need for a redeemer to deliver us from guilt.

In the first movement of my sermon, represented by point I, I worked through the text. I discussed the meaning of "redeemer" and argued that Job envisioned someone who would stand up now to declare his innocence rather than the risen Messiah at Job's resurrection. Then I made a transition to my second point—the big idea—like this: "Now, if you are disappointed that Job 19:25–27 does not say what you thought it said, let me encourage you by pointing you to the grand story of redemption in which Job is located." I told my listeners that if they are troubled by Job's claim to innocence when Scripture tells us that we have all sinned (Rom. 3:23), they need to keep in mind that Job is speaking as a believer about the way he has lived before God. He is affirming what God had already said about him (Job 1:8). Thus, I do not believe that Job is claiming to be a special case, a good guy who never did anything wrong in his life. Rather, he is arguing (albeit from a misapplication of the Retribution Principle) that his suffering is not appropriate in light of his godly lifestyle. That is, he hasn't done anything to deserve what he is facing. I told my listeners that Job needed a redeemer to deliver him from his guilt just as much as you and I do. It is through faith in Jesus, our Redeemer, that we are delivered from the guilt of sin and receive a right standing with God. I cited Romans 4:18–25 and noted that Abraham's experience applies to everyone who believes (Rom. 4:25). This work of God is called "redemption" (Rom. 3:24).

What I did, then, was challenge the popular understanding of Job 19:25–27 while acknowledging that Job's statement about his redeemer reminds us of another Redeemer that we need. Job was looking for vindication; we need God's gift of justification. This was and is an important message in a culture that believes in "justification by death." The popular idea, which I have heard at almost every funeral for a nonbeliever, is that all people—except the really wicked ones—go to heaven when they die. Deceased people who have had no time for the Lord in their lives are eulogized as good people who are playing the front nine at the big golf course in the sky. But when we truly understand God's justice, we understand our need for the redemption that he provides through Jesus Christ.

Job 29:1–42:6

This is another huge swath of text. Trying to preach it in one sermon might seem like trying to overcome Leviathan (pardon the pun). Yet there is value in seeing how the speeches of Job and Elihu build to the climax: the speeches of the Lord, who finally takes the stage after endless chapters of human argumentation. My title for this sermon is "Questioning the Wisdom of God," and the main points of my outline are as follows:

    I. Job continues to insist on his innocence and demands an answer from the Almighty (chaps. 29–31).

    II. Elihu argues that Job's self-righteousness is the cause of his suffering (chaps. 32–37).

    III. The Lord says that Job's challenge is inappropriate because Job lacks the wisdom and the power that belong to God alone (38:1–42:6).

    IV. (*Big Idea*) We must trust in the wisdom of God when we suffer because his ways are beyond our understanding and control.

You can figure out how I developed these sections of text from my comments above on the speeches of Job, Elihu, and the Lord.

One way to introduce a sermon on this passage is to ask your listeners to think about a situation they are facing that causes them to doubt God's wisdom. Ask why your listeners can trust a God who seems silent when his people suffer. A few years ago, I received an email from a church leader in the northeast part of Nigeria. I had met him when he visited our church during a trip to the United States. After he returned home, I reached out to him to ask how the churches were doing in the area where he was serving the Lord. His reply was disconcerting. He described the way Islamic jihadists had taken over villages, destroyed churches, and killed villagers. It makes me wonder how we can trust the wisdom of God when people face this kind of suffering. This passage provides the answer.

After working through the text, I spent some time developing the big idea of my sermon. I argued that God does not owe us explanations. Even if he provided them, they would not comfort us the way we hope, since God's ways are beyond us—as chapters 38–41 make clear. We have already learned why Job suffered. Can you imagine the Lord explaining to Job that he allowed him to suffer to prove that there is such a thing as "disinterested righteousness"—that people actually worship God for who he is, not just what he gives? I am not sure it would have provided comfort to Job. We want to know the answers to our "why" questions, but the answer to "why" is "who." We have a God who promises that "our present sufferings are not worth comparing with the glory that will be revealed in us" (Rom. 8:18). So we must endure suffering as Scripture calls us to do. First Peter 2:21 says, "To this you were called, because Christ suffered for you, leaving you an example, that you should follow in his steps."

There are a couple further questions to think about when preaching Job 29:1–42:6. First, would it be acceptable to preach Job 32–37, the Elihu speech, on its own? Ken Shigematsu has suggested this, noting that while "Elihu responds to Job's suffering by repeating some of the same simplistic arguments as Job's three friends," he also "offers a more enlightened perspective of how God speaks to humanity and refines people through suffering."[43] His big idea for this sermon is that "God can reveal himself and refine us through suffering." This can work, of course. However, such an approach will require us to remind our listeners—repeatedly!—that while Elihu's theology is "largely accurate," he has a "flawed understanding

43. Shigematsu, *Job*, 195.

of how God's policies work."[44] We would need to work hard at pointing out the simplistic arguments to which Shigematsu refers, thus pointing out where Elihu distorts the truth as well as where he gets it right.[45]

A second question concerns whether we might preach Job 31, his oath of innocence, as a profile of a blameless, upright person. After all, Job 31:1—"I made a covenant with my eyes not to look lustfully at a young woman"—is often cited as an example of what men should do. The problem is, of course, that Job's words in chapter 31 function as a demand for God, the Almighty, to answer Job. Personally, then, I would not preach it like this, even in a sermon series on Job. If you do, you must admit to your listeners that you are using Job's words in a different way than he did. It's one thing to borrow his language in verse 1 as a strategy for dealing with lust. But it's another thing to preach the chapter wholesale in a way that differs from the intent of Job and the author of this book that bears his name.

Job 42:7–17

My fifth and final sermon from the book of Job unpacks the narrative epilogue. I title it "The Problem of Good." Here are the main points in my sermon outline:

I. God's response to Job's friends reaffirms that we cannot reduce God to a predictable deity who is confined by fixed formulas (vv. 7–9).

II. God's response to Job reaffirms that (*Big Idea*) whatever God gives us is a gift of his grace, not a reward for our righteousness (vv. 10–17).

In the first movement, I explained to my listeners that Job's friends did not speak to God as Job did. They did not repent, as Job did, for presuming to know how God is supposed to run the world. Twice, for emphasis, the Lord said to them, "You have not spoken to me truthfully" (my translation). Essentially, the Lord asked the friends to humble themselves by going to Job for prayer (42:8). When they did, the Lord accepted Job's prayer (42:9), indicating that the Lord dealt graciously with his friends. At this

---

44. Walton, *Job*, 376.
45. Walton is a helpful guide because he does this well in his section on "Elihu's Theology" (*Job*, 376–82).

point, I reflected on how God is free to act in ways that make no sense to us and is free to withhold explanations. We cannot assume that if we are "good people," we will not suffer. Nor can we assume that when we or anyone else suffers, it is because we or they have done wrong. We do not like mystery. We want a predictable world, one that is governed by a flow-chart. If we do A, God will do B. Now, it is *generally* true that if we live by wisdom, we will experience peace and blessing. This is what the book of Proverbs teaches us. But our only recourse when we face unexplained tragedy and undeserved sorrow in life is to trust in the wisdom of God. We will set ourselves up for disappointment with God unless we constantly remind ourselves that though God is good, he is also free to do what he does without explaining it to us.

Then, in the second movement of the sermon (point II), I dealt with two objections. The first objection is that restoring Job's prosperity does not make up for what Job lost. Elie Wiesel was a Holocaust survivor. He and his family were taken to Auschwitz when he was a teen, and his mother and sister were murdered there. Eventually, he and his father were transferred to Buchenwald, where his father died after being beaten. Years later, Wiesel said that he was "preoccupied with Job, especially in the early years after the war."[46] Everywhere he looked, he saw Job-like figures. Then, he says that he was offended by Job's resignation to his situation. Wiesel writes, "He should not have given in so easily. He should have continued to protest, to refuse the handouts. He should have said to God: Very well, I forgive You, I forgive You to the extent of my sorrow, my anguish. But what about my dead children, do they forgive You? . . . By accepting Your inequities, do I not become Your accomplice? Now it is my turn to choose between You and my children, and I refuse to repudiate them. I demand that justice be done to them."[47]

We can hear the heartache in Wiesel's soul when he suggests that Job should have asked, "But what about my dead children?" We must be clear when we preach the epilogue of the book that God's restoration of Job's prosperity does not make up for what he lost. Nothing in the text teaches this. Job's restoration was not intended to erase Job's pain. Life in God's kingdom does not work this way. In 1975, my four-year old cousin, Mark, was killed in a tractor accident on a farm in Pennsylvania. God blessed my

46. Wiesel, *Messengers of God*, 233.
47. Wiesel, *Messengers of God*, 234.

uncle and aunt with several other children. But that did not make up for
their loss. A few years ago, my mother asked her sister, Mark's mother,
"So after forty years, how often do you think about Mark?" My aunt
answered, "Every day." God's restoration of Job was a gift of his grace,
not a reward for Job's righteousness that would somehow erase the pain.
This would be too simplistic.

The narrative epilogue of the book of Job is a great reminder that we
serve a God who loves to bless his people. That is his policy. He does it
because he is good. We will all do well to heed the words of an old hymn:
"Ponder anew what the Almighty can do, when with his love he befriends
you." Even better, might we pray for "power, together with all the Lord's
holy people, to grasp how wide and long and high and deep is the love of
Christ" (Eph. 3:18).

Helpful Resources for Studying and Preaching

If we follow the strategy of preaching larger blocks of the book of Job,
then our "go-to" commentaries may well be those that best synthesize the
message of the book without getting bogged down in too many details.
For this reason, my favorite Job commentaries are John Walton's volume
in the NIV Application Commentary, Francis Andersen's volume in the
Tyndale Old Testament Commentaries, and Barry Webb's volume in the
Evangelical Biblical Theology Commentary. Another useful commentary
in this vein is the volume by Daniel J. Estes in the Teach the Text Commentary series. For a bit more detail, both John Hartley's volume in the
New International Commentary on the Old Testament and Tremper Longman's volume in the Baker Commentary on the Old Testament Wisdom
and Psalms are excellent. The three volumes by David J. A. Clines in the
Word Biblical Commentary are remarkable, yet more detailed than most
preachers will want or need for sermon preparation.[48] Another volume
that provides more detail than most preachers need is C. L. Seow's massive
volume on Job 1–21. It is one page shy of a thousand pages! Christopher
Ash's volume on Job in the Preaching the Word series is helpful because
it reads more like a sermon manuscript than a commentary. Sometimes,

48. The Word Biblical Commentary has been published by Word Books and Thomas Nelson,
but the current publisher is Zondervan Academic.

though, I feel that his Christ-centered focus eclipses the concern of the book of Job. For example, the introduction begins, "The book of Job raises three big questions: What kind of a world do we live in? What kind of church should we want? What kind of Savior do we need?"[49] Of course, these are important questions, but they are not the questions that should come to mind when we read the book of Job. By now, we know that the big questions raised by the book of Job are about God's policies. With this caveat aside, Ash's book is quite helpful.

You will also find the Bible Project resources on Job to be useful. These include the Book Overview video on Job as well as the video on Job in the Wisdom Series videos in the Book Collections.[50]

There are two more volumes I highly recommend for everyone who preaches the book of Job. The first is *Wrestling with Job*, by the father-son duo Bill Kynes and Will Kynes. The book grew out of a sermon series preached by the father, Bill, and they are outstanding expositions. In fact, they might provide a suggestion as to how you can preach the book of Job in a nine-part sermon series. Second, the slim volume by John Walton and Tremper Longman, *How to Read Job*, promises what it delivers. It provides a succinct summary of Job's literary features, its characters, its theological message, and its application for Christians.

Another helpful resource is Ken Shigematsu's chapter on Job in *The Big Idea Companion for Preaching and Teaching*. He provides the grist for a five-part sermon series. Some preachers might find Archibald MacLeish's play *J.B.* helpful. It is based on the story of Job and won the 1959 Pulitzer Prize for drama. The drama, set to verse, is about an American millionaire who refuses to turn his back on God after he is stripped of his family and wealth at God's command. It was originally published in 1958 but is still in print. The chapter on Job in *Messengers of God: Biblical Portraits and Legends*, by Holocaust survivor Elie Wiesel, is thought provoking as well.

---

49. Ash, *Job*, 17.
50. You can access these resources at https://bibleproject.com/.

5

Preaching Ecclesiastes

My wife, Priscilla, and two of our kids, Anna and Luke, enjoy putting together puzzles. I do not. I recall Christmas seasons when the three of them worked on a thousand-piece puzzle with the pieces scattered over a card table in our living room. Occasionally, they cajoled me into helping them. This would last only a few minutes. That is how long it would take for me to get frustrated. I would stare at random puzzle pieces. Some were bland, and others had a splash of color. I had a vague idea of where the pieces with a straight edge fit. But for the most part, I had no idea how the pieces fit together to make the picture on the puzzle box top. This is how life works—except that we do not get to see the box top with the picture we are trying to create. Life is a series of events from birth to death that often do not make sense. To make matters worse, life roars by like a train. One moment you see it, then it is gone. Or, to switch metaphors, time resembles a river. It keeps flowing to the sea. Then it is gone forever.[1] We tell high school graduates to follow their dreams and make the world a better place. If we are honest, we should tell them that one day, they will say, "My life makes no sense." The truth is, life is not a puzzle you can solve.

This is where the book of Ecclesiastes can help. It stands in the great wisdom tradition of Israel. Michael Fox says that it "is a strange and

---

1. This metaphor comes from the lyrics to the song "Time," by The Alan Parsons Project.

disquieting book" and gives voice to "the pain and frustration engendered by an unblinking gaze at life's absurdities and injustices."[2] He further observes that it "is the closest the Bible comes to philosophy, which is the intellectual and rational contemplation of fundamental human issues."[3] Fox even portrays Qohelet, the main character in the book, as frustrated "that the mass of disjointed deeds and events [of life] cannot be drawn together into a coherent and significant picture."[4] Craig Bartholomew describes the book as taking its readers "on a roller-coaster ride as its main character, Qohelet, sets out to explore the meaning of life." Thus, it is a sign "of God's desire to meet us where we are and to lead us to full life in Christ amid the brokenness of the world."[5]

So, then, while the book of Proverbs helps us understand how to live so that life makes sense, and while the book of Job helps us understand how to live when life falls apart, the book of Ecclesiastes helps us understand how to live when life is fleeting and makes no sense. My big idea for Ecclesiastes is this: *Life is not a puzzle you can solve but a gift you can enjoy in the fear of God.*[6] We need to preach that message to listeners who feel the weight of a life that is both transient and frustrating.

Studying Ecclesiastes

The book of Ecclesiastes gets its name from the Septuagint's title, ΕΚΚΛΗ-ΣΙΑΣΤΗΣ (*ekklēsiastēs*), which is the Greek translation of the Hebrew title, קהלת (*qohelet*). This is the name of the book's main character (see 1:2). It means "the convener"—it refers either "to one who gathers an assembly to address it or to one who gathers words for instruction" (see 12:9–11).[7] Thus, "Qohelet" is a nickname rather than a proper name. English versions translate it as either "the Teacher" (NIV, CSB, NRSV, NET) or "the Preacher" (ESV, NASB, KJV). Although Jewish tradition identified Solomon as the author, modern evangelical commentators generally believe that

2. Fox, *Ecclesiastes*, ix.
3. Fox, *Ecclesiastes*, xi.
4. Fox, *Ecclesiastes*, xxx.
5. Bartholomew, *Ecclesiastes*, 17.
6. This is my adaptation of the big-idea proposal for Ecclesiastes that I heard several decades ago from Frank Ames, a Hebrew Bible scholar and professor at Denver Seminary: "Life is not a puzzle you can solve but a mystery you can enjoy in the fear of God."
7. Bartholomew, *Ecclesiastes*, 18.

a careful reading of the book disputes this.[8] Thus, George Athas considers the reference to "son of David, king in Jerusalem" in verse 1 as a reflection of "the exploits of numerous kings of Judah, not just Solomon."[9]

Thankfully, our understanding of Ecclesiastes is not dependent on a precise identification of its author—any more than we need to know the identity of the author of the books of Samuel or the author of the Letter to the Hebrews in the New Testament. The best way to understand Ecclesiastes is to examine its structure, its perspective, and its key words and concepts. Only then can we understand it truly and proclaim it faithfully.

The Structure of Ecclesiastes

Commentators generally agree with Craig Bartholomew that while Ecclesiastes is "carefully crafted," it does not have a logical, discernible structure, since Qohelet "moves from subject to subject" and "often doubles back on himself, picking up earlier themes."[10] Iain Provan says that the book is "resistant to linear, systematic treatment."[11] Michael Fox says, "The question of an overarching structure and cohesiveness is one of the most vexing issues in the study of Ecclesiastes," and "it is hard to find some design that would organize the book's components and guide the reader in comprehending the parts and the whole."[12]

Nevertheless, despite "the lack of an organized literary structure, the book displays a deep cohesiveness. This shows above all in the constant presence of a single consciousness mediating all the book's observations, counsels, and evaluations."[13] Athas says that "Qohelet's train of thought begins in orderly fashion," but after 3:8 "the train of thought seems to meander haphazardly, making it notoriously difficult to discern a deliberate structure beyond that point."[14] However, there is intentionality behind this. Athas considers this "a rhetorical device to demonstrate his [Qohelet's] motto that all is meaningless." Thus, the "form of his discourse—or rather, its lack of form—helps create his message."[15]

---

8. See Provan, *Ecclesiastes, Song of Songs*, 26–31; Bartholomew, *Ecclesiastes*, 46–54.
9. Athas, *Ecclesiastes, Song of Songs*, 22.
10. Bartholomew, *Ecclesiastes*, 82–83.
11. Provan, *Ecclesiastes, Song of Songs*, 34.
12. Fox, *Ecclesiastes*, xv.
13. Fox, *Ecclesiastes*, xvi.
14. Athas, *Ecclesiastes, Song of Songs*, 40.
15. Athas, *Ecclesiastes, Song of Songs*, 41.

There is a prologue (1:1–11) and an epilogue (12:9–14) that frame the book, introducing the Teacher and then summarizing his message. The result is the division of the book into three main parts:[16]

    I. Introduction by the third-person narrator (1:1–11)

    II. The words of Qohelet (1:12–12:8)

    III. Epilogue by the third-person narrator (12:9–14)

Although I have not seen reference to this in the commentaries, it seems as though the beginning and the ending of the book form a chiastic structure:

    A An introductory statement about Qohelet (1:1)

      B A declaration of the theme of the book (1:2)

        C A poem about the enigma of life (1:3–11)

        C′ A poem about the end of life (11:7–12:7)

      B′ A declaration of the theme of the book (12:8)

    A′ A concluding statement about Qohelet (12:9–14)

Attempts to outline the body of the book—the words of Qohelet (1:12–12:8)—vary from commentator to commentator, and none of them stand out as the "right approach." Perhaps Iain Provan's outline lends itself the best of all to a sermon series because it outlines the book of Ecclesiastes in fourteen units:[17]

- Introduction (1:1–11)
- Wisdom, pleasure, and joy (1:12–2:26)
- A time for everything (3:1–22)
- Achievement and oppression (4:1–16)
- True worship (5:1–7)
- The pursuit of wealth (5:8–6:12)
- Wisdom is a shelter (7:1–12)
- The universe beyond our grasp (7:13–29)

16. Bartholomew, *Ecclesiastes*, 83.
17. Provan, *Ecclesiastes, Song of Songs*, 43.

- Dealing with an unjust world (8:1–17)
- Living in the face of death (9:1–12)
- The way of wisdom (9:13–10:20)
- The mysterious God (11:1–8)
- In the days of youth (11:9–12:8)
- Qohelet was a wise man (12:9–14)

The Perspective of Ecclesiastes

One of the challenges of understanding Ecclesiastes is to reconcile the seemingly negative statements with the seemingly positive statements. One example is the side-by-side perspectives in Ecclesiastes 2:22–25: "What do people get for all the toil and anxious striving with which they labor under the sun? All their days their work is grief and pain; even at night their minds do not rest. This too is meaningless. A person can do nothing better than to eat and drink and find satisfaction in their own toil. This too, I see, is from the hand of God, for without him, who can eat or find enjoyment?" Work is grief and pain, yet we can find satisfaction in it and even enjoyment. This sounds like a contradiction. How are we to understand the message of Ecclesiastes? What is its perspective?

A Positive Perspective

One option is to view the book's perspective and message as positive. Michael Eaton takes this approach. He writes, "The Preacher has held before his readers two ways of life: the vicious circle of a pointless world, temporary pleasures, fruitless work, futile wisdom, inevitable death, versus an enjoyable life taken daily from the hand of God, in the 'assurance of faith' that he deals appropriately with righteous and unrighteous."[18] This view presents Qohelet as optimistic, "characterizing his theology as a positive biblical form of *carpe diem* ('Seize the day!')."[19] However, the more I read Ecclesiastes, the more convinced I am that Qohelet holds to the pessimistic statements he shares. That is, it appears as though he is presenting a pessimistic outlook on life as his own view, not the view of others which he wants to refute.

18. Eaton, *Ecclesiastes*, 76–77.
19. Athas, *Ecclesiastes, Song of Songs*, 37.

A Pessimistic Perspective

Most commentators view Ecclesiastes as basically pessimistic.[20] Tremper Longman takes this approach. He argues that the "theological message of Qohelet's autobiography (1:12–12:7)" is "Life is full of trouble and then you die."[21] Longman understands the passages that encourage enjoyment (2:24–26; 3:12–14; 5:18–20; 8:15; 9:7–10) as describing a limited type of joy that is "hardly enthusiastic." Thus, "Qohelet expresses resignation rather than affirmation."[22] He calls people to "enjoy the temporal pleasures that lighten the burden" in "the darkness of a life that has no ultimate meaning."[23] However, Longman believes that the narrator, whose voice is heard at the beginning (1:1–11) and the end (12:8–15) of the book, offers a different perspective and is the one who offers the correct theological perspective.[24] He concludes, "Just as in the book of Job, most of the book of Ecclesiastes is composed of the nonorthodox speeches of the human participants of the book, speeches that are torn down and demolished in the end."[25]

The alternative, presented by the narrator at the end of the book, is to live in a right relationship with God ("fear God"), keep his commandments, and remember that God will bring every deed into judgment. This is a summary of the message of the entire Old Testament.[26] However, while the book of Job has a significant proportion of "nonorthodox speeches," the Lord himself makes this clear at the end of the book (Job 42:7–8). This is not the case at the end of Ecclesiastes. It takes a lot of effort to temper the narrator's commendation of Qohelet (the Teacher) in 12:9–10.[27]

---

20. See Bartholomew, *Ecclesiastes*, 93.

21. Longman, *Ecclesiastes*, 34.

22. Longman, *Ecclesiastes*, 34.

23. Longman, *Ecclesiastes*, 35.

24. Longman, *Ecclesiastes*, 36–37.

25. Longman, *Ecclesiastes*, 38.

26. Longman, *Ecclesiastes*, 39.

27. Longman says that the narrator's evaluation in 12:9 "is somewhat complimentary but very reserved" and that although he refers to Qohelet as wise and describes him as "an industrious person," his description "lacks any honorifics or terms of respect" (*Ecclesiastes*, 277). Taking this leap requires us to conclude that wisdom in Qohelet does not have the "moral overtones" that it does in the book of Proverbs, where it "is inextricably bound with righteousness and godliness" (277). While it is true that "wise" (חָכָם, *hakam*) can refer to evil sages as well as good ones throughout the canon (e.g., 2 Sam. 13:3), the context of these instances makes it clear that the term is being used without positive moral overtones—in either a neutral or a negative way. I do not find such clarity in the epilogue to Ecclesiastes.

A Balanced Perspective

There is another way to understand the perspective of the book of Ecclesiastes. Commentators like Craig Bartholomew believe that Qohelet holds the positive and the pessimistic views in tension. He says that holding to a view that takes Ecclesiastes as "fundamentally positive, affirming joy, or basically pessimistic" is "to ignore the literary juxtaposition of contradictory views that is central to the book and the life-death tension it embodies."[28] Bartholomew offers this conclusion: "Ecclesiastes thus exhorts Israelites struggling with the nature of life's meaning and God's purposes to pursue genuine wisdom by allowing their thinking to be shaped integrally by a recognition of God as creator so that they can enjoy God's good gifts and obey his laws amid the enigma of his purposes."[29] Notice how Bartholomew understands the intended outcome of Ecclesiastes. It calls God's people to enjoy God's good gifts *and* obey his laws. In Longman's view, the "joy" passages in Ecclesiastes are part of a wrong way to live life that turns to pleasure and enjoyment as a kind of escape. Instead, the call is to obey God's laws.

In the view that Ecclesiastes presents a balanced perspective, or holds the positive and pessimistic perspectives in tension, there is no disagreement between the narrator (who speaks at the beginning and end of the book) and Qohelet. They are in lockstep. Thus, the speeches of Qohelet do not resemble the nonorthodox speeches of Job's friends. Rather, as Iain Provan says, "Qohelet contrasts with Job's friends. These 'comforters' present to us a rather different picture of how to handle 'wisdom'—a less critical, less thoughtful, and in the end much less helpful treatment."[30] Furthermore, Provan says that the parts of Qohelet's discourse that have "a more troubled and gloomy tone" are "designed to gain a hearing for Qohelet's more positive advice by dispelling false consciousness about the world and by undermining false dreams and hopes."[31] Thus, Qohelet calls his readers to "focus on living each moment of life joyfully before God rather than on the pursuit of wisdom, wealth, or any other human end that comes under the heading 'chasing after wind.'"[32]

28. Bartholomew, *Ecclesiastes*, 93.
29. Bartholomew, *Ecclesiastes*, 95.
30. Provan, *Ecclesiastes, Song of Songs*, 36.
31. Provan, *Ecclesiastes, Song of Songs*, 38.
32. Provan, *Ecclesiastes, Song of Songs*, 39.

Knut Heim offers a twist on a balanced perspective, arguing that the book "was composed in Jerusalem in the final decades of the third century BC" as "resistance literature in the form of political satire."[33] He believes that the phrase "under the sun" is a "cypher for Egypt," meaning "subject to the Egyptian foreign regime."[34] The historical background, then, is Israel being ruled by the Egyptian Ptolemaic kings. Thus, argues Heim, the book of Ecclesiastes "affirms the illusory nature of life *under the sun*, that is, under foreign rule, while at the same time promoting a positive, hopeful outlook on life conducted within the trajectory of Jewish religion and tradition."[35] If this view is correct, it is very subtle. Heim offers support but admits that his arguments do not provide conclusive proof, since "Qoheleth had to be careful"—presumably careful not to rile up the foreign oppressor.[36]

Key Words and Concepts in Ecclesiastes

Our understanding of key words and concepts in Ecclesiastes will lead us to one of the perspectives described above. So, we need to take a brief look at the book's vocabulary.

Vapor. The word הֶבֶל (*hebel*), "vapor," occurs thirty-eight times in Ecclesiastes,[37] and is by far its most important word for understanding the book's message. It features prominently in the theme statement or motto at the book's beginning and end (1:2; 12:8). It is a concrete word meaning "warm breath, vapor,"[38] yet it is used metaphorically throughout the book. The challenge is to determine what the metaphor represents. A straightforward translation of 1:3 would read:

> "Vapor of vapors,"
> says the Qohelet.
> "Vapor of vapors.
> All is vapor."

The term is used in two primary ways in Ecclesiastes. First, it means "fleeting, temporary," referring to what is here one moment and gone the next—"including actions that are 'passing' in the sense that they make no

33. Heim, *Ecclesiastes*, 4, 8.
34. Heim, *Ecclesiastes*, 6.
35. Heim, *Ecclesiastes*, 8.
36. Heim, *Ecclesiastes*, 8.
37. Bartholomew, *Ecclesiastes*, 105.
38. *HALOT*.

permanent impact or impression on reality." That is, "their effects do not last."[39] Second, it can refer to what is enigmatic or elusive in that "it resists our attempts to capture it and contain it, to grasp hold of it and control it."[40] Craig Bartholomew argues that although the word is used "with a variety of nuances," including a negative connotation in some instances, its "core meaning or reference" is to something that "cannot be grasped and is thus *enigmatic* or *incomprehensible*."[41] After all, a breath or vapor is real. It is not meaningless; it simply cannot be grasped.[42]

Admittedly, הֶבֶל (*hebel*) is a difficult word to translate in the book of Ecclesiastes, where it is used metaphorically. However, our English translations have created confusion by translating it as "meaningless" (NIV, NLT) or "futility/futile" (CSB, NET). The translation "vanity" (ESV, NASB, KJV) might be slightly better, but it too is unhelpful without qualification and explanation. Robert Alter makes a good point: "The problem is that all of these English equivalents are more or less right, and abstractions being what they are, each one has the effect of excluding the others and thus limiting the scope of the Hebrew metaphor."[43] Exactly! Perhaps Bartholomew's suggestion of "enigma/enigmatic" is the best approach aside from translating it literally as "vapor" or "breath."

Gain. The Hebrew word יִתְרוֹן (*yitron*) occurs ten times in Ecclesiastes, and these are its only occurrences in the Old Testament.[44] It "is a commercial term meaning 'profit'" and refers in Ecclesiastes to "surplus returns from one's investment of work."[45] The question raised in 1:3 and 3:9 is "whether labor and life are of any *benefit* at all."[46]

Under the sun. The Hebrew expression תַּחַת הַשָּׁמֶשׁ (*tahat hashamesh*), "under the sun," occurs twenty-nine times in Ecclesiastes, appearing only here in the Old Testament.[47] There is nothing mysterious about this

---

39. Provan, *Ecclesiastes, Song of Songs*, 51.
40. Provan, *Ecclesiastes, Song of Songs*, 52.
41. Bartholomew, *Ecclesiastes*, 106.
42. Bartholomew, *Ecclesiastes*, 106.
43. Alter, *Hebrew Bible*, 3:675.
44. The word יִתְרוֹן (*yitron*) occurs in Eccles. 1:3; 2:11, 13 (2x); 3:9; 5:9 (v. 8 in Hebrew text); 16 (v. 15 in Hebrew text); 7:12; 10:10, 11.
45. Fox, *Ecclesiastes*, xxi.
46. Bartholomew, *Ecclesiastes*, 108.
47. The expression תַּחַת הַשָּׁמֶשׁ (*tahat hashamesh*) occurs in Eccles. 1:3, 9, 14; 2:11, 17, 18, 19, 20, 22; 3:16; 4:1, 3, 7, 14; 5:13 (v. 12 in Hebrew text), 18 (v. 17 in Hebrew text); 6:1, 12; 8:9, 15 (2x), 17; 9:3, 6, 9 (2x), 11, 13; 10:5.

expression. It simply "refers to life in this present world and is synony-mous with the phrases 'under heaven' (e.g., 1:13) and 'on earth' (e.g., 8:14)."[48] However, as noted earlier, Knut Heim has challenged this view and understands the expression as a cypher that cryptically refers to being subject to the Egyptian Ptolemaic kings. His strongest argument for this understanding is that the title "the Sun" was commonly used for Egyptian pharaohs and that "the Ptolemaic kings carried the designation 'son of the Sun' in their official throne cartouches."[49] Even if Heim's understanding is correct, it does not change the common interpretation as much as it provides a more specific understanding of the difficulties that the readers of Ecclesiastes were experiencing in their life on earth.

Chasing after the wind. The expression "chasing after the wind," either רְעוּת רוּחַ (*re'ut ruah*) or רַעְיוֹן רוּחַ (*ra'yon ruah*) in Hebrew, is used metaphorically in Ecclesiastes.[50] According to Iain Provan, "To chase the wind is to seek to grasp hold of and control something beyond our grasp and uncontrollable."[51] The expression is frequently paired with the word הֶבֶל (*hebel*) in Ecclesiastes, thus underlining the same truth with a different metaphor.[52]

Preaching Strategies

Like the other wisdom books, the book of Ecclesiastes is a "must-preach" book. It speaks to people whose lives do not make sense and who thus feel either confusion, frustration, or despair. To help us preach Ecclesiastes effec-tively, we will explore sermon series options, address the matter of preaching Christ in Ecclesiastes, and consider some thoughts on key sermon texts,

Sermon Series Options

The size of the book of Ecclesiastes—twelve chapters—allows for a sermon series that covers the entire book. One way to divide the book into preaching passages is to use Iain Provan's outline (see above) and

---

48. Provan, *Ecclesiastes, Song of Songs*, 54.
49. Heim, *Ecclesiastes*, 8.
50. The expression רְעוּת רוּחַ (*re'ut ruah*) occurs in Eccles. 1:14; 2:11, 17, 26; 4:4, 6; 6:9. The expression רַעְיוֹן רוּחַ (*ra'yon ruah*) occurs in Eccles. 1:17; 4:16. All of these instances are preceded by הֶבֶל (*hebel*) except for 1:17 and 4:6.
51. Provan, *Ecclesiastes, Song of Songs*, 53.
52. Provan, *Ecclesiastes, Song of Songs*, 53.

preach the book in fourteen sermons. Similarly, Sidney Greidanus breaks up the book into fifteen preaching units.[53] For a comparison between the two breakdowns, see table 5.1. You can decide, based on your own study and commentary work, where to begin and end the preaching units in sections of the book where the outlines by Provan and Greidanus differ. Philip Ryken breaks down the book of Ecclesiastes into twenty-six preaching units in his commentary for expositors,[54] while Calvin Choi selects twelve key passages for preaching, basically one text from each chapter of Ecclesiastes.[55]

Table 5.1

Two Approaches to a Sermon Series on Ecclesiastes

Iain Provan's Breakdown	Sidney Greidanus's Breakdown
1. Introduction (1:1–11)	1. No Gain from All Our Toil (1:1–11)
2. Wisdom, Pleasure, and Joy (1:12–2:26)	2. The Teacher's Search for Meaning (1:12–2:26)
3. A Time for Everything (3:1–22)	3. God Set the Times (3:1–15)
4. Achievement and Oppression (4:1–16)	4. Working in a Wicked World (3:16–4:6)
5. True Worship (5:1–7)	5. Working Together (4:7–16)
6. The Pursuit of Wealth (5:8–6:12)	6. Worshiping in God's House (5:1–7)
7. Wisdom Is a Shelter (7:1–12)	7. The Love of Money (5:8–6:9)
8. The Universe beyond Our Grasp (7:13–29)	8. How to Handle Adversity (6:10–7:14)
9. Dealing with an Unjust World (8:1–17)	9. How to Act in a Paradoxical World (7:15–29)
10. Living in the Face of Death (9:1–12)	10. Use Wisdom but Know Its Limitations (8:1–17)
11. The Way of Wisdom (9:13–10:20)	11. Enjoy Life! (9:1–12)
12. The Mysterious God (11:1–8)	12. Because of the Harm Inflicted by Folly, Use Wisdom (9:13–10:20)
13. In the Days of Youth (11:9–12:8)	13. Take Risks Boldly but Wisely! (11:1–6)
14. Qohelet Was a Wise Man (12:9–14)	14. Remember Your Creator! (11:7–12:8)
	15. Fear God, and Keep His Commandments! (12:9–14)

53. Greidanus, *Ecclesiastes*, viii–ix.
54. P. Ryken, *Ecclesiastes*, 7–8.
55. Choi, "Ecclesiastes," 240–43.

Your ministry context will help you determine whether a longer series on the book is feasible. My concern is not so much people's attention spans as whether a breakdown into such small units might keep them from feeling the overall flow of the argument in the book. Furthermore, I want to expose people to as much of the Bible as possible over the course of my preaching ministry in a local church. Taking half a year in Ecclesiastes and two or three years in the Gospel of Matthew, for example, will keep me from ever preaching other books in the canon. I am not suggesting that there is a right or wrong answer, but simply that each preacher or preaching team needs to weigh the upsides and downsides to a sermon series of any length.

If you are looking for a shorter series that covers the sweep of thought in Ecclesiastes, though not every passage, you might consider a five-week series that includes the following sermon texts.

- Ecclesiastes 1–2
- Ecclesiastes 3:1–15
- Ecclesiastes 4:1–12
- Ecclesiastes 9:13–10:20
- Ecclesiastes 11:7–12:14

Below we will consider how to preach each of these five texts. In addition to helping us with these specific texts, this discussion will guide us in thinking about how to preach other passages in the book. Before we explore these five texts, we should turn our attention to another challenge.

Preaching Christ in Ecclesiastes

Sidney Greidanus describes the challenge of preaching Christ in Ecclesiastes. He says, "Ecclesiastes contains not even one 'messianic text'; there is no promise of the coming Messiah. How does one preach Christ from a book that has no messianic texts?"[56] Those who rely on typology will experience frustration. It is next to impossible to find anything that prefigures Jesus or any aspect of his ministry. But as I have already argued, Christ-centered preaching should be understood as locating any passage of Scripture in the larger story of the Bible—a story whose hero is Jesus

---

56. Greidanus, *Ecclesiastes*, 24.

Christ. I will make some suggestions for doing this in the following discussion of some key sermon texts in Ecclesiastes.

Some Thoughts on Key Sermon Texts

There is a real possibility that few, if any, of your listeners have ever heard a sermon on a text from the book of Ecclesiastes. Thus, you will need to unpack every passage you preach in a clear, compelling way. When you announce the series, communicate the basics about the book. You might use a paragraph like this, either in a promo video, an announcement on your church's website, or an email.

> Life resembles chasing the wind. We can never quite control it or figure it out. It is not a puzzle we can solve. Like a vapor, or a puff of air, life is mysterious, elusive, and fleeting. It is here one moment, gone the next. However we try to cope with life, we seem to come up empty. Wisdom and knowledge have limits. Wealth and pleasure fail to satisfy. Work is tedious. Death is inevitable. But the book of Ecclesiastes points out the way forward. It tells us how to cope when our pursuits of knowledge, wealth, pleasure, and work leave us empty, frustrated, and disillusioned. The book of Ecclesiastes tells us that life is not a puzzle we can solve but a gift we can enjoy in the fear of God.

Here are some suggestions for preaching the five key passages I identified above. The sermons you prepare need to be built on a solid exegetical base. Then you need to think creatively about how best to communicate the ideas, including the big idea, in each one.

Ecclesiastes 1–2

This sermon will obviously set the tone for your series on the book of Ecclesiastes. Rather than doing an introductory sermon on the entire book, I use the introduction of my first sermon to introduce the book, especially because Ecclesiastes has a clear prologue (1:1–11). I suggest reminding your listeners in your sermon's introduction that while the book of Proverbs helps us understand how to live so that life makes sense, and while the book of Job helps us understand how to live when life falls apart, the book of Ecclesiastes helps us understand how to live when life is fleeting and makes no sense. Below is my preaching outline for Ecclesiastes 1–2.

I. Life is as fleeting and uncontrollable as a vapor (1:1–2:23).

    A. The book's *title* introduces the Teacher (1:1).

    B. The book's *theme* is "Everything in life is *hebel*" (1:2).

    C. The book's *underlying question* is "What is left over at the end of one's life?" (1:3).

    D. A *poem* expresses the theme and the question by looking at nature (1:4–11).

    E. The book's theme holds true even in the best ways we can spend our lives (1:12–2:23).

        1. The pursuit of wisdom/knowledge is *hebel* (1:12–18).

        2. The pursuit of pleasure is *hebel* (2:1–11).

        3. The pursuit of morality is *hebel* (2:12–16).

        4. The pursuit of work is *hebel* (2:17–23).

II. However, you can enjoy life as a gift of God (2:24–26).

    A. The conclusion sounds a bit like hedonism: just pursue pleasure (2:24a).

    B. But the conclusion is to enjoy life as a gift from God, even though it is *hebel* (2:24b–26).

    C. Thus, (*Big Idea*) although life is as fleeting and uncontrollable as a vapor, you can enjoy it as a gift of God.

There is a time to teach your listeners a Hebrew word and a time to refrain from teaching your listeners a Hebrew word. A sermon on Ecclesiastes 1–2 is one of the former times. The word to teach them, of course, is הֶבֶל (*hebel*). Point out that it is used as a metaphor, and it is difficult to translate. The best way to explain it is probably not to find the perfect word by which to translate it. Rather, help your listeners visualize the meaning of *hebel*. You can ask them to picture smoke from the candles on their birthday cake once they blow them out, or their breath on a cold winter day. Both the smoke and the cloud of mist will disappear quickly. They are fleeting—here one moment, gone the next. Also, they cannot grab a handful of smoke or mist and put it in a box. It is uncontrollable. An even more vivid way to get the point across is to purchase a fog machine. (These are surprisingly inexpensive!) You can shoot puffs of *hebel* (fog) and then demonstrate how it quickly disappears and how you are unable to get ahold of it and put it in a box or move it from one location to another.[57]

You might be tempted to slow down and preach a series on each one of the pursuits that Ecclesiastes identifies as *hebel* (see the outline above). However, each of these pursuits diagnoses the problem. The initial solution statement does not come until 2:24–26. So, if you preach these pursuits individually, you need to arrive at 2:24–26 in each sermon. Actually, this might not be a bad approach because it will reinforce the rather surprising solution: enjoying life as a gift from God.

One critical element for preaching Ecclesiastes 1–2 according to the above outline is an effective transition between points I and II. You might say something like this: "Where does this leave you? Being told that life is fleeting and uncontrollable like a vapor can easily lead to despair. How, then, should you live? If everything is *hebel*, then life seems rather pointless." You might even share your own struggle with these kinds of feelings or reference a song or movie or story that expresses them.

When it comes to preaching Christ, you have the opportunity to proclaim the truth that true happiness, or the good life, is described in the Sermon on the Mount (see Matt. 5:3–12). As Jonathan Pennington says, "Jesus is a philosopher of happiness."[58] Rather than looking for satisfaction or meaning or fulfillment or happiness in pursuits that only amount to *hebel*, the full life we want is found in Jesus Christ (John 10:10). Yet the twist is that "his authoritative declarations about what true happiness is" begin with attitudes that are counterintuitive.[59] Declare to your listeners that the wisdom, knowledge, and happiness that God gives (Eccles. 2:26) are found only in Jesus—the one in whom all the treasures of wisdom and knowledge are hidden (Col. 2:3). You might also point out that the Greek term ματαιότης (*mataiotēs*), which is used to translate the Hebrew word הֶבֶל (*hebel*) in the Greek translation of the Old Testament, appears in Romans 8:20. Although "creation was subjected to frustration [ματαιότης, *mataiotēs*]," it will be brought into the freedom and glory of the children of God when we are raised with Christ (see Rom. 8:20–23). Our risen Lord will one day bring about the ultimate reversal of *hebel*!

57. I got this idea several years ago from Chris Dolson and Tim Mackie when they served together on the preaching team at Blackhawk Church in Madison, Wisconsin.
58. Pennington, *Jesus the Great Philosopher*, 206.
59. Pennington, *Jesus the Great Philosopher*, 206.

Ecclesiastes 3:1–15

This is a classic text that contains one of the best-known poems in the Bible. More importantly, it expands the idea communicated in chapters 1–2. Here are the major movements in a sermon outline on this text.

I. Life is a series of times—favorable and unfavorable from birth to death (vv. 1–8).

II. God has burdened us with the awareness that we belong to a larger story without letting us see how he makes everything beautiful in its time (vv. 9–11).

III. (*Big Idea*) Life is not a puzzle we can solve but a gift we can enjoy in the fear of God (vv. 12–15).

I have already indicated that I see point III as the big idea for the book of Ecclesiastes as well as for this passage. Admittedly, there is a risk in using the puzzle metaphor because it is external to Ecclesiastes. But I believe that it nicely captures the teaching of Ecclesiastes 3:1–15. Of course, we always wrestle with word choice when we formulate a big-idea statement, so there are some other options. One is to swap the word "mystery" for the word "puzzle." Another option is to word the big idea like this: "Although you may not be able to make sense of your life, it is a gift you can enjoy in the fear of God."

Now, here are some thoughts about preaching this passage. When you reflect on the poem in verses 1–8, point out that verse 1 states the general principle, and then verses 2–8 flesh it out by presenting the activities of life in a series of opposites.[60] The list is descriptive rather than prescriptive. For example, verse 3 is not telling people that it is appropriate to kill. Rather, it is simply observing that killing and healing are events in human life. Older listeners will remember the 1960s song "Turn! Turn! Turn!" which was based on this poem and was popularized by the Byrds, an American folk rock group. A good commentary will help you understand possible meanings of some of the more obscure language, like that of scattering and gathering stones (v. 5a).

The second movement, verses 9–11, is utterly profound. Following the survey of the times of one's life (vv. 1–8), it returns to the question first

---

60. These pairs of activities are merisms. They describe activities or events that are opposites and include everything else in between.

raised in Ecclesiastes 1:3, asking what workers gain from their toil. This is a rhetorical question because Qohelet offers an observation rather than an answer. He has seen the burden that God has laid on the human race (3:10). Then, in verse 11, he describes this burden. God "has made everything beautiful in its time" (v. 11a). Iain Provan observes that we should understand this "in the sense of 'beautifully fitting,' given the emphasis of Ecclesiastes 3:1–8, rather than in the sense of 'intrinsically beautiful.' There is an elegance about how life works, as 'time' succeeds 'time.'"[61] Perhaps both ideas are in play here.

Yet, God has done something else besides making everything beautiful in its time. He has also "set eternity in the human heart" so that "no one can fathom what God has done from beginning to end" (v. 11b). The burden, then, is that God has given human beings a sense of eternity—that we belong to a larger story, yet we do not have the ability to figure it out. This reminds me of a job I had for one year in Montana as a ranch hand. I loved the days when I had a focused task such as plowing a field or moving cattle. But I found myself frustrated on days when I was given a series of disjointed tasks and had no idea of what the big picture was (though the rancher did). This is where the puzzle analogy might be helpful. Life is like a box of puzzle pieces, only there is no picture on the box top to tell you what kind of picture the pieces will make when assembled.

In the third movement, verses 12–15, Qohelet offers his conclusion on the matter. So what should we do? He returns to the advice he gave in 2:24–26. Only this time he adds more detail. Not only are we to enjoy life as "the gift of God" (3:13), but also we are to recognize that God has set up life—with its frustrations and mysteries—so that we will fear God (3:14). Here is a prominent theme in the wisdom books. Proverbs began with the fear of the Lord (1:7), and Ecclesiastes will end with it (12:13). This is an attitude of reverence and awe.

If you use the puzzle imagery, consider handing out a puzzle piece to everyone. Simply buy a five-hundred- or one-thousand-piece puzzle (and multiple boxes of the same puzzle if you have a large congregation), and have your ushers hand out a piece to everyone who enters your sanctuary or worship center. Make sure not to have the box top visible. Instruct the ushers to say to people, "Hang onto this. You'll get an explanation before

---

61. Provan, *Ecclesiastes, Song of Songs*, 90.

our worship is finished." Alternatively, you could hand these out at the beginning of the sermon. But handing these out before the service will create a bit of anticipation. At the appropriate point in your sermon, remind your listeners that the puzzle piece they received does not make sense on its own. They have no idea what kind of picture their piece and all the other puzzle pieces make when properly assembled. Then remind them that the events of their lives are a series of puzzle pieces that don't make sense on their own. Only God can put them together. When he does, a beautiful picture will emerge. This is what God does with all of the pieces of their lives that make no sense at the time. I took this approach a decade ago when I preached a sermon series on Ecclesiastes. A few years after the sermon series, a church member told me he had found his puzzle piece while cleaning out his desk drawer, and he remembered that life is not a puzzle we can solve but a gift we can enjoy in the fear of God.

Perhaps the best way to locate this text within the larger story of Scripture and its hero, Jesus Christ, is to connect it to the apostle Peter's sermon in Acts 3:11–26. In his sermon, Peter says that heaven must receive Jesus the Messiah "until the time comes for God to restore everything" (v. 21). This time of restoration is the time when God will make everything beautifully fitting. The great chapter on resurrection, 1 Corinthians 15, talks about the end as well—the time when the risen Christ fully establishes his reign (vv. 24–28). The implication is that Christ's followers should give themselves fully to the work of the Lord, knowing that our labor is not in vain (v. 58). Serving Christ is not an empty pursuit, given that it somehow contributes to his final victory and the establishment of his reign. A third potential connection is to Romans 8:28, where God promises that "in all things God works for the good of those who love him." This is, at the very least, a faint echo of God's promise to make everything beautifully fitting in its time. Reading Romans 8:28 in context makes it clear that it is all dependent on the work of Christ.

Ecclesiastes 4:1–12

This is a fascinating chapter that gives us some insights on how we can keep our lives together in a world of broken relationships. Yet even after revealing the solution, Qohelet is quick to remind us that the solution has its limits in a world of *hebel* in which there is much "chasing after the wind." Here is one possible preaching outline for the chapter.

I. Human relationships break down for a variety of reasons (vv. 1–8).

   A. They can break down because of oppression (vv. 1–3).

   B. They can break down because of envy (vv. 4–6).

   C. They can break down because of loneliness (vv. 7–8).

II. (*Big Idea*) You can keep your life together in a world of broken relationships by pursuing life together (vv. 9–12).

III. However, life together has its limits due to living in a world of *hebel* (vv. 13–16).

IV. The way we restore and experience community is through the gospel of Jesus.

The first movement, verses 1–8, describes the problem in terms of three causes. Here we must help our listeners feel the anguish represented by "the tears of the oppressed" in verse 1. Invite your listeners to see the tears of a teen girl who is bullied at school because her clothes are not in style. Invite your listeners to see the tears of an eight-year-old boy who has been abused by a relative and pulls the covers up over his chin at night. Invite your listeners to see the tears of a single mom who is being harassed by a collection agency for bills she cannot pay. Invite your listeners to see the tears of starving villagers whose children have bloated bellies as they wait for food that sits rotting on a dock because a corrupt government refuses to let a relief agency distribute it. It might be helpful to point out the literary art in verses 1–3, where "under the sun" brackets the content inside and where the declaration that the dead are happier than the living is hyperbole—deliberate exaggeration for the sake of effect. In verse 4, the reality that envy is at the root of achievement is another example of *hebel*. In this context, *hebel* has the sense of "absurd" or "frustrating." One way to capture the *hebel* of loneliness in verses 7–8 is by describing or showing Samuel Beckett's play *Breath*.[62] This play is only thirty-five seconds long, opening with a cry, ending with a cry, and in between an inhale and an exhale. There are no characters. Beckett's script calls for the curtain to open and the stage to be "littered with miscellaneous rubbish."[63]

---

62. Philip Ryken uses this play as an illustration in his exposition of Eccles. 12:8–14 (*Ecclesiastes*, 274), but I believe that it fits just as well here in Eccles. 4:7–8.

63. Julie Bates, "Samuel Beckett's Miscellaneous Rubbish," *Irish Times*, August 30, 2017, https://www.irishtimes.com/culture/books/samuel-beckett-s-miscellaneous-rubbish-1.3202335. A number of videos of a "performance" of this play are available on YouTube or similar platforms.

The second movement, in Ecclesiastes 4:9–12, provides the solution. Life together, or community, will replace oppression, envy, and loneliness with cooperation. This is the way God designed life to work (see Gen. 2:18). Solitude is good, but loneliness is not. Community enables us to prosper (v. 9) and to survive (vv. 10–12a). Famous pairs offer one example of this. Think of Lewis and Clark, Fred Astaire and Ginger Rogers, or Barnes and Noble. You might consider illustrating Ecclesiastes 4:12, "A cord of three strands is not quickly broken," with three dowel rods tied together. Have someone come up to the platform and give them a single dowel rod—one that is not too difficult to break. Then hand the same person three dowel rods that are taped or tied together. It will be much harder, maybe impossible, for the person to break them.

The big idea of the passage is in the second movement, and it seems like a great place to stop. After all, Qohelet has provided us with a satisfying solution to a troubling problem. But Qohelet presses on and qualifies his solution in a third movement, verses 13–16. His sobering words in this movement prevent us from concluding that if we have community, then all will be well. The reality is that in the end, the benefits of community are all *hebel*—fleeting and frustrating. When I preach on Ecclesiastes 4, I devote a final movement to exploring how we can restore and experience genuine life together in a broken world. We all know that as soon as we surround ourselves with other people, the comfort and support that this provides quickly give way to envy and oppression. The only way out is through knowing Christ. He has modeled for us how to forgive others (Eph. 4:32) and how to put their interests ahead of our own (Phil. 2:1–11).

Ecclesiastes 9:13–10:20

This section of Ecclesiastes is an extended meditation on living wisely in a world that ignores wisdom. Chapter 10 consists of proverbial wisdom—that is, the kind of maxims or short sayings for which the book of Proverbs is famous. Here is a potential preaching outline for this section.

I. (*Big Idea*) The power we need for living is found not in strength but in godly wisdom (9:13–10:3).

   A. Qohelet shares an impressive example of how wisdom is better than strength (9:13–16a).

    B. However, our world despises wisdom, and fools destroy it
       (9:16b–10:3).
  II. Godly wisdom is desperately needed to overcome folly, especially
     in leadership (10:4–20).
    A. There is a desperate need for wise reactions (v. 4).
    B. There is a desperate need for wise leadership (vv. 5–7, 16–17).
    C. There is a desperate need for wise preparations and precautions
      (vv. 8–11).
    D. There is a desperate need for wise words (vv. 12–15, 20).
    E. There is a desperate need for wise work—that is, diligence (vv.
      18–19).

In the first movement (9:13–10:3), Qohelet describes how a poor man saved his city during a siege by acting wisely. This led Qohelet to say, "Wisdom is better than strength" (9:16a). Yet he follows this with the observation that "the poor man's wisdom is despised, and his words are no longer heeded" (9:16b). Then Qohelet shifts to proverbial wisdom in 9:17 to contrast wisdom and folly. This contrast continues through 10:3, observing that our world despises wisdom and fools destroy it. While the proverbial sayings continue in 10:4 and following, Qohelet touches on various areas in life where wisdom is needed. The proverbs—and their ideas—are woven throughout this section and do not occur in neat, tidy packages. Craig Bartholomew argues that Ecclesiastes 10 deals with a challenge to the biblical notion of two ways (see Ps. 1). He writes, "What Qohelet demonstrates in this chapter is that denial of the biblical two ways does not eradicate them but transmutes them into an idolatrous two ways, which Proverbs would itself call folly."[64] The "idolatrous two ways" consist of wealth and power. We know from "Qohelet's earlier reflections (cf. 2:1–11)" that "to absolutize wealth and power is no answer to the question of life and its meaning."[65]

Finding a connection to Jesus and his gospel is not difficult. He is the wisest person who ever lived on this planet (Matt. 12:42; Col. 2:3), and his gospel provides the wisdom we need for living. The apostle Paul tells us to conduct ourselves in a manner worthy of the gospel (Phil. 1:27), and he

---

64. Bartholomew, *Ecclesiastes*, 332.
65. Bartholomew, *Ecclesiastes*, 333.

affirms that while the gospel is foolishness to the world, that foolishness is wiser than the world's wisdom (1 Cor. 1:18–25).

Ecclesiastes 11:7–12:14

The book of Ecclesiastes ends with a poem reminding us that the joy of life ends in death (11:7–12:8), and this is followed by the third-person narrator's epilogue (12:9–14). It is a sobering reflection that calls the reader to "rejoice" and "remember" (11:8 ESV). According to Craig Bartholomew, these are "the two verbs that dominate the poem. . . . 'Rejoice' is the imperative that governs 11:9–10, and 'remember' is the imperative that governs 12:1–7."[66] My title for this sermon is "The Tunnel at the End of the Light." Here is my preaching outline for Ecclesiastes 11:7–12:14.

   I. The problem: Even though life is a gift to enjoy, darkness is coming (11:7–8).
      A. Light is a metaphor for the goodness of life—a gift to enjoy (11:7–8a).
      B. Darkness is a metaphor for the brokenness of life—a reality to remember (11:8b).
   II. The solution: (*Big Idea*) The best way to enjoy life when you are young is to remember your Creator, who will judge you after you are old and die (11:9–12:14).
      A. Enjoy life when you are young, knowing that God will bring you into judgment (11:9–10).
      B. Remember your Creator before you get old and die (12:1–8).
      C. Epilogue: Fear and obey God, who ultimately will judge your deeds (12:9–14).

A simple yet effective way to begin this sermon is to say, "You may have heard the old saying that there is a light at the end of the tunnel. No matter how dark it seems, you'll soon end up in daylight. However, when you look at life as a whole, the opposite is true. There is a tunnel at the end of the light. There are days of darkness ahead—even death. So how should you live, knowing that there is a tunnel at the end of the light? The

---

66. Bartholomew, *Ecclesiastes*, 343.

final section of the book of Ecclesiastes gives us the answer. Look with me at Ecclesiastes 11:7–12:14." Of course, you can flesh this out a bit. But sometimes, shorter introductions are the most effective. This one creates interest, raises a need, and orients listeners to the Scripture text. That's all a good introduction needs to accomplish.

The sermon outline is simple, moving from problem to solution. Point II is the big idea, and I recommend preaching it inductively. In other words, do not reveal the big idea until you have worked through subpoints A, B, and C. As always, you will need to clarify what Qohelet is saying and not saying. For example, the call to "follow the ways of your heart and whatever your eyes see" (11:9b) is neither hedonistic ("Live it up now!") nor cynical ("You might as well live it up now because you'll pay in the end anyway!"). Rather, it is a call for following your desire with a healthy awareness of judgment. Also, we need to cast a positive light on God's judgment. It is by judgment that God removes everything that causes *hebel*. Furthermore, it's important to tell your listeners that 12:2–7 is a metaphor of aging toward death, utilizing "day of the Lord" imagery and overtones. The imagery is vivid. As Zack Eswine says, "In Ecclesiastes, death is a piece of tornado from which no proverbial basement can shelter us."[67] Finally, show your listeners from the context that 12:12 is not a rejection of new books. The point is this: Do not overdo it when it comes to reading wisdom or you will be overwhelmed with all the ideas you encounter; instead, fear God and keep his commandments.

So, at the end of the book, the narrator is reinforcing the teaching of Qohelet. He tells us not to let *hebel* rob us of our youth by plunging us into darkness, bitterness, loneliness, or despair. Our purpose in life is not simply to get through each day. The final conclusion about fearing God reminds us of the book's big idea, that life is not a puzzle we can solve but a gift we can enjoy in the fear of God.

One way to connect Ecclesiastes 11:7–12:14 to the larger story of Scripture and its hero, Jesus, is to focus on the final judgment. George Athas provides an example of how to do this in the following reflection:

> As he talked to the philosophers at the Areopagus in Athens, Paul made the claim that God "has set a day when he will judge the world with justice by

67. Eswine, *Recovering Eden*, 9.

the man he has appointed. He has given proof of this to everyone by raising him from the dead" (Acts 17:31). Jesus' resurrection is the first verdict of the final judgment day. As he walked out of his tomb, the eschatological clock struck twelve. It is just that it has not stopped chiming yet. But soon it will. We must not be fooled into thinking our actions have no consequences or that God pays us no heed. Since God created a single humanity, our actions inevitably have repercussions for our relationship with him and with each other. God's love for us does not undermine his righteousness and justice, so perfect is his love. Life should be justly enjoyed as God intended. If we do not know God, and Jesus Christ, whom he has sent (John 17:3), we forego true and lasting satisfaction. The prospect of judgment is frightening.[68]

Appendix E contains a sample sermon on Ecclesiastes 11:7–12:14. It follows the outline provided above and attempts to capture the pathos of the final poem and the ethos of the epilogue.

Helpful Resources for Studying and Preaching

My favorite commentaries for studying and preaching the book of Ecclesiastes include Iain Provan's *Ecclesiastes, Song of Songs* in the NIV Application Commentary and Craig Bartholomew's volume *Ecclesiastes* in the Baker Commentary on the Old Testament Wisdom and Psalms. Both are sensitive to the literary artistry of the book and to the theological message it communicates. Both hold the positive and the pessimistic viewpoints in tension. I appreciate Bartholomew's candor and humility when he says the content of Ecclesiastes "is like an octopus—just when you think you have all the tentacles pinned down, you notice one still waving around!"[69] I suspect that most preachers will agree with this comment. George Athas's volume *Ecclesiastes, Song of Songs* in the Story of God Commentary shares a balanced perspective similar to that of Provan and Bartholomew when it comes to the book's positive and pessimistic viewpoints. He too is good on the book's theological message. Tremper Longman's volume on Ecclesiastes in the New International Commentary on the Old Testament is "vintage Longman." He is an outstanding exegete and Old Testament scholar, and his work is as excellent as one can find from the viewpoint that

---

68. Athas, *Ecclesiastes, Song of Songs*, 220.
69. Bartholomew, *Ecclesiastes*, 13.

the book's perspective is more negative. Knut Heim's volume in the Tyndale Old Testament Commentaries, as noted above, is insightful, whether or not his provocative suggestion that life "under the sun" refers to living under the oppression of Ptolemaic kings is correct.

For a homiletical commentary, Philip Ryken's volume on Ecclesiastes in the Preaching the Word series is outstanding. You will find a lot of great supporting material—illustrations, literature, and so on—in his careful expositions. *Preaching Christ from Ecclesiastes* by Sidney Greidanus is also an excellent resource. He is a superb exegete, and his Christ-centered focus does not preclude him from presenting the challenge or ethical thrust of the text and applying it to the lives of believers.

Once again, you will benefit from the Bible Project resources on Ecclesiastes as well as the chapter on Ecclesiastes in *The Big Idea Companion for Preaching and Teaching.* The Bible Project resources include the Book Overview video as well as the video on Ecclesiastes in the Wisdom Series videos in the Book Collections.[70] As previously noted, Calvin Choi's chapter in *The Big Idea Companion for Preaching and Teaching* provides basic suggestions for twelve sermons from the book of Ecclesiastes, roughly one per chapter.

Finally, there are two fine popular-level expositions that you can put into the hands of your listeners during a series on Ecclesiastes. The first is Zack Eswine's *Recovering Eden: The Gospel according to Ecclesiastes.* The second is *Living Life Backward: How Ecclesiastes Teaches Us to Live in Light of the End* by David Gibson.

---

70. You can access these resources at https://bibleproject.com/.

6

Preaching Song of Songs

Our final stop on a tour of the Old Testament poetic books is the little book known as Song of Songs. Its opening words, "the song of songs," make the claim that it is the best love song ever.[1] Othmar Keel says that this expression "is a superlative," like "king of kings" (Dan. 2:37) or "holy of holies" (Exod. 26:33).[2] However, preachers tend to avoid Song of Songs. Let's face it: its lyrics seem silly, embarrassing, confusing, and even devoid of theology. These are the reasons why preachers avoid it or at least struggle with it if they muster the courage to preach it. Let's explore them a bit further.

First, the lyrics of Song of Songs seem a bit silly to our Western, late-modern ears. My wife, Priscilla, and I asked our friend Dave to sing *Annie's Song* at our wedding. This is a love song written in the early 1970s by John Denver for his wife, Annie. Like Song of Songs, it captures the power and delight of love by using images from nature. I can still use some of the lines forty years after our wedding when I write an anniversary card to my wife. I can tell her that she still fills up my senses like the mountains in springtime or like a walk in the rain. Those images still work. But some of the lyrics in Song of Songs make it sound like a silly love song. For example, the lover extols the beauty of his darling by saying, "Your hair

---

1. See van der Merwe, Naudé, and Kroeze, *Hebrew Reference Grammar*, 272. They translate the Hebrew expression שִׁיר הַשִּׁירִים (*shir hashirim*) in Song 1:1 as "the most beautiful song."
2. Keel, *Song of Songs*, 38.

is like a flock of goats descending from the hills of Gilead" (4:1). In our current culture, that might not be well received by a woman who is having a bad hair day. Then the lover says, "Your teeth are like a flock of sheep just shorn, coming up from the washing" (4:2). We can understand the metaphor that follows: "Your lips are like a scarlet ribbon; your mouth is lovely" (4:3a). But the next metaphors make no sense to us: "Your temples behind your veil are like the halves of a pomegranate. Your neck is like the tower of David, built with courses of stone; on it hang a thousand shields, all of them shields of warriors" (4:3b–4). If you are a man, you might not want to tell the one you love that she has things hanging from her neck. The reason why these kinds of lyrics seem silly is that they do not make sense to us. This is really the problem. We are not sure, at least on first reading, what these metaphors mean.

Furthermore, the lyrics of Song of Songs are somewhat embarrassing and border on being erotic. If you continue reading in Song of Songs chapter 4, you will hear the lover say to his darling, "Your breasts are like two fawns, like twin fawns of a gazelle that browse among the lilies" (4:5). Near the end of the book, the young woman asserts, "I am a wall, and my breasts are like towers" (8:10). Imagine reading those lines to your congregation when you get up to preach. As Barry Webb says, "There is an intimacy about the book which is both delightful and embarrassing."[3]

Another reason for our struggle with Song of Songs is that we are not always sure who is speaking. Generally, we can tell whether a man or a woman is speaking. But one look at the headings supplied by the translators of our English versions shows disagreement as to exactly who is speaking at various places throughout the book. For example, is the speaker in 1:8 to be identified as "Friends" (NIV) or "Man" (CSB)? Does 1:17 continue the words of the woman (CSB), or is it now the man speaking (NIV)?

Finally, we struggle with Song of Songs because the book is not overtly theological. The lyrics do not mention God except for one possible reference in 8:6, where scholars debate whether the יָה (*yah*) at the end of the word "flame" is an abbreviated form of the divine name "Yahweh," or whether it is an intensive adjectival suffix that should be translated as "mighty." We will consider this in due course.

3. Webb, *Five Festal Garments*, 18.

Studying Song of Songs

If we plan to preach Song of Songs, there are three questions we must consider carefully. These three questions arise from reading the book, but then they turn around and shape the way we read it as we move forward. We need to ask: (1) What is the role of Solomon? (2) What is the book's literary strategy? (3) What is the book's purpose? Leading Old Testament scholars disagree on the answers to these questions, but we need to settle on the answers to the best of our ability. After we consider them, we will look at a couple additional issues.

The Role of Solomon

This issue surfaces immediately in verse 1. A straightforward translation of the Hebrew text is "The Song of Songs which is to Solomon." The question is how to understand the Hebrew preposition לְ (*le*), which is prefixed to the name Solomon and is commonly translated as "to."[4] Tremper Longman lists the four main possibilities:

1. *To Solomon:* The book is dedicated to Solomon.
2. *By Solomon:* Authorship.
3. *Concerning Solomon:* Solomon is the subject matter of the book.
4. *Solomonic:* In the Solomonic/wisdom literary tradition.[5]

The first option is possible only if Solomon is presented in a positive light in the book. In this case, says Richard Hess, "Solomon, as the king and symbol of wisdom and love, becomes an image for the male lover in the poem. Thus the female speaker, who dominates the poem, dedicates it to her Solomon, a figure who embodies her greatest desires for the fulfillment of love."[6]

The second option, Solomonic authorship, "has been the common Jewish and Christian view up until modern times."[7] However, Michael Fox points out that "none of the Tannaim mention Solomonic authorship to

4. Van der Merwe, Naudé, and Kroeze explain, "The preposition לְ does not have a specialized meaning. It indicates a very general relationship between two entities that can at best be described as '*x* as far as *y* is concerned'" (*Hebrew Reference Grammar*, 348).
5. Longman, *Song of Songs*, 3.
6. Hess, *Song of Songs*, 39.
7. Provan, *Ecclesiastes, Song of Songs*, 235.

justify canonization."[8] Furthermore, as Iain Provan observes, "Solomon only appears in this book in third-person references, and none of the first-person speeches are explicitly connected with him."[9] If Song of Songs portrays Solomon in a negative light, then it is even more unlikely that he is the book's author.

While the title in Song of Songs 1:1 could mean that it was composed in the wisdom literary tradition of which Solomon was a key figure (option 4),[10] several recent leading evangelical scholars prefer the third option and translate verse 1, "The Song of Songs which *concerns* Solomon." Thus, the book "is *about* Solomon to some extent."[11]

The main controversy regarding the role of Solomon in Song of Songs is whether the book portrays him in a positive or a negative light, or both. Franz Delitzsch represents past generations of Old Testament scholars who viewed Solomon as a positive figure, at least at the end of the book. He conjectures that the Shulammite, "a country maiden of humble rank, who, by her beauty and by the purity of her soul, filled Solomon with a love for her which drew him away from the wantonness of polygamy, and made for him the primitive idea of marriage, as it is described in Gen. iii. 23ff. [sic], a self-experienced reality."[12] Apparently, this repentance was short-lived. Delitzsch says, "This sunny glimpse of paradisaical love which Solomon experienced, again became darkened by the insatiableness of passion," yet "the providence of God has preserved" this particular poem.[13] Furthermore, Delitzsch believes Solomon is a type of Christ, "of whom it can be said, 'a greater than Solomon is here' (Matt. xii. 12)."[14]

However, the current leading commentators do not believe that Song of Songs portrays Solomon in a positive, or entirely positive, light. There are

8. Fox, *Song of Songs*, 250. The Tannaim were Jewish rabbis during the mishnaic period (the first two centuries AD).

9. Provan, *Ecclesiastes, Song of Songs*, 235.

10. Robert Alter says that the attribution to Solomon follows "a practice of attributing Late Biblical Books to famous figures from earlier Israelite history" (*Hebrew Bible*, 3:587).

11. Provan, *Ecclesiastes, Song of Songs*, 235. See also Athas, *Ecclesiastes, Song of Songs*, 250. Tremper Longman says that his translation—"The Song of Songs, which *concerns* Solomon"—is "purposively ambiguous in terms of Solomon's relationship to the Song" (*Song of Songs*, 7). Iain Duguid says that the title (Song 1:1) simply indicates "a more general relationship between the content of the Song and the biblical character" (*Song of Songs*, 20).

12. Delitzsch, *Song of Songs and Ecclesiastes*, 3. The Genesis reference is a misprint. It should be "Gen. ii. 23ff."

13. Delitzsch, *Song of Songs and Ecclesiastes*, 3.

14. Delitzsch, *Song of Songs and Ecclesiastes*, 3.

three places where Solomon shows up in the book, aside from the title in Song of Songs 1:1: (1) 1:5, where the woman likens her dark color to the curtains of Solomon; (2) 3:7–11, where Solomon's carriage is described; and (3) 8:11–12, where Solomon's vineyard is in view.

Commentators are essentially unanimous that Solomon is portrayed negatively in his final mention in 8:11–12, although some take a more positive stance regarding his appearance in 3:7–11. Longman says that "for the most part Solomon appears in a positive light in chapter 3 and a negative one" in chapter 8.[15] In 8:11–12 he is "one who buys and sells love" and is portrayed in a negative light.[16] Similarly, Fox views 3:7–11 as the Shulammite using the image of King Solomon on the day of his wedding to imply that she and her beloved "are like king and queen on their wedding day, reclining in a splendid royal pavilion."[17] Yet he thinks it likely that 8:12 makes fun of Solomon, the great king "who possessed so many women that he could not keep their 'fruit' to himself."[18] Likewise, Hess believes that the references to King Solomon in 3:7–11 "represent the images that the male and female possess in the eyes of one another."[19] The female lover views herself and her male lover as queen and king. But in 8:11–12, Hess says, the "true and committed love of this couple contrasts dramatically with the harem of Solomon. He can have the great wealth and the appearance of great pleasure that is demonstrated by, and (supposedly) comes with, his harem. However, the female regards her body and her love as her own and of greater worth than all of Solomon's wealth."[20]

Other commentators see the picture of Solomon in both 3:7–11 and 8:11–12 as consistently negative. Provan understands 3:7–11 as an image of "Solomon driving around in his pretentious chariot-bed." He "cuts a rather pathetic figure, inhabiting a lonely world of materialism and sexual conquest . . . that is implied by the military overtones of verses 7–8."[21] Thus, 3:6–11 is "a dark and bitter satire concerning Solomon and his string of sacrificial female victims."[22] In 8:11–12, the woman rebuffs

---

15. Longman, *Song of Songs*, 219.
16. Longman, *Song of Songs*, 41.
17. Fox, *Song of Songs*, 127.
18. Fox, *Song of Songs*, 175.
19. Hess, *Song of Songs*, 124.
20. Hess, *Song of Songs*, 247.
21. Provan, *Ecclesiastes, Song of Songs*, 303.
22. Provan, *Ecclesiastes, Song of Songs*, 304.

Solomon's claim of ownership of her—as a vineyard—and declares that she is not a vineyard that can be entered by the payment of a fee, "even if the fee-paying visitor who brings with him 'his thousand pieces of silver' is the mighty Solomon."[23] Bruce Waltke adopts a similar stance, viewing all three references to Solomon in Song of Songs as negative: representations of exploitation (1:5), of the desert where nothing flourishes (3:6–7), and as a powerful king who has a harem but lacks love and intimacy.[24] Likewise, George Athas concludes that, rather than the "wise Solomon," the image of Solomon is that of a "serial womanizer" who fell into idolatry because of his love for foreign women and his large harem.[25] The woman encounters Solomon in a dream in 3:7–11, and then in 8:11–12 he appears in person in "the moment of doom that the couple has been dreading."[26]

Thus, Solomon is either the groom or male lover in the book (two-character view), the idealized lover (but not a character) in the relationship between the male lover and the female lover, or an intruder or villain whose presence threatens the relationship between the male lover and the female lover (three-character view). This brings us to the most controversial issue that divides present-day commentators. It is an issue that determines how we understand the purpose and message of the book of Song of Songs.

The Book's Literary Strategy

There is general agreement about the main message of Song of Songs, but behind this is a great debate over the book's literary strategy, whether it is a love poem or collection of love poems or a drama cast in poetry. Before we enter the debate, we should note the main divisions of Song of Songs. After the title in 1:1, there are six main sections:[27]

- 1:2–2:7
- 2:8–3:5
- 3:6–5:1
- 5:2–6:3

23. Provan, *Ecclesiastes, Song of Songs*, 371.
24. Waltke, *Old Testament Theology*, 164.
25. Athas, *Ecclesiastes, Song of Songs*, 269.
26. Athas, *Ecclesiastes, Song of Songs*, 354.
27. See Duguid, *Song of Songs*, 53; Hess, *Song of Songs*, 5. However, Longman divides the book into twenty-three poems (*Song of Songs*, viii).

- 6:4–8:4
- 8:5–14

Tremper Longman is clearly an advocate for the approach that understands Song of Songs to be an anthology or collection of love poems.[28] These poems are "only loosely connected by recurrent refrains, a consistency of persona, and repetition of themes and metaphors."[29] He argues against the dramatic approach, suggesting it has "the same fatal shortcomings as the allegorical approach."[30] There are no textual clues, only "dialogue with absolutely no stage directions" and no narrative voice that helps readers make sense of the characters' speeches.[31] Similarly, Richard Hess offers this blunt assessment: "The Song is not a drama or a sequential narrative."[32] Rather, it is a love poem—a "poetic unity"—that consists of six stanzas.[33]

Iain Duguid takes a somewhat mediating view. While he does not see a "dramatic storyline" or a "straightforward sequential narrative" in Song of Songs,[34] he thinks that there is "a broad development and logical flow" to the poem that leads up to and away from the marriage between the male and female lovers.[35]

Other commentators see the poem as a drama. Michael Fox regards Song of Songs "as a dramatic poem" whose action "is brought out by the agency of the speakers."[36] In this way it resembles Egyptian love songs.[37] Iain Provan also views Song of Songs as a drama, although he clarifies that this does not imply that it was written "for enactment by actors, whether in the royal court or in worship"; rather, it "has a clearly dramatic form— something recognized already by Origen in the third century and by the Greek translators of Codex Sinaiticus (fourth century) and Codex Alexandrinus (fifth century), who added marginal notes to the text intended to indicate the speakers and the persons addressed."[38] Provan adopts a

28. Longman, *Song of Songs*, 43, 58.
29. Longman, *Song of Songs*, 48.
30. Longman, *Song of Songs*, 42.
31. Longman, *Song of Songs*, 42.
32. Hess, *Song of Songs*, 34.
33. Hess, *Song of Songs*, 34–36.
34. Duguid, *Song of Songs*, 37, 53.
35. Duguid, *Song of Songs*, 54.
36. Fox, *Song of Songs*, 258.
37. Fox, *Song of Songs*, 256.
38. Provan, *Ecclesiastes, Song of Songs*, 245.

three-character view that goes back to the medieval Spanish exegete Ibn Ezra. He distinguished between the "king" (Solomon) and the "shepherd," with King Solomon as a "dark force" in the drama who threatens the love relationship between the woman and her shepherd-lover.[39] Provan suggests that the woman was already a member of the king's harem, yet she continues to express her love for her shepherd-lover and disdain for King Solomon.[40] The drama ends with the woman establishing her independence from both her brothers and Solomon before she invites her lover to run away with her.[41]

George Athas also views Song of Songs as a drama with a love triangle between a young shepherd, a young woman, and King Solomon, who is presented negatively. However, he differs from Provan in his understanding of the predicament facing the woman.[42] Athas views the young woman and shepherd boy as madly in love. "However, the woman's older brothers have pledged her in marriage to Solomon, which will benefit them economically and socially, turning the woman's relationship with her beloved shepherd into a forbidden romance." The story is resolved when the woman takes drastic action before time runs out and sleeps with her beloved shepherd "as a means of dealing with the supreme injustice of being forced into Solomon's bed."[43] Athas likens her unorthodox approach to Tamar in Genesis 38. Her desperate act of sleeping with the shepherd will force her brothers to marry her to the shepherd or else "see her branded as a promiscuous woman and executed."[44] Athas suggests that even after she has slept with the shepherd, her brothers try to pass her off as a virgin so they can benefit economically from her marriage to Solomon. Yet the shepherd shows up at the end, and the woman urges him to flee—an abrupt end that leaves us wondering what happens and how the woman and her shepherd-lover experience justice.[45]

It is difficult to arrive at a conclusion when such careful, solid scholars disagree on the book's approach. Personally, I lean toward seeing Song of Songs as a drama. However, it is wise to exercise caution about the exact

---

39. Provan, *Ecclesiastes, Song of Songs*, 246.
40. Provan, *Ecclesiastes, Song of Songs*, 246, 266.
41. Provan, *Ecclesiastes, Song of Songs*, 365.
42. Athas, *Ecclesiastes, Song of Songs*, 256.
43. Athas, *Ecclesiastes, Song of Songs*, 258.
44. Athas, *Ecclesiastes, Song of Songs*, 258.
45. Athas, *Ecclesiastes, Song of Songs*, 258.

details in the scenarios proposed by Provan and Athos. It is challenging to decide whether the woman has already been taken by Solomon or has been promised to him by her brothers. There is also uncertainty as to whether the woman simply rebuffs Solomon at the end of the drama by refusing to join his harem (Provan) or whether she has taken a more drastic step of sleeping with her shepherd-lover before leaving Solomon's harem (Athas). Here I side with Provan's view, yet I do so with exegetical humility. So much depends on how we understand the details, specifically the metaphors and images. To what degree are they explicitly sexual? All of this discussion leads to the ultimate issue: What is the purpose, and thus the meaning, of Song of Songs?

The Purpose of Song of Songs

The oldest understandings of Song of Songs were allegorical. Jewish rabbis viewed it as depicting the relationship between Yahweh and his people, while the church fathers interpreted it as speaking of the relationship between Christ and his church.[46] This conveniently allowed preachers to avoid the embarrassment of preaching about matters of sex, especially when their listeners were monks who had taken a vow of celibacy.[47] However, as Longman notes, "There is absolutely nothing in Song of Songs itself that hints of a meaning different from the sexual meaning."[48] The result of allegorical interpretation is a rather arbitrary spiritualization of the details. For example, the bride's two breasts in 4:5 and 7:8 have been variously understood as the church from which we feed, the Old and New Testaments, love of God and neighbor, the blood and the water from Christ's side, and the outer and inner person.[49] While Song of Songs certainly can anticipate the themes of God's love for his people and Christ's love for his church, the allegorical approach is not the proper pathway to this destination.

Furthermore, I agree with Hess that Song of Songs is "not a manifesto for free love, nor is it a description of the married relationship."[50] Also, I believe Webb is right that it is "neither a philosophical treatise about

46. Duguid, *Song of Songs*, 25.
47. Duguid, *Song of Songs*, 26. For a helpful discussion of the history of allegorical interpretation, see Longman, *Song of Songs*, 20–38.
48. Longman, *Song of Songs*, 36.
49. Longman, *Song of Songs*, 37.
50. Hess, *Song of Songs*, 35.

love, nor a sex manual."[51] These approaches strike me as unnecessarily reductionistic. It's not that Song of Songs has nothing to teach us about sex or marriage; rather, it has a larger concern.

I believe that the purpose of Song of Songs is to declare the power of exclusive, committed sexual love. To be sure, this can point to the love relationship between God and his people. After all, the Old Testament prophets spoke of a marriage between God and his people (e.g., Isa. 54:4–10; Ezek. 16:8–34), and according to the apostle Paul, the marriage union between husband and wife points to the marriage between Christ and his bride, the church (Eph. 5:21–33). But the love relationship between God and his people or between Christ and his church is simply an extension of the book's main purpose.[52] As Hess argues, "Physical love remains the focus of the Song, and this must never be lost in any identification of the major theme."[53] Longman describes the purpose of the book as celebrating and offering caution about human love.[54] Provan describes Song of Songs as "a story of love redeemed," which contrasts with "love gone awry"—the misuse of love as a commodity that is "practiced as an expression of power, manipulation, and control."[55] Duguid says it well: "Song of Songs is best understood as a wisdom piece about two idealized people, a man and a woman, whose exclusive and committed love is deep but, like all loves in this fallen world, far from perfect. Their idealized love story is contrasted with the alternative Solomonic model of 'love' that we see in 1 Kings 11, a model that views marriage primarily as a commercial and political transaction, a means to wealth, security, or political advancement."[56] Thankfully, it is possible to arrive at a similar conclusion about the book's message—its focus on the power of exclusive, committed sexual love—whether we work from the view that the book is a love poem or a collection of love poems, or whether we consider the book a love song with a developing story.

51. Webb, *Five Festal Garments*, 18.
52. For this reason, I am not entirely satisfied with Webb's view that the "Song of Songs is there to stop love going out of our relationships, with God and with one another" (*Five Festal Garments*, 35). I see this as an implication of the book's message, but not the central message itself.
53. Hess, *Song of Songs*, 33.
54. Longman, *Song of Songs*, 67.
55. Provan, *Ecclesiastes, Song of Songs*, 247, 249.
56. Duguid, *Song of Songs*, 36.

Two Additional Interpretive Issues

Before we consider how to preach Song of Songs, we need to consider two additional issues that have a bearing on how we understand and interpret the book. The first concerns the level of eroticism in Song of Songs. How many of the images are explicitly or implicitly sexual? The second concerns the presence or absence of God. It seems like the writer lets God make a cameo appearance, but that is all.

The Eroticism of Song of Songs

One of the challenges in understanding Song of Songs is trying to determine how sexually suggestive its imagery is. The book is chock-full of images and metaphors, particularly descriptions of bodily features. Keel observes, "One of the central experiences of love is the lover's tendency to see all things beautiful and desirable as reminders of the beloved, finding in her or him their unity and meaning."[57] To what extent are these images sexual? Webb describes the imagery in Song of Songs as "very sensuous,"[58] and Longman concludes that it is "a kind of erotic psalter."[59] Duguid notes that Song of Songs "explodes straight into action with the woman's passionate declaration, 'Let him kiss me with the kisses of his mouth!' (1:2), without the slightest explanation of who the speaker is or the identity of her lover." Hess observes how "the female of the Song expresses sexual metaphors of moist and succulent fruit, which creates a . . . picture, one of fruitfulness and the many sensual pleasures of touch, taste, and aroma."[60] However, Duguid offers this caution: "The supposedly explicit erotic nature of the language of the Song has been vastly overstated. To be sure, many commentators have found erotic euphemisms behind almost every image of the book, but many of these are as fanciful as the thoughts of any medieval allegorist. To find erotic referents in the shape of a henna bush or the fact that the hair on the bridegroom's head is wet with dew is far from self-evident."[61]

---

57. Keel, *Song of Songs*, 24. He notes that this form occurs frequently in modern Arab love poetry and is referred to as a *wazf*. A *wazf* is "an Arabic love song in which the lover praises the physical attributes of his or her partner" (Hess, *Song of Songs*, 31).

58. Webb, *Five Festal Garments*, 17.

59. Longman, *Song of Songs*, 43.

60. Hess, *Song of Songs*, 29.

61. Duguid, *Song of Songs*, 33.

The best practice, I suggest, is to consult multiple commentators to see if they agree that a particular metaphor or image has sexual connotations. If not, be cautious about turning the detail into an explicit sexual innuendo. As the old saying goes, do not make a mountain out of a mole hill. Or, do not envision a castle where Scripture simply envisions a condo. The imagery for physical love in Song of Songs is as subtle as it is bold.

The Role of God in Song of Songs

The only reference to God in the book is in Song of Songs 8:6, where love issues "flashes of fire" (NRSV). These flashes of fire are further described by the Hebrew expression שַׁלְהֶבֶתְיָה (shalhebetyah). The question is whether the suffix יָה (yah), the shortened form of יהוה (yhwh), should be translated as a direct reference to Yahweh—thus, "flame of the Lord" (so ESV, NASB)—or as an intensifier that results in a translation like "mighty flame" (NIV), "almighty flame" (CSB), or "raging flame" (NRSV).

Longman opts for the latter because God's name has not been previously mentioned in Song of Songs. In fact, the charge in 2:7 and 3:5 given to the daughters of Jerusalem, "by the gazelles and by the does of the field," seems to be a deliberate avoidance of using God's name. Thus, "the force of the word is to say that it is a 'god-awful' flame, i.e., burning hot."[62] Athas takes a similar view, suggesting that a direct reference to Yahweh makes no sense because it would portray him as "a wreaker of havoc on the lives of unsuspecting victims."[63] Likewise, Alter believes that יָה (yah) is used in this instance "as an intensifier, with no theological implication." This is consistent, he says, with the rest of the book, in which God is neither mentioned nor is an issue.[64]

However, Webb makes a good case for understanding יָה (yah) as a reference to God. He presents three lines of reasoning.[65] First, the shortened form of God's name is used here in close relationship to "jealousy" and "fire," both of which are closely associated with Yahweh in Scripture.[66] Second, an allusion to Yahweh is fitting at a point where the poem "moves

62. Longman, Song of Songs, 213.
63. Athas, Ecclesiastes, Song of Songs, 350.
64. Alter, Hebrew Bible, 3:615.
65. Webb, Five Festal Garments, 25.
66. For example, Deut. 4:24 says, "For the Lord your God is a consuming fire, a jealous God." Psalm 79:5 likewise uses the two terms in combination to describe the Lord. On the

transparently into wisdom mode, since the very first principle of Old Testament wisdom is the fear of Yahweh."[67] Third, the love described in Song of Songs as a whole is rooted in Yahweh, the one whose very nature is love. Hess adds an additional reason for taking the shortened form יָהּ (*yah*) as direct mention of Yahweh, as is frequently done in the book of Psalms: "The absence of any direct reference to God, except at this point, suggests that here the erotic love of the Song reaches a level of the love that transcends all and through which God is known. . . . The greatest physical pointer to such love is the committed sexual intimacy between a husband and wife."[68] Finally, Duguid notes that there are several other more-direct ways of expressing a superlative in Hebrew, "so a climactic reference to God seems plausible." He then suggests that "the most elegant translation, retaining something of the ambiguity of the original, is 'an Almighty flame.'"[69]

Preaching Strategies

The way you feel about preaching Song of Songs may resemble the way you feel about getting a colonoscopy. It is unpleasant and a bit disconcerting. Yet we fail to preach the whole counsel of God if we deliberately ignore this book. Below are some ideas to help you preach this marvelous, though daunting, book.

Preparing to Preach Song of Songs

When you plan to preach a book of Scripture, it is always a good idea to read through it a few times. The length of Song of Songs makes this quite doable. Let me suggest a couple of practices as you do so. First, read the book in a reader's edition of the Bible, which has neither verse divisions nor headings. As you read, try to identify the various speakers—the woman, the man, and the friends. Second, read through the book once as if it is a collection of poems. Then read through it again as if it is a developing drama. You might want to consult a commentary that is representative of each approach for a broad outline of the suggested structure. Read

---

Lord's jealousy, see Exod. 20:5; Deut. 6:15; Josh. 24:19; Ezek. 16:38; Zeph. 3:8. On the Lord's association with fire, see Exod. 3:2; 13:21; 24:17; 2 Sam. 22:9; Ps. 18:8; Isa. 30:27, 30; 33:14.
   67. Webb, *Five Festal Garments*, 24.
   68. Hess, *Song of Songs*, 240.
   69. Duguid, *Song of Songs*, 155.

the book in line with that particular structure. Then ask yourself which approach makes the most sense to you.

At some point, you will have to determine how many weeks to devote to Song of Songs. If you plan to preach through the entire book, then a six-part series on the six main sections of the book (see above) would work well. You can include the title (1:1) along with the first section. Or, if you accept the view that Song of Songs unfolds as a drama, you can follow Iain Provan's divisions and preach the text in seven sermons[70] or the breakdown provided by George Athas and preach the text in four sermons.[71] The challenge of preaching through the entire book is that all but the final section have no mention of God. The way to deal with this is to tie the themes in these sections to the larger storyline of Scripture, especially what it says about love and even sexuality. For example, passages in Song of Songs related to commitment and loyalty in love would interface well with Proverbs 5, which warns against adultery and calls for intoxication with the love of one's spouse.

If you preach a single sermon, your options include a stand-alone sermon, a sermon in a series on marriage, a sermon in a series on the wisdom books, or a sermon in a five-week series on the Megillot, or Five Scrolls. Barry Webb's book *Five Festal Garments: Christian Reflections on the Song of Songs, Ruth, Lamentations, Ecclesiastes, and Esther* will help you do the latter. As he explains, the five shortest books in the Writings—the third major division of the Hebrew Bible—are known as "the Scrolls," or Megillot in Hebrew.[72] Eventually, they were adopted as readings for five of the major festivals in Judaism.

- Song of Songs → Passover
- Ruth → Feast of Weeks
- Lamentations → Ninth of Ab
- Ecclesiastes → Feast of Tabernacles
- Esther → Festival of Purim

Aside from Ruth, these tend to be neglected books. So you will do yourself and your congregation a favor by devoting a week to each one of them.

---

70. Provan, *Ecclesiastes, Song of Songs*, 256.
71. Athas, *Ecclesiastes, Song of Songs*, 264.
72. Webb, *Five Festal Garments*, 14.

In *Five Festal Garments*, Webb shows how each of these five books of Scripture relates to the Christian gospel, but he does so without flattening out each book's distinctive teaching and approach.[73]

A final consideration in preparing to preach Song of Songs is your audience. As Richard Hess says, "The Song of Songs is an adult book."[74] Preaching it with children present is a challenge, although I have done it. What better place is there for children to hear about marital love than in Christian worship? You should alert parents ahead of time that you will be preaching Song of Songs. They can decide what to do with their children. But do not apologize for preaching this important, yet neglected, book of Scripture.

An Outline for Preaching Song of Songs in a Single Sermon

To give you an idea of how you might preach this book in a single sermon, I have provided a sermon outline and a few comments below. You can also find a sample sermon based on this approach in appendix F. I lean toward the approach that sees a drama unfolding in Song of Songs, so my outline reflects that approach. I am closer to Provan than Athas in my understanding of the drama.

    I. Opening scene: A young woman and a young man express their passionate love for each other, despite the interference of the king (1:2–17).

    II. Carriage scene: Solomon emerges as a pathetic figure, lost in a lonely world of materialism and sexual conquest (3:6–11).

    III. Closing scene: The young woman expresses the power of her love for the young man, rejects Solomon, and invites the young man to "come away" with her (8:5–14).

    IV. (*Big Idea*) Marital love has a God-given power and delight that sex without boundaries can never achieve.

If you are sympathetic to the "unfolding drama" approach to Song of Songs, this outline will work whether you understand the young woman to be pledged in marriage to Solomon by her brothers or already part of his harem. The big idea emerges out of the closing scene—the epilogue

---

73. Webb, *Five Festal Garments*, 14–15.
74. Hess, *Song of Songs*, 11.

of the book in 8:5–14—and reflects my understanding that the "mighty flame" in 8:8 is "the flame of Yah(weh)."

Theological Insights to Communicate

A single sermon or a sermon series on Song of Songs provides a terrific opportunity to present some theological insights related to love, sex, and marriage. Here are four that wise preachers will do well to highlight as they work their way through the book.

Sex Is a Beautiful Gift from God

Even though there is minimal reference to God in Song of Songs, the devotion of a book in the canon to physical love reminds us how God designed men and women as sexual beings (Gen. 1:27) and created marriage to provide the intimacy and support that the man lacked by himself. Solitude is good, but loneliness is not. When we highlight this theological insight, we will want to be sensitive to those who are single and not diminish their place in God's kingdom. After all, Jesus was single, and the apostle Paul expressed singleness as positive and as a preference (1 Cor. 7:7–8).

This Beautiful Gift Is Something to Celebrate

This is one of the entailments of the truth that sex is a beautiful gift from God. Unfortunately, as Tremper Longman observes, "The Church has a tendency to make the topic of sexuality a taboo; it is rarely spoken about or discussed in the context of Christian fellowship."[75] However, Song of Songs opens with a desire for passionate kissing (1:2), not the longing for a good meal or a prayer time. The young woman wants physical intimacy. Perhaps there is something we can learn from the woman in Puritan New England who went to her pastor and then to the whole congregation with a complaint that her husband was neglecting their sex life. The church ended up excommunicating the man![76]

This Beautiful Gift Needs Boundaries for Protection

Like participation in the running of the bulls in Spain, sexual expression without boundaries is both thrilling and dangerous. Even though Song of

---

75. Longman, *Song of Songs*, 59.
76. See L. Ryken, *Worldly Saints*, 39.

Songs does not explicitly limit sex to a monogamous relationship between a husband and a wife, this is certainly the assumption and the expectation provided by the book's canonical context—both the wisdom books (e.g., Prov. 5) and the entire canon. Iain Duguid is right that "the Song confronts hedonism, the view that celebrates sexuality in any and every form of expression, heterosexual or homosexual, faithful or adulterous, as a means of satisfying an appetite, or even as a means of access to the divine."[77] Encouraging people to fulfill their sexual desires in a way that is true to them, as long as they don't hurt anyone else, is tantamount to teaching children how to play "safely" in traffic. Sooner or later, harm will happen.

Do Not Awaken Love Until the Time Is Right

There is a refrain in Song of Songs that occurs three times: "Do not arouse or awaken love until it so desires" (2:7; 3:5; 8:4). Richard Hess explains the meaning: "The joys of physical love and the arousal to that ecstasy are not to be toyed with. . . . Love is such a powerful emotion and carries such enormous power that it must not be misused."[78] Over almost four decades in pastoral ministry, I have often encouraged couples to get married sooner rather than later. Our culture prolongs adolescence and sets the expectation that a couple will wait to get married until they have had the time to fulfill their personal dreams or taken the time to grow up. I remember overhearing a conversation my youngest son had with a group of middle-school buddies. One of them said, "Yeah, my plan is to go to college, then move to Wrigleyville [near Wrigley Field in Chicago] and live the bachelor life. Then I'll get married around thirty." I thought that was a rather telling perspective from a thirteen-year-old. However, there are times when it is wise to wait to get married. Although marriage will be a crucible that refines you, it might be wise to mature, to experience travel or work, or to deal with personal issues that will cause difficulty in a marriage. The challenge is to keep love from being aroused while you wait. Unfortunately, large segments of the Christian church are recovering from the well-intentioned but damaging strategies of the purity culture. Perhaps a sermon or a series on Song of Songs will provide an opportunity for conversations about healthy approaches that help young adults not to arouse or awaken love until the time is right.

77. Duguid, *Song of Songs*, 40.
78. Hess, *Song of Songs*, 82–83.

Preaching Christ from Song of Songs

The New Testament never quotes or alludes to Song of Songs.[79] This might be a bit surprising, given the way that the Christian church over the centuries has read the book as an allegory of Christ's love for the church. While the allegorical approach is not a satisfactory way of reading Song of Songs,[80] we must ask of Song of Songs—as with any Old Testament book—how it speaks of Christ (Luke 24:27, 44) and fits into the overall storyline of Scripture. I like the way Iain Provan frames the question, asking "what this drama about good human relationships and bad ones has to say about the love of God for the church, and about the true love of the church for God in the midst of the temptations that face her in the world."[81] Furthermore, the fact that Ephesians 5:21–33 describes the marriage union between husband and wife as pointing to the marriage between Christ and his bride, the church, gives us a precedent for drawing parallels between the physical love between the young man and young woman in Song of Songs and the love between Christ and his bride, the church. Those who think that this exercise is inappropriate or irreverent need to remember how God himself does this in a provocative way in Ezekiel 16. Some of the graphic sexual imagery there might make readers blush or cringe.[82] Yet God saw fit to describe his relationship with his people as a spouse, particularly one who was spurned.

Thus, we can utilize various lines from Song of Songs and either direct them to or refer them to Christ. One of the most popular is the adaptation of lines from Song of Songs 2:4 and 2:16 in a popular chorus where believers sing of Christ, "I am my beloved's and he is mine, yes his banner over me is love." We must never lose sight of the straightforward reference of these words to a human lover, yet we can use them in alignment with the way marriage union points to Christ (Eph. 5:21–33).

Perhaps the most productive approach, though, is to think about marital love in light of the larger story of the Bible. It is only in the power of the gospel that we can love our spouses. After all, Ephesians

---

79. This is based on the absence of any entries for Song of Songs in the Index of Quotations and the Index of Allusions and Verbal Parallels from the Old Testament at the end of *The Greek New Testament* (fifth revised edition), published by the United Bible Societies.

80. See Duguid, *Song of Songs*, 35–38.

81. Provan, *Ecclesiastes, Song of Songs*, 255.

82. See, for example, Ezek. 16:8, 25–26.

5:25 tells husbands to love their wives "just as Christ loved the church and gave himself up for her." "What is more, on the cross," says Iain Duguid, "Jesus suffered and died for our many failures to love properly. The wages of the sinful abuse of our sexuality, whether in singleness or marriage, were paid once for all by Jesus through his death in our place." Furthermore, "Christ rose triumphant from the grave for the sake of his beloved, whom he now clothes in the wedding garments of his perfect righteousness."[83] No wonder we are to love him with an undying love (Eph. 6:24)! The culmination of our union with Christ is our wedding to him when we feast at the marriage supper of the Lamb (Rev. 19:6–8). To use the categories of C. S. Lewis in his essay "The Weight of Glory," the greatest moments of joy and ecstasy—and the memory of them—are "good images of what we really desire," but "not the thing itself; they are only the scent of a flower we have not found, the echo of a tune we have not yet heard, news from a country we have never yet visited."[84] Duguid says it so well: "The love that is so beautifully described in the Song of Songs is the love for which we were truly made, and for whose consummation we continue to long."[85]

Helpful Resources for Studying and Preaching

By now, you can probably figure out which commentaries are my favorites for studying and preaching the book of Song of Songs. Iain Provan's *Ecclesiastes, Song of Songs* in the NIV Application Commentary is outstanding, and my own view of the book as a poetic drama has been shaped by Provan more than by any other commentator. However, I have benefited greatly from several other excellent commentaries on Song of Songs, including the one by Richard Hess in the Baker Commentary on the Old Testament Wisdom and Psalms, Tremper Longman's volume in the New International Commentary on the Old Testament, and the contribution by Iain Duguid in the Tyndale Old Testament Commentaries. I also like the thoughtfulness and theological depth of the volume by George Athas in the Story of God Bible Commentary. You do not have to agree with his approach to the book to benefit from his keen pastoral insights. Barry

---

83. Duguid, *Song of Songs*, 52.
84. Lewis, "The Weight of Glory," 30–31.
85. Duguid, *Song of Songs*, 52.

Webb's chapter on Song of Songs in *Five Festal Garments* provides a concise, sensible overview of the book.

For a homiletical commentary, Douglas O'Donnell's volume on Song of Songs in the Preaching the Word series is warm and thoughtful. He takes the view that Solomon is the author. His expositions contain a lot of great supporting material and ideas for how to frame sensitive topics and how to apply the book's teaching. Eric Ortlund's essay "The Wisdom of the Song of Songs: A Pastoral Guide for Preaching and Teaching" promises exactly what it delivers and is definitely worth consulting. It is available online for free.[86] Craig Glickman has written a popular-level book, *Solomon's Song of Love*, which is grounded in solid scholarship. It models how to communicate the message of the book to the kind of people who will listen to you preach.

You probably also expect me to say that you will benefit from the Bible Project resources on Song of Songs, and this is true. The Bible Project resources include the Book Overview video as well as the video on Song of Songs in the Wisdom Series videos in the Book Collections.[87] Pablo Jiménez has a chapter on Song of Songs in *The Big Idea Companion for Preaching and Teaching*. He offers basic suggestions for seven sermons from Song of Songs, and these sermons tend to apply the poems in the book to our relationship with God rather than to marital love.

Finally, for a popular-level exposition that you can put into the hands of your listeners during a series on Song of Songs, I recommend Philip Ryken's fine book *The Love of Loves in the Song of Songs*. It is both readable and affordable.

---

86. See the bibliography for full details. The article appeared in *Themelios*, a journal now published by The Gospel Coalition. You can access it at https://www.thegospelcoalition.org /themelios/.

87. You can access these resources at https://bibleproject.com/.

7

A Final Word

Familiarity breeds contempt. That old saying may be true in some cases, but not always. Often, the opposite is true. Familiarity breeds confidence. This is the case when it comes to preaching the Old Testament poetic books. Frankly, they are intimidating because they are unfamiliar. But the more you get to know them, the more you will grow to love them and appreciate the message they have for the church. At some point, your attitude toward preaching them will turn from obligation to desire. You will feel compelled to preach them.

I believe that Psalms, Proverbs, Job, Ecclesiastes, and Song of Songs can help the Christian church navigate the massive cultural shift we are currently experiencing in Western civilization and in the Christian church. The forces behind this were set in motion decades, if not centuries, ago. Now these forces are coming home to roost. Recent technological advancements, including those accelerated by the COVID-19 pandemic, have happened at a dizzying pace. Social media has both connected people and disoriented them. The Christian church is reeling from abusive leaders. The new sexual ethic is brazen and intolerant. The quality of public discourse has eroded as leading politicians try to sway voters with fearmongering rather than with reasoned, rational arguments. Partisan politics divides Christ-followers, and it seems that any believer who uses the J-word ("justice") is quickly accused of being "woke." I could go on, but you get the picture. This is the world in which we live, and we—the Christian church—can find our way forward in it much more effectively if we are steeped in the poetic books of the Old Testament.

The book of Psalms helps us talk to God in this crazy moment. It tells us who to celebrate (the Lord, the maker of heaven and earth) and why to celebrate (because of who God is and because of what God has done). It helps us talk to God when life is tough and we are angry, stressed, or depressed. I do not know how I would be able to pray, praise, or grieve without the help that these songs provide. The psalms became the soundtrack for Jesus's life, especially during his suffering. We need them to be the soundtrack for our lives as well. So commit to preaching Psalms.

The book of Proverbs helps us live so that life can go as well as it possibly can in a fallen, broken world. We need help managing our money and our emotions. We need help making and keeping friends. We need to develop skill in our work habits, our decision-making, and in the way we use our words. Sticks and stones may break your bones, but words will hurt you and the people around you even more. We live in an educated society where lots of people have mastered a narrow slice of life. They know the ins and outs of investment banking, range management, or information technology. But they have not graduated from the first grade when it comes to living with their family and friends. So commit to preaching Proverbs.

The book of Job helps us trust God and his wisdom when we suffer. It does not answer the question of why the righteous suffer. Instead, it tells us to focus on "who" (God) instead of "why" (an acceptable answer). In my experience, answers do not heal broken hearts. The only way forward in our pain and frustration is, in the words of a hymn writer, "trusting in my Father's wise bestowment."[1] I need to learn, and to help others learn, to trust God's justice rather than to assume or insist that he operate by a strict application of the Retribution Principle. So commit to preaching Job.

The book of Ecclesiastes helps us enjoy life as God's gift even though it is fleeting and often does not make sense. The older I get, the more confusing life feels. I am in my early sixties, so that means I am in the final quarter of my life if I live into my eighties. The years hurry by, like a swiftly flowing river on its way to the sea. And I know that there is a tunnel looming at the end of the light. As I look back, I see God's hand in my life. Yet I don't know exactly what he is doing to connect all the

---

1. Linda Sandell, "Day by Day."

pieces of my life—my work, my experiences, my relationships. Oh, how I need grace to trust him more, especially trust in the truth that he makes everything beautiful in its time. Others need that same confidence. So commit to preaching Ecclesiastes.

Song of Songs helps us revel in the joy of marital love. We don't need a sex manual as much as we need a vision of the wonder of exclusive, committed love in an age that celebrates sex without boundaries. Sex is like nitroglycerin. It can promote healing, or it can blow things up. Unfortunately, in recent decades, the Christian church's attempts to pursue sexual purity have blown up in its face. The culture of sexual purity has unwittingly created false expectations about marriage as sexual nirvana for couples who are "pure." It has also caused disillusionment, despair, guilt, and ultimately rebellion against Scripture's vision for romantic love. We need to recapture the wonder of this gift of God. So commit to preaching Song of Songs.

If you think that you can benefit from reading some sermon manuscripts, I have provided six of them in appendices A through F. All but one are lightly edited manuscripts from sermons I preached at CrossLife Evangelical Free Church in Libertyville, Illinois, where I served as senior pastor for seventeen and a half years. The manuscript from Job 28 is from a sermon I preached at North Suburban Evangelical Free Church in Deerfield, Illinois. My practice was to preach without notes, except a few that I write in my Bible. I was able to do this only because I prepared these manuscripts. Doing so was a way of thinking through what I wanted to say and how I wanted to say it. I did not memorize these manuscripts, but I internalized them. I should say that they are manuscripts, not transcripts. I tried to write them for the ear, not the eye. But inevitably, I am quite sure that I worded a few things differently when I stood up to preach. Hopefully, these sample sermons will give you an idea of how to take everything you've learned in this volume and craft an actual sermon.

Here is a brief description of the six sermons: Appendix A is on Psalm 87, a psalm of praise or thanksgiving. Appendix B is on Psalm 137, a psalm of lament that contains perhaps the harshest prayer of imprecation in the Psalter. Appendix C is on Proverbs 31:1–9, words of wisdom from "the other Proverbs 31 woman." Appendix D is on Job 28:1–28, a text that provides a window into the message of the entire book. Appendix E is on Ecclesiastes 11:7–12:14, the book's final section, which contains a final sobering poem and then the epilogue of the book. And appendix F is on Song of Songs, covering the entire book by looking at three key passages. Please note that I put the big idea of each sermon in bold text. This helped me identify it easily and make sure I repeated it sufficiently.

All right, it is time to rediscover and pay attention to the poetic books in the Old Testament. So, take up and read them. Then preach them. Who knows what God's Spirit might do in your life and in the lives of those to whom you preach?

Appendix A

Sample Sermon on Psalm 87

This manuscript is an example of a sermon on a thanksgiving psalm, a subtype of praise psalm. It is also a good example of how a psalm that seems odd or obscure can be surprisingly fruitful for preaching. I placed the big idea of this sermon, as well as the other five sample sermons, in bold print. Notice how I worked the big idea into the conclusion a handful of times without making it explicit. Obviously, the sermon flowed inductively, since the big idea emerged at the end. The purpose of the sermon is to help listeners view the people around them, locally and globally, as potential members of God's family, not as enemies, thus resulting in praying for and working for the salvation of those we might ordinarily consider enemies.

The Shocking Truth about God's Favorite Place

Psalm 87

Take a moment to think about your favorite place on earth. Do you have one? This is a place you love, a place you like to share with your family and friends. It might be a beach, a city, a national park. Do you have a place like that which stirs up good memories? It's hard for me to narrow it down to one. It might be my grandparents' farm in Pennsylvania. Or

Moraine Park in Colorado's Rocky Mountain National Park. Or Madison Junction in Yellowstone National Park. Or Washington, DC. I love those places. They hold memories and stir something deep inside me.

Did you know that God has a favorite place on earth, a place he loves? It's a city. But what you find in that city is shocking. In fact, it's disturbing at first. But then it's deeply moving and wonderful. What you find there may change your perspective on the whole world and how to pray for it. So let's find out what it is. Please find Psalm 87 in your Bible or on your Bible app. This song has three movements, and a little musical marker, "Selah," at the end of the first two movements tips us off to this (although the NIV leaves it untranslated).

The first movement is in verses 1–2: *He has founded his city on the holy mountain. The* LORD *loves the gates of Zion more than all the other dwellings of Jacob.* So what is God's favorite place on earth? It's Jerusalem, or Zion. This is the place God has chosen to live. It is "his city," and he loves it more than any other place. The "gates" are the most prominent part of a city wall, so they represent the city. Now, we are not exactly sure what the term "Zion" means. Suggestions include "defense, dry, bald." But it became a term of endearment in the Old Testament. Portland, Oregon, is known as the "Rose City," and that is endearing—assuming you love roses. Well, that is how "Zion" is used in this psalm.

Verse 3 describes this city as the "city of God," and we learn that "glorious things" are said about it. We will get to these "glorious things" starting in verse 3. But there's a "Selah" at the end of this verse. So we can pause here for a moment to reflect on what we've just been told. We know from other Scriptures that the temple in Jerusalem is the place of God's presence. Although heaven and earth could never confine God, he chose Zion as the place where he would share his presence with his people. So then, Zion is the glorious city where God shares his presence with his people.

But then we come to the second movement, beginning in verse 4 and running through verse 6. What we discover is shocking, at first. Yet the more we reflect on it, the more wonderful it becomes. Listen to verses 4–6: *"I will record Rahab and Babylon among those who acknowledge me—Philistia too, and Tyre, along with Cush—and will say, 'This one was born in Zion.'" Indeed, of Zion it will be said, "This one and that one were born in her, and the Most High himself will establish her." The* LORD *will write in the register of the peoples: "This one was born in Zion."*

At first hearing, these words are quite disturbing. There are enemies within the gates of the city! Rahab—not the character "Rahab" in Joshua—is a poetic name for Egypt. It is the name of a mythological sea monster referred to in the book of Job (9:13; 26:12) and in Isaiah (51:9). For whatever reason, it was associated with Egypt. Then there is Babylon. Both of these nations were oppressors. Egypt, of course, was the land in which Israel was in slavery for about four hundred years. Babylon was the great empire that took Judah, the Southern Kingdom, into captivity and destroyed the holy city in the process. What is the destroyer of the holy city doing within its gates? How can this be one of the "glorious things" that are spoken about the city?

Then there is Philistia. The Philistines were not a world power. But they occupied a strip of land along the Mediterranean coast that we refer to today as the Gaza Strip. The Philistines harassed Israel throughout the reigns of Kings Saul and David, as well as prior to that in the days of Samson. Then there are Tyre and Cush. One Bible scholar calls these two nations "enticers." Tyre and Cush were places of commerce. Tyre was a city-state to the north of Israel, and it was synonymous with wealth. Ezekiel 28 condemns it for pride, violence, and dishonest gain. "Cush" is the ancient name for the modern region of Ethiopia, Eritrea, and parts of Sudan. Back in Old Testament times, it was a wealthy region.

All right, this is by no means a perfect analogy, but this is something like saying that one of the glorious things about Washington, DC—our nation's capital—is the presence of North Korea, China, Russia, and Iraq. These were or are considered enemy nations and threats to world peace and stability.

This is where it gets glorious, though. These nations are not enemies that have infiltrated the city and are about to start an uprising. No, these are nations that "know me" (the NIV's "acknowledge" is not strong enough) and were "born in Zion" (v. 4). What?! That's a strong claim. A few years ago, when you drove through Colorado, you'd see cars with bumper stickers that said "Native." Colorado residents wanted to distinguish themselves from the outsiders who had moved in. Oregonians were even more blunt. Years ago, when I lived in Oregon, I saw bumper stickers that said, "Welcome to Oregon. Now go home." Well, God is saying to these former enemies, you can put a "Native" bumper sticker on your car because I consider you "born in Zion."

Verse 5 repeats this to make sure we understand it is true. *Indeed, of Zion it will be said, "This one and that one were born in her, and the Most High will establish her."* In other words, the presence of these former enemies will not destroy the city. Rather, God will make the city secure. Verse 6 makes the picture even more astonishing: *The LORD will write in the register of the peoples: "This one was born in Zion."* The Lord's writing the names of people from Egypt and Babylon and Philistia and Tyre and Cush may be a reference to God's "book of life." In Psalm 69:28, David prays that his enemies might be "blotted out of the book of life and not listed with the righteous." So then, in Psalm 87, God is writing in this "register"—presumably the "book of life"—that "this one is born in Zion."

Now, in what sense were these former enemies "born in Zion"? This is undoubtedly a reference to spiritual birth. The proof of this rebirth is given in the final movement of Psalm 87, in verse 7. Notice the "Selah" after verse 6. That ends the second movement, which says that one of the glorious things said about the city of God is that former enemies are now Zion-born. With that, the final movement of Psalm 87 says, *As they make music they will sing, "All my fountains are in you"* (v. 7).

What is going on here is that the diverse people who gather in Zion—those from enemy nations—express joy over the gift of God's presence. A fountain, or spring of water, is a metaphor for a source of life and blessing. And the metaphor is applied in Scripture to God's gift of salvation and himself! Isaiah 12:3 says, "With joy you will draw water from the wells of salvation." And in Jeremiah 2:13, the Lord describes himself as "the spring of living water."

So then, Psalm 87 is saying that **one of the glories of God's city is the presence of former enemies within its gates**. A glory of God's city is the presence of people who formerly were enemies but are now citizens by virtue of birth. That's astounding! Psalm 87, then, reflects God's heart for lost people—those who are far from him, those who are his enemies and the enemies of his people.

These themes, of course, continue into the New Testament. First, there is the wonder of God's gift of the new birth. In John 3:3, Jesus says, "Very truly I tell you, no one can see the kingdom of God unless they are born again." A few statements later, in John 3:6, Jesus says that "the Spirit gives birth to spirit." When asked, "How can this be?" Jesus goes on to talk about his death. He says, "The Son of Man must be lifted up, that everyone who believes may have eternal life in him" (John 3:14–15). The Letter of James identifies one of the Father's "good and perfect gifts" that comes down from above as the gift of the new birth. James 1:18 says, "He chose to give us birth through the word of truth, that we might be a kind of firstfruits of all he created."

This is good news. But it gets even more radical. Revelation 5:9 says that Jesus purchased with his blood "persons from every tribe and language and people and nation." And throughout his ministry on earth, you see Jesus reaching across boundaries to love and share the good news with people that others considered enemies—because of their race, their lifestyle, their occupation. He loved his enemies. So, **one of the glories of God's city is the presence of former enemies within its gates.**

How, then, does Psalm 87 shape the way that we pray? Let me suggest two ways. First, it reminds us to pray for the nations—specifically, for people in those nations to turn in repentance and faith to Jesus Christ. A good place to start would be the nations in which our mission partners serve: South Africa, France, Mali, the Dominican Republic, Costa Rica, Bosnia, Bolivia. For years, I've used a resource called *Operation World*, a thick book with information about every nation in the world and how to pray for it. Now, that resource is available on the Prayermate app on your smartphone.

Second, in addition to praying for the nations, let's pray for those we consider "enemies." To be honest, people are not the enemy. There are people who are deceived by the enemy, and this turns them into enemies. Quite frankly, it's easier to pray for North Korea than to pray for a person at your workplace who is making life miserable for you. Instead of putting people down, put them down on your prayer list. Never assume that someone is too lost to be beyond the reach of God's grace. **One of the glories of God's city is the presence of former enemies within its gates.**

Here's a final thought. When Psalm 87 was written, Zion was God's favorite place on earth. That is where the temple was. It was the place of God's presence. But where is the temple today? Where is the place of God's presence? It is the church! In fact, Ephesians 2:12 says that formerly we were "excluded from citizenship in Israel" and were "foreigners to the covenants of the promise." Then, Ephesians 2:13 says, "But now in Christ Jesus you who once were far away have been brought near by the blood of

Christ." Furthermore, we're being built together to become a holy temple, "a dwelling in which God lives by his Spirit" (Eph. 2:21–22). Thank God for the new birth, the privilege of being Zion-born. Thank God that he is still bringing his enemies into his presence through the new birth. Let's pray for that to happen among the nations and even among people that we would otherwise consider enemies. When God's enemies receive the gift of the new birth and end up in the community of faith, it's simply glorious.

Sample Sermon on Psalm 137

This manuscript provides an example of how to preach a lament psalm, and more specifically, one that contains a prayer of imprecation. The imprecation in this psalm is without a doubt the most offensive one in the psalms. Once again, notice how I repeated the big idea a couple times to make sure my listeners got it, even though I did not say, "Now, here is my big idea." The purpose of this sermon is to teach people how to express their grief in prayer when they have been victimized by violence, abuse, discrimination, or any other form of injustice.

A Victim's Prayer

Psalm 137

There are times when it seems impossible to pray. If you've been betrayed or abused, what do you say to God? "Thank you for all your blessings"? If you've been a victim of violence, what do you say to God? It's hard enough to face devastating illness or a tragic accident. But there's another layer of pain when you face a personal attack. How do you pray when you're a victim?

There is a psalm that teaches us how to pray when we are victimized, when we're betrayed, abused, or victims of violence. It's Psalm 137. Please find Psalm 137 in your Bible or on your Bible app. Derek Kidner says that "every line of it is alive with pain." I believe that its three parts provide a model for praying when we are victims—either as a community (as is the case in Ps. 137) or as an individual. Psalm 137 begins in verses 1–3 with an expression of grief. It reads, *By the rivers of Babylon we sat and wept when we remembered Zion. There on the poplars we hung our harps, for there our captors asked us for songs, our tormentors demanded songs of joy; they said, "Sing us one of the songs of Zion!"*

These are words of "lament," and Psalm 137 is a lament psalm. This is where we begin in our prayer when we have been victimized. We express our grief through lament. That might seem surprising, since God calls his people to live lives of praise. In fact, the previous two psalms are psalms of praise. Psalm 135 begins and ends with the Hebrew words *Hallelu Yah*—"Praise the LORD." And in between, Psalm 135 describes what God has done. Then, Psalm 136 calls God's people to give thanks to him for his goodness and his wonders. And it recites those wonders, telling the story of how God led his people from Egypt and into the promised land. Every other line you see the refrain "His love endures forever." As the hymn we often sing says, "Streams of mercy never ceasing call for songs of loudest praise."[1]

But that is not the mood of Psalm 137. It begins with lament, an expression of grief. Specifically, it is grief over being captives in a foreign land. In 586 BC, the Babylonian army finally breached the walls of Jerusalem and destroyed the city. Men were slaughtered; women were raped; babies were thrown over the city wall. That's what happened in these kinds of sieges. Then, the people were carted off into captivity. So here they are, by the rivers of Babylon—the Euphrates and the Tigris and the canals that flowed from them. It's in the region of southern Iraq. And in this psalm God's people are weeping over what they have lost. They remember their home, and that they have been displaced. And instead of singing, they've hung up their harps. To make matters worse, their captors taunted them. "Sing a happy song! Sing one of the songs of Zion!" (v. 3). "Sing that Mount Zion is the joy of the whole earth" (Ps. 48:2). This is a taunt, and perhaps even a challenge to "get over it."

---

1. Robert Robinson, "Come, Thou Fount of Every Blessing."

Friend, when you're a victim, and you're wondering how to pray, begin by expressing your grief. This psalm and other psalms of lament give you permission to do that. Now, you'll notice that the first movement of Psalm 137 doesn't give you the exact words to cry out when you weep, but other psalms do. For example, in Psalm 88:14 the psalmist says, "Why, LORD, do you reject me and hide your face from me?" Those are bold, blunt words. And in verse 18, "You have taken from me friend and neighbor—darkness is my closest friend." Those words are raw and real. Yes, you can pray that way. Start by telling God how angry and hurt and frustrated you are, and that you wonder why he doesn't seem to care.

Some of you need to hear this because you've been told to "suck it up and smile." You've been told to keep quiet unless you have something positive to say. And yet, people who have experienced trauma need the opportunity to speak truthfully to God about what they feel. There are times when we cannot sing, "His love endures forever." All we can do is cry out in pain.

Psalm 137 and all the psalms of lament are for the woman who learned about her husband's unfaithfulness on Christmas Eve. This psalm is for the boy who pulled up the covers over his head at night, praying that his dad wouldn't come in and beat him. This psalm is for the girl who wanted to vomit when she sees her uncle because she knows what he has done to her and what he will do again if he gets her alone. This psalm is for the woman whose husband made her get an abortion and who has dealt with the pain for decades. These are real people. I've known all of them. None of them are from our church or in the area. But all of them are believers. How can they pray as victims who have been abused and betrayed and traumatized? The place to begin is to express their grief to God. To lament.

There's a second way that we pray, and it's modeled for us in verses 4–6: *How can we sing the songs of the LORD while in a foreign land? If I forget you, Jerusalem, may my right hand forget its skill. May my tongue cling to the roof of my mouth if I do not remember you, if I do not consider Jerusalem my highest joy.* Now, there is a disconnect here. On the one hand, God's people did not feel like singing praise while in a foreign land. How could they? Yet, on the other hand, they could not forget God. Notice that in verses 5–6 they are praying judgment on themselves if they forget Jerusalem and fail to remember her—if they do not consider Jerusalem their highest joy. So what they are saying is, "I don't feel at all like singing

songs of praise to God, but I must because Jerusalem is my highest joy."
Why was it their highest joy? Because it was the place of God's presence.
The place where he lived among his people.

When we are victims, we begin our prayer by expressing our grief to
God (vv. 1–3). But then, we remember our highest joy (vv. 4–6). Our
highest joy is the experience of God's presence in our lives. As Hebrews
12:22 reminds us, we are citizens of Jerusalem by virtue of our trust in
Christ. I have talked and prayed with a lot of victims over the years, and
what stands out is how their well-being depends on whether or not they
remember their highest joy. Oh, it is easy to become bitter and hardened
when you've been betrayed or abused or violated. But I have watched
faithful believers get through the moment because they did not let their
experience define them. Rather, they didn't forget their highest joy—the
greatness and goodness of their God—even though they were victimized.

Friends, when we are victims, the way to pray is to express our grief to
God and to remember our highest joy (his presence), and then there is a
final way to pray that is modeled in verses 7–9: *Remember, LORD, what
the Edomites did on the day Jerusalem fell. "Tear it down," they cried,
"tear it down to its foundations!" Daughter Babylon, doomed to destruction, happy is the one who repays you according to what you have done
to us. Happy is the one who seizes your infants and dashes them against
the rocks.*

Well, that doesn't sound very Christian. It sounds vindictive and cruel.
How could a child of God ever pray that without later coming back to
confess hatred? I would argue, though, that this is part of the model that
we need to follow when we pray as victims. Even though it seems vindictive,
what it does, in the strongest language possible, is turn over the matter
to God to let him deal with it as he sees fit. It is a prayer for God to bring
about justice. As Derek Kidner observes, what the psalmist says in verses
7–9 "comes to us white-hot."[2] Yet, this is a plea for God to deal with the
perpetrator. As Old Testament scholar Walter Brueggemann says, "It is
an act of profound faith to entrust one's most precious hatreds to God,
knowing they will be taken seriously."[3]

Notice that verses 7–8 single out both the perpetrator, Babylon, as well
as the bystanders (the Edomites). In the case of the Edomites, they stood

2. Kidner, *Psalms 73–150*, 460–61.
3. Brueggemann, *Message of the Psalms*, 77.

by and cheered. Sometimes, though, we feel betrayed by the bystanders who are silent. Those who do nothing while we are abused or violated. We have to trust God for justice in both cases.

But how are we to understand verse 9? If the psalmist had ended with verse 8, it would be a lot easier to use this as a model, to simply pray, "Remember, God, what people have done to me and those who stood by and either cheered or did nothing." However, verse 9 is simply revolting. The picture makes you want to vomit, doesn't it? Yet that's the point. Do you realize that this is what was done to Israel? Verse 9 comes from a community that experienced the trauma of their city, Jerusalem, being burned and destroyed. Women were raped, and babies were thrown over the city wall. Verse 9, then, is a raw cry for justice! "Do to them what they did to us!" Notice that the psalmist is not saying, "This is what I'm going to do." Rather, the psalmist is using the language of war to say, "Repay them, God, for their evil deeds." I realize that the language is shocking and troublesome. Yet it's a commitment to leave vengeance with God.

This psalm, then, gives us a model for how to pray when we are betrayed, abused, or violated. **When you're a victim, the way to pray is to express your grief, remember your highest joy, and trust God for justice.** I would say that this psalm is not out of step with the New Testament, yet the New Testament takes it a step further, telling us, "Bless those who persecute you" (Rom. 12:14), and "Do not repay anyone evil for evil. . . . Do not take revenge, but leave room for God's wrath" (Rom. 12:17, 19). And it is the gospel that enables us to do this. Because Jesus Christ died for our sins and for the sins of the whole world (1 John 2:2), one of two things will happen to those who abuse or traumatize us. If they decide to let Christ bear their sin, he will forgive them because justice has been accomplished at the cross. If they refuse God's gracious offer to let Christ bear their sin, they will bear the curse for it themselves.

Several years ago, Marietta Jaeger wrote a book titled *The Lost Child*. It tells the story of how she and her family drove to Montana for vacation in the summer of 1973. And while they were camped there one night, her seven-year-old daughter, Susie, was abducted while sleeping in her tent. To make a long, tragic story short, Susie became a victim of a serial killer. What strikes me about the story, though, is the way she responded. It was not easy. But through her grief, she committed herself to her faithful Creator, and she remembered that God was her highest joy. Marietta did not find out for a year what had happened to her daughter. Six months after the abduction, she said she continued to pray, even though there were times when it felt like God was absent.[4] But she persisted. She said, "This marvelous God was absolutely irresistible. I could not turn away from Him. My whole being was drawn to Him."[5] None of this happened overnight. But it was the result of praying continually—even in a time of deep despair and grief. Friends, when you're a victim, don't give up on prayer. **When you're a victim, the way to pray is to express your grief, remember your highest joy, and trust God for justice.** And he will be there for you.

4. Jaeger, *The Lost Child*, 60.
5. Jaeger, *The Lost Child*, 61.

Sample Sermon on Proverbs 31:1–9

I preached this sermon in a sermon series on "generous justice." It also happened to be Mother's Day. You'll notice that the introduction was fairly brief. It may not seem as riveting as a sermon introduction should be, but sometimes "less is more." I think that the topic is compelling enough to create interest without needing a story or quote or another attention-grabbing element. The purpose of this sermon is to influence believers to use their privileges to serve others, not themselves. Although moms were the direct audience, my hope is that others who "overheard" what I had to say to moms realized that God is calling them, as sons or daughters, to do what their mom taught them or should have taught them.

What a Godly Mom Taught Her Son about Justice

Proverbs 31:1–9

We are in a sermon series on "generous justice," and today we're going to learn from Scripture how moms have a key role to play in teaching their children to pursue justice for others—to care for those who are in need, who are poor, oppressed, marginalized.

Our text this morning is Proverbs 31:1–9. Please find this text in your Bible or on your Bible app. This is what one mother taught her son about justice. I call her "the other Proverbs 31 woman" because when you think of Proverbs 31, you think of the marvelous poem in verses 10–31 that shows us what wisdom looks like when fleshed out in a person's life. Today, though, we're looking at verses 1–9. Now, you have to be patient with this text. At first, it might sound a bit odd, maybe even a bit crass, or childish. But when you understand the message that this mom is conveying to her son, it's profound! All right, this is what Scripture says in Proverbs 31:1–9:

> *The sayings of King Lemuel—an inspired utterance his mother taught him.*
>
> *Listen, my son! Listen, son of my womb!*
> *Listen, my son, the answer to my prayers!*
> *Do not spend your strength on women,*
> *your vigor on those who ruin kings.*
>
> *It is not for kings, Lemuel—*
> *it is not for kings to drink wine,*
> *not for rulers to crave beer,*
> *lest they drink and forget what has been decreed,*
> *and deprive all the oppressed of their rights.*
> *Let beer be for those who are perishing,*
> *wine for those who are in anguish!*
> *Let them drink and forget their poverty*
> *and remember their misery no more.*
>
> *Speak up for those who cannot speak for themselves,*
> *for the rights of all who are destitute.*
> *Speak up and judge fairly;*
> *defend the rights of the poor and needy.*

Probably the greatest "former president" we have ever had is Jimmy Carter. His presidency was not remarkable, but his postpresidential years have been. He devoted his life since his presidency to social justice, particularly working with Habitat for Humanity to provide affordable housing to people who are willing to work. His mother, Lillian, is responsible for this. Jimmy Carter's father, James Sr., a successful farmer, taught him to work hard. His mother, a nurse, taught him compassion for the poor and marginalized. In Plains, Georgia, racial segregation was the rule of the day. But Lillian Carter fought it. She nursed their African American neighbors, even when she and her family had no money. She cared about justice for those in need. And that's what the mother in Proverbs 31 does.

According to verse 1, this mom is a queen whose son becomes king. We don't have a clue as to who "Lemuel" was. Some think he was Solomon. His name means "belonging to God," so it could be a nickname. But probably he was a king outside of Israel who believed in the God of Israel—the Lord of heaven and earth. Whoever he was, his mom, the queen mother, taught him something important. "Inspired utterance," or "oracle," translates a Hebrew word that means "burden" or "heavy word." As you can see in verse 2, she is passionate about her son receiving this "heavy word." She says, "Listen, my son!" Or some translations say, "What, my son?" That could be in the sense of "What should you do, my son? Let me tell you." She's saying, "You're the one I love. I gave birth to you. I asked God for you." That last phrase, which in our Scripture reading is "the answer to my prayers" or "the son of my vows," reminds us of Hannah in 1 Samuel 2:1–10 and so portrays this mom as a godly mom.

Now, in the following verses, she shares her "burden" or "heavy word" negatively and positively. First, in verses 3–7, she expresses it negatively. Initially, her advice sounds rather simplistic, even crass: "Don't chase women and don't drink beer." But if you think that is all this lesson is about, you have missed the point. This mother's concern is how her son is going to use his power as a person of influence and privilege. The Bible doesn't tell us, but I suspect that her son grew up in the affluent suburbs of a prominent city, went to a high school where 30 is an "average" score on your ACT test, and then landed in a top-tier college and went to law school or business school. Okay, the text doesn't say anything about that. But this son grew up in the royal family. He was destined to be king. He grew up like our kids grow up in the north suburbs of Chicago. The wealth and privilege and opportunities are staggering. And the temptation is to use that wealth and privilege for self-indulgence, self-gratification.

That's why King Lemuel's mom's message to him was "Do not use privilege to serve yourself." In verse 3, when she says, "Do not spend your strength on women," this is not sexist language. The concern is that Lemuel will try to use his position to sleep with any woman he wants to—even to build a large harem. This was something kings did, but it was a distortion of power. Again, this is not a put-down of women. What's remarkable is that the model for wisdom in the final section of the book, Proverbs 31:10–31, is a woman, not a prince or a king. Now, notice the consequence of living for sexual gratification. Verse 3 says that kings who give their strength to women can get destroyed. I think of David, who ruined his career because of an adulterous relationship, and Solomon, who ruined his career because of all the wives he acquired—idol-worshiping wives who led him astray.

In verses 4–7, King Lemuel's mom turns to another concern: the abuse of alcohol. In the Bible, wine can be seen as a source of joy. Here are a few Scripture passages you can look at later: Deuteronomy 14:26; Psalm 104:14–15; Isaiah 25:6–8; Isaiah 55:1. But wine can also be misused. That is clear from the following passages: Proverbs 20:1; Proverbs 23:20–21, 29–35; Isaiah 5:11–12, 22; Ephesians 5:18; 1 Corinthians 6:10; and Galatians 5:19–21.

The cause for concern is that the abuse of alcohol can be self-destructive. I think of Elah, king of Israel, who was getting drunk when Zimri, one of his officials, assassinated him (1 Kings 16:9–10). Yet King Lemuel's mother has a larger concern here. It is not just about how self-indulgence can affect Lemuel personally. Notice who ultimately gets hurt: the people who are counting on his leadership—specifically, the oppressed. The rights of the afflicted are at stake. That's the larger concern. No wonder Lemuel's mother was the founder of MADR. You've heard of MADD—Mothers Against Drunk Driving. Lemuel's mom is the founder of MADR—Mothers Against Drunk Ruling. She knows what that can do to the people whose rights her son's rule is supposed to protect. I don't think that the problem she raises is one of taking advantage of the poor in a moment of drunkenness. Rather, it is a lifestyle of self-indulgence that treats poor people either as obstacles (who get in the way) or as opportunities (who can be exploited for personal gain).

Jon Krakauer's book *Missoula: Rape and the Justice System in a College Town* shows how the binge-drinking culture fuels the horrible mistreatment of women. He chose Missoula, Montana, not because it is unique but as an example of what happens in almost all college towns across the nation. Drunkenness often causes those who are more powerful—either physically, socially, or politically—to take advantage of those who are less powerful. This is what Ahab and his wife, Jezebel, did in 1 Kings 21. They used Ahab's power as king to frame Naboth and take possession of his vineyard—the vineyard Ahab coveted and Naboth wouldn't sell.

Now to dramatize the point, the mom says in 6–7, *Let beer be for those who are perishing, wine for those who are in anguish! Let them drink and forget their poverty and remember their misery no more.* Please understand that the queen mother is not recommending a "free beer for the poor program." No, she is using sarcasm to awaken Lemuel to the duties that go with his class and status. She is saying, "Don't use your power to serve yourself." And that's her warning. Don't use your privileges to indulge yourself.

In verses 8–9, she shifts from negative (a warning) to positive (a challenge). The queen mother calls her son to speak up for those who can't speak up for themselves, to speak up for the rights of the destitute, to defend the rights of the poor and needy—in other words, to pursue social justice. This is what God wants people in places of privilege to do. He puts people in positions of leadership to care for those who are not. He gives people influence or wealth to use for the good of the community—particularly those who are less fortunate. The wise mother is calling her son to do what Solomon said about the king in Psalm 72:12–14: "For he will deliver the needy who cry out, the afflicted who have no one to help. He will take pity on the weak and the needy and save the needy from death. He will rescue them from oppression and violence, for precious is their blood in his sight."

The words of the queen mother in Proverbs 31:8–9 are not the first words about doing justice in Proverbs. Elsewhere, for example, Proverbs says, "Whoever oppresses the poor shows contempt for their Maker, but whoever is kind to the needy honors God" (14:31). And, "The generous will themselves be blessed, for they share their food with the poor" (22:9). And, "A ruler who oppresses the poor is like a driving rain that leaves no crops" (28:3). Nor is Proverbs 31:8–9 the last time we read something like this in Proverbs. In the final poem of the book, in which a woman is the supermodel of wisdom, we read, "She opens her arms to the poor, and extends her hands to the needy" (31:20).

I'm thankful that my kids' mom, my wife, insisted that our kids look out for the welfare of the kids who were despised or ignored by others. She would say, "Reach out to that boy over there, the one everyone else is picking on. Reach out to the girl over there who is ridiculed because she is out of style and does not have the social skills everyone else does." That is what Proverbs 31:1–9 is calling moms and, may I suggest, other influential people to do. **A mom who fears the Lord teaches her kids to use their privileges to serve people in need rather than to serve themselves.**

When I read the words of King Lemuel's mom, I think about the greatest king who ever lived, a king whose kingdom was all about meeting the needs of the destitute, the widow, the orphan, the marginalized, the poor. I am referring, of course, to King Jesus. At the beginning of his earthly ministry—his reign as king—he stood up in a place of worship in his hometown and read some words from Isaiah the prophet that he applied to himself. Luke 4:18–19 records those words: "The Spirit of the Lord is on me, because he has anointed me to proclaim good news to the poor. He has sent me to proclaim freedom for the prisoners and recovery of sight for the blind, to set the oppressed free, to proclaim the year of the Lord's favor." When everyone looked at him, waiting for him to continue reading or to give the sermon for the day, he simply said, "Today this Scripture is fulfilled in your hearing" (Luke 4:21).

Jesus was the kind of king that King Lemuel's mother wanted Lemuel to be—**a king who used his privileges to serve people in need rather than to serve himself.** But not only that, Jesus calls those in his kingdom—people who call him their king—to do the same. Once, at a dinner banquet, Jesus said to his host, "When you give a banquet, invite the poor, the crippled, the lame, the blind, and you will be blessed" (Luke 14:13–14a).

Friends, **a mom who fears the Lord teaches her kids to use their privileges to serve people in need rather than to serve themselves.** But how can we teach our kids to do this, and how can we do what our mothers teach us when we struggle with selfishness and with using our strength to satisfy ourselves? It is through the power of the gospel. Jesus Christ paid the price for our sins in order to bring us to God, and Scripture says that our Lord Jesus Christ "was rich, yet for your sake he became poor, so that you through his poverty might become rich" (2 Cor. 8:9). He made the ultimate sacrifice so that through faith in him, he could make us rich by bringing us to God! Have you become rich? Have you placed your faith in Jesus Christ? Have you given your life to Christ? The riches that he offers to poor folks like me, who need forgiveness and purpose and family and meaning and life, are a free gift. That's the gospel.

Once you've responded to the gospel and accepted Christ, then you live out the gospel by using your strength to serve people in need. Not out of guilt, but out of gratitude. Not to earn points with God, but because God has made you rich. Moms, you do not have to be perfect. You don't have to be supermoms. Just teach your kids what really matters. Point them to Jesus, the one who was rich, yet for our sake became poor. Then teach them to follow Jesus's example, to **use their privileges to serve people in need rather than to serve themselves.**

Sample Sermon on Job 28:1–28

I prepared this sermon to serve as a window into the book of Job. It allowed me to focus on one chapter while providing an overview of the entire book. I tried to set up Job 28 in a compelling way, summarizing the chapters that precede it without saying, "Let me give you some background information so you can understand Job 28." Background information is important. But introducing it as such is a rather boring approach. The challenge is to communicate the background to Job 28 with a bit of intrigue. The outline that I followed for the chapter itself is from point III of my outline (in chap. 4) for a sermon on Job 3–28. The sermon is inductive, as the big idea emerges toward its end.

How to Respond to Undeserved Suffering

Job 28:1–28

A few years ago, some extended family members felt that God had let them down, that he was causing them to experience suffering they did not deserve. These family members are with the Lord now, so I feel free to share their story. I do not do so in a critical way, because I know my own heart, and I realize that I would be tempted to respond in the same way.

This is what happened. This couple was in their seventies, and they had been devoted followers of Jesus Christ for many years. But then life began to unravel. The husband was diagnosed with cancer. Then he developed problems with his eyesight. One day, he and his wife were in a car accident. Thankfully, they escaped serious injury, but their car was totaled. When the couple shared the news with relatives, one of them said, "Why is this happening to us? We've tried to be good Christians. Why would God do this to us? It's not fair." Part of me thought, "They should know better than to respond that way." Yet another part of me realized that this kind of attitude can easily bubble up in my life when I face what I perceive to be undeserved suffering. Sometimes I have said, or at least thought, "God, why are you giving me all this grief? I've tried to be faithful to you, and this is what I get?" Have you ever been there or felt that way? If so, this sermon is for you.

There is a man in the Bible who faced undeserved suffering. His name was Job. Yes, I know that all of us deserve judgment for our sin. None of us is perfect. All of us have sinned and fall short of God's glory. Yet Job did not deserve his suffering. We know that because God says so. This morning we're going to look at Job 28 because it is a chapter that helps us understand how we should respond to undeserved suffering. Please find Job 28 in your Bible or on your Bible app. I believe that this chapter is a remarkable interlude where we can find wisdom to cope with our suffering. Some of the headings in your Bible attribute this chapter to Job. But I don't believe that's correct. Remember, the headings are not part of the inspired text, so I'm not arguing with the Bible! I'm arguing with some of its translators. We will talk about that in a moment.

But as we prepare to look at Job 28, this stunning chapter that helps us understand how to handle undeserved suffering, we have to ask how we got here. The book of Job opens with two chapters of narrative—the story about how Job ended up in suffering. Job was a man who enjoyed the good life. He had it all. Job 1:3 says of him, *He was the greatest man among all the people of the East.* He had a large family, he was extremely wealthy, and he was godly. In 1:1, the book's author says, *This man was blameless and upright; he feared God and shunned evil.* Then God himself affirms this in 1:8, saying, *"He is blameless and upright, a man who fears God and shuns evil."*

God makes this observation to Satan, and Satan replies in Job 1:9 with the question that drives the book: *"Does Job fear God for nothing?"*

Satan's point is that Job worships God because God has showered him with blessings. But take it all away, Satan argues, and Job surely will curse God to his face (1:11). So God allows Satan to make Job's life miserable—within limits. The result is breathtaking. Through an enemy attack, fire from heaven, and a windstorm, Job loses his wealth, his servants, and his children. Yet the author tells us in 1:22, *In all this, Job did not sin by charging God with wrongdoing.* When God points this out to Satan, Satan replies, *"But now stretch out your hand and strike his flesh and bones, and he will surely curse you to your face"* (2:5). So God now allows Satan to inflict physical suffering on Job, but he orders Satan to spare Job's life. I can't imagine the misery Job faced as Satan afflicted him with painful sores (2:7). It was so bad that *Job took a piece of broken pottery and scraped himself with it as he sat among the ashes* in a state of mourning (2:8). But even though Job's wife told him, *Curse God and die!* (2:9), Scripture says, *In all this, Job did not sin in what he said* (2:10).

Now, remember that while Job is suffering, God is the one who is on trial. Satan has claimed that it's not a good policy to bless the righteous, since that is the only reason they worship God. However, Job proves that people can follow God for who he is, not only for his gifts.

But the story is far from over. Job is in great grief, and his three friends show up. Sometimes we are too hard on the friends. Let us give them some credit. They show up and say nothing for seven days (2:11–13). But then, in response to Job's lament in chapter 3, they launch into a lengthy dialogue with Job about his suffering in chapters 4–27. If you've read through the book of Job, this is the section that gets tedious and makes you want to stop reading. And that is by design! I think that we're supposed to get worn out by reading the back-and-forth exchanges between Job and his friends. Basically, chapters 4–27 argue that Job is experiencing retribution from God—that he is suffering because of a specific sin. The friends are putting Job on trial.

What's interesting is that Job adopts the same perspective that his friends do, assuming that suffering is always related to a specific sin. So Job puts God on trial, arguing that since he has done nothing wrong, his suffering is undeserved. Now, we know that there is truth to what we might call the "retribution principle." God gives people what they deserve. As Galatians 6:7 says, "Do not be deceived: God cannot be mocked. A man reaps what he sows." However, this is a general principle, not a specific one that explains every bad thing that happens to God's people or even to those who do not fear him.

Anyway, the dialogue in chapters 4–27 is tedious and frustrating to read. I feel like we're cheating a bit to jump right to Job 28 without experiencing the frustration of reading the chapters that lead up to it. These chapters have a unique design. There are three rounds of speeches. In each one, Eliphaz speaks, Job responds, Bildad speaks, Job responds, Zophar speaks, and Job responds. At least, that's what happens in the first two rounds. In round one, Job 4–14, the basic message of the friends is "Admit you're wrong, and deal with your sin." Then, in round two, Job 15–21, the challenge is "Consider the fate of the wicked, and realize that you're one of them." Then, in round three, Job 22–27, the friends level an accusation: "God is rebuking you for your great wickedness."

It is in round three that something remarkable happens. Eliphaz speaks, and Job replies. Then Bildad speaks, and Job replies. And then, in chapter 28, instead of Zophar speaking, we get a stunning poem about wisdom. Some versions of the Bible have a heading that identifies this as Job's speech. One (the ESV) says, "Job Continues: Where Is Wisdom?" But this makes no sense. As one commentator, John Walton, observes, Job's speech in chapter 27 exudes "a pessimistic, fatalistic despair.[1] And if we think that Job has suddenly adopted a proper response to God's involvement in his circumstances, read chapter 29. When Job continues his discourse in 29:1, he shows no hint of the convictions expressed in chapter 28. Chapter 29 throws us back into the ongoing dispute over why Job is suffering and what he needs to do about it. I believe, then, that Job 28 is an interlude or hymn by the author of the book. And it helps us understand how to respond to undeserved suffering.

There are three parts to the argument in this chapter. The first part, in verses 1–11, begins by observing that human beings know where to find hidden things like precious metals. This is poetry, yet it is building an argument. This is what verses 1–11 say:

> *There is a mine for silver*
> *   and a place where gold is refined.*
> *Iron is taken from the earth,*
> *   and copper is smelted from ore.*

1. Walton, *Job*, 30.

Mortals put an end to the darkness;
    they search out the farthest recesses
    for ore in the blackest darkness.
Far from human dwellings they cut a shaft,
    in places untouched by human feet;
    far from other people they dangle and sway.
The earth, from which food comes,
    is transformed below as by fire;
lapis lazuli comes from its rocks,
    and its dust contains nuggets of gold.
No bird of prey knows that hidden path,
    no falcon's eye has seen it.
Proud beasts do not set foot on it,
    and no lion prowls there.
People assault the flinty rock with their hands
    and lay bare the roots of the mountains.
They tunnel through the rock;
    their eyes see all its treasures.
They search the sources of the rivers
    and bring hidden things to light.

That is exquisite poetry, isn't it? It pictures the amazing feat we call mining. Even in the ancient world, mining was an important industry, and people figured how to "cut a shaft" (v. 4) and tunnel into the deepest, darkest places of the earth to find precious metals. Presumably, they descended on ropes into hidden places to dig out treasure. Even birds of prey, with their keen eyesight, and lions, with all of their strength and majesty, are unable to go where humans go when it comes to finding treasure. Perhaps you remember the thrilling rescue of thirty-three Chilean miners in 2010 who were trapped 2,300 feet underground. It reminds us what a remarkable exploit mining really is.

However, verses 12–19 provide a contrast. Even though human beings have had spectacular success in figuring out how to mine precious metals from the depths of the earth, they simply cannot find wisdom. According to verses 12–19, wisdom is elusive. Listen to the second movement in this poem.

But where can wisdom be found?
    Where does understanding dwell?

> *No mortal comprehends its worth;*
>   *it cannot be found in the land of the living.*
> *The deep says, "It is not in me";*
>   *the sea says, "It is not with me."*
> *It cannot be bought with the finest gold,*
>   *nor can its price be weighed out in silver.*
> *It cannot be bought with the gold of Ophir,*
>   *with precious onyx or lapis lazuli.*
> *Neither gold nor crystal can compare with it,*
>   *nor can it be had for jewels of gold.*
> *Coral and jasper are not worthy of mention;*
>   *the price of wisdom is beyond rubies.*
> *The topaz of Cush cannot compare with it;*
>   *it cannot be bought with pure gold.*

No matter how human beings have mastered the art of mining, tunneling into the dark reaches of the earth to find treasure, they simply cannot find wisdom. Here we need to remind ourselves that the word "wisdom" means "skill." It is the skill of living life the way God designed it to work. In Proverbs, wisdom is about adapting to the patterns God has made so that life goes smoothly. But there is a skill of living life in a way that copes with suffering and hardship. But this kind of wisdom is elusive. The first line of verse 13, *No mortal comprehends its worth*, seems to say that wisdom cannot be bought. Then, the second line of the verse, *It cannot be found in the land of the living*, is a rather bold statement that seems to contradict everything we know about the pursuit of wisdom by Solomon and others who had a hand in writing the book of Proverbs. When you read Proverbs, and the description of Solomon in 1 Kings 4:29–34, you get the sense that wisdom can be discovered and learned by human beings. However, what the second line of Job 28:13 affirms is that wisdom does not have its source in human beings.

Verse 14 continues the vivid picture. The deep and the sea are the most inaccessible places in the "land of the living." They are personified here, confessing this about wisdom: *"It is not in me. . . . It is not with me."* Furthermore, wisdom is too costly for purchase with precious metals or jewels. At one level, this is quite discouraging, because we are so used to dealing with problems by spending money. If I can afford a new roof for my house or a new computer system for my business or a particular treatment for an autoimmune disease, then I can purchase a solution to my problem. But when it comes to the wisdom needed to cope with suffering, no amount of money can buy it. No human ingenuity can discover it.

This brings us to the final movement of our poem, verses 20–28. These verses begin by raising again the question that occupies this chapter. Look at verses 20–22:

> *Where then does wisdom come from?*
> *Where does understanding dwell?*
> *It is hidden from the eyes of every living thing,*
> *concealed even from the birds in the sky.*
> *Destruction and Death say,*
> *"Only a rumor of it has reached our ears."*

The poet personifies Death and Destruction. They are the most powerful forces in the universe, and they admit that they do not know where wisdom can be found. And then the answer comes in verses 23–27.

> *God understands the way to it*
> *and he alone knows where it dwells,*
> *for he views the ends of the earth*
> *and sees everything under the heavens.*
> *When he established the force of the wind*
> *and measured out the waters,*
> *when he made a decree for the rain*
> *and a path for the thunderstorm,*
> *then he looked at wisdom and appraised it;*
> *he confirmed it and tested it.*

So where can we find wisdom? Only God knows where it is found. Wisdom is the exclusive domain of God. He knows the path to wisdom and the place to which this path leads. He is a God who sees! *He views the ends of the earth and sees everything under the heavens* (v. 24). And what he sees when he looks at the force of the wind and the rain and the storm is wisdom. God's creative work reflects wisdom—his wisdom. Now, the wind and the rain can bring about good. Yet in the book of Job, a "mighty wind" resulted in the collapse of the house of Job's oldest son, and he and his siblings were killed (1:19). Perhaps this is a reminder that

our understanding of how justice and wisdom interface is beyond us. It
is something only God understands.

So where does this leave us? How does this help us cope with undeserved
suffering? How then shall we live? God speaks in verse 28, the final verse
of the poem, and supplies the answer:

> *And he said to the human race,*
>   *"The fear of the Lord—that is wisdom,*
>   *and to shun evil is understanding."*

All right, what is the answer? How do we respond to undeserved suffering? Friends, **the way to respond to undeserved suffering is to trust in
the wisdom of God**. This answer is rooted in the fear of God. To fear
God is to worship him, to hold him in awe and reverence, and to trust
him—even though he does not reveal to us why we are suffering. Notice
the final line of God's words to the human race: "To shun evil is understanding." When we suffer, we are tempted to cope with it through sin.
That can be cursing God directly. Or it can be our pursuit of cocaine for
the soul—complaining, wallowing in bitterness, turning to pornography,
or medicating ourselves with drugs and alcohol. Instead, we are to trust
in God's infinite wisdom, knowing that he is good and just and loving.
**The way to respond to undeserved suffering is to trust in the wisdom of
God.** That's the message of this interlude in Job 28.

Yet, whatever relief chapter 28 provides, chapter 29 throws us back
into the ongoing dispute. In chapters 29–31, Job continues to insist on
his innocence and demands an answer from the Almighty. Then another
character enters the stage. In chapters 32–37, Elihu confronts Job. Unlike
the three previous friends, he does not accuse Job of committing a big sin
that led to his suffering. Rather, Elihu argues that Job's self-righteousness
is the cause of his suffering. Then, in chapter 38, the Lord speaks. Finally!
In Job 38:1–42:6, the Lord hammers Job with question after question.
At one point, Job even says, "All right, I'll shut up now" (40:3–5). But
God continues the questioning. Through his questions, the Lord says that
Job's challenge is inappropriate because Job lacks the wisdom and the
power that belong to God alone. Thus, the point is that Job must trust
in the wisdom of God when he suffers, because God's ways are beyond
Job's understanding and control. You can see, then, how the interlude

on wisdom in Job 28 foreshadows what God says in chapters 38–42. According to Job 28, **the way to respond to undeserved suffering is to trust in the wisdom of God.**

At the end of the book of Job, the Lord rebukes Job's three friends. He expresses anger at them because they "have not spoken the truth about me, as my servant Job has" (42:7). I believe that the reference here is to Job's confession in 42:1–6, where he repented and acknowledged that he was wrong to speak of things he did not understand. Yet the three friends did what the Lord told them and asked Job to pray for them. How humbling! The Lord accepted Job's prayer on their behalf, and then the Lord "restored his fortunes and gave him twice as much as he had before" (42:10). He made Job wealthier than ever and gave him more children. There's no suggestion that this made up for the pain of the prior deaths of his children. This is simply the Lord returning to his policy of blessing the righteous, after it is clear that righteous people worship God for who he is, not just because of what he does for us.

Friends, when it comes to suffering, God does not owe us explanations. Even if he provided them, they would not comfort us the way we hope, since God's ways are beyond us. Several years ago, four families lost loved ones in an accident involving a driver's education car. The instructor and three students were killed when the car hit an icy patch on a highway and veered into the path of a semitrailer. One of the boys and his family belonged to the church I served as pastor in Montana. The horrific accident caused the age-old question to resurface: "Why? God, why would you let this happen?" The boys and their families were all believers in Jesus. Why would God allow such suffering?

It is appropriate to turn to the book of Job for perspective. However, the book of Job never tells us why the righteous suffer. It does not explain to us the intricacies of God's justice. Rather, it tells us what the righteous can do when they face undeserved suffering. **The way to respond to undeserved suffering is to trust in the wisdom of God.** We have a God who promises that "our present sufferings are not worth comparing with the glory that will be revealed in us" (Rom. 8:18). So we must endure suffering as Jesus did. The author of 1 Peter 2:21 says, "To this you were called, because Christ suffered for you, leaving you an example, that you should follow in his steps." And a few sentences later, we read that when Christ suffered, "he entrusted himself to him who judges justly" (2:23). That's what we are called to do.

So when we are suffering, instead of accusing God of being unfair, and instead of asking, "Why is this happening to me?" the question we should ask is, "How should I respond to this undeserved suffering?" The answer is **to trust in the wisdom of God**. We trust God not because we understand how his justice relates to our suffering but because we affirm his wisdom. Our Savior, to whom we turn for help in times of need, is the one in whom all the treasures of wisdom and knowledge are hidden (Col. 2:3). I can trust my Savior when I suffer, knowing that he is infinitely wise.

Sample Sermon on Ecclesiastes 11:7–12:14

This is the final sermon I preached in a series on the book of Ecclesiastes. The introduction is notably brief. It relies on a twist on an old saying to create interest and to raise a need for the sermon. Then it orients listeners to the Scripture text. That is all a good introduction needs to accomplish. As we noted in chapter 5, this sermon attempts to capture the pathos of the book's final poem (11:7–12:8) and the ethos of its epilogue (12:9–14).

The Tunnel at the End of the Light

Ecclesiastes 11:7–12:14

You have heard the old saying that there is a light at the end of the tunnel. Right? No matter how dark it gets, you will soon end up in daylight. There is light at the end of the tunnel. However, when you look at life as a whole, the opposite is true. There is a tunnel at the end of the light. There are days of darkness ahead—even death. The last time I checked statistics, the mortality rate is 100 percent. So how should you live, knowing that there is a tunnel at the end of the light? The final section of the book of

Ecclesiastes gives us the answer. Look with me at Ecclesiastes 11:7–12:14. Please find this text in your Bible or on your Bible app.

The book of Ecclesiastes concludes with a poem in 11:7–12:8, and then the narrator's epilogue in 12:9–14. Both the poem and the epilogue help us understand how to live life in light of the reality that there is a tunnel at the end of the light. The first two verses of the poem, 11:7–8, state the problem:

> *Light is sweet,*
>> *and it pleases the eyes to see the sun.*
> *However many years anyone may live,*
>> *let them enjoy them all.*
> *But let them remember the days of darkness,*
>> *for there will be many.*
>> *Everything to come is meaningless.*

The problem is that even though life is a gift to enjoy, darkness is coming. Notice the contrast between light and darkness. In the Bible, light is a metaphor for the goodness of life—a gift we are supposed to enjoy. My wife's sister and family live in Wasilla, Alaska. We have visited them a couple times during the summer, and we have learned why Alaska is called "the land of the midnight sun." The light is sweet, and it always makes me happy to see so much of it. That's the Teacher's counsel in verse 8: enjoy those years of sunlight. If you have been tracking with the message of Ecclesiastes, you know that life is not a puzzle you can solve but a gift you can enjoy in the worship of God. Verse 8 re-echoes that message.

But there is another side to this—a dark side. Remember that the days of darkness are coming. The word "remember" is a key word in this final poem. Remember that the days of darkness are coming. I have not visited Alaska in the winter, and frankly, I don't want to do so. There are days of darkness. In December in Wasilla, the sun rises around 10:00 a.m. and sets around 3:30 p.m. It is dark most of the day. But the darkness in this poem is an even more serious matter. It is a metaphor for the brokenness of life. The "days of darkness" in verse 8 refer to death and everything that leads up to it, such as oppression, aloneness, or abuse.

Thus, "everything to come is meaningless." Now, recall that the word "meaningless" is a translation of the Hebrew term *hebel*—a vapor or a breath. It is hard to capture it with one English translation. Often, the metaphor expresses that life is fleeting—that is, here one moment and gone the next. Think of the breath you exhale on a zero-degree day. You can see it, but not for long. Sometimes, the idea is that you can't control life. Try stuffing that breath, before it disappears, in a box. Or try moving it a few feet to the right or left. It doesn't work. You cannot control it. I think the idea of "uncontrollable" fits here. You can't control the days of darkness that are coming. You cannot make them days of light. The problem, then, is that even though life is a gift to enjoy, darkness is coming.

What is the solution, then? What can we do about it? The Teacher fleshes out the solution by describing it in three different ways. The first description is in 11:9–10:

> You who are young, be happy while you are young,
>   and let your heart give you joy in the days of your youth.
> Follow the ways of your heart
>   and whatever your eyes see,
> but know that for all these things
>   God will bring you into judgment.
> So then, banish anxiety from your heart
>   and cast off the troubles of your body,
>   for youth and vigor are meaningless.

This counsel is addressed to those who are young, and it is jarring after the sober request in verse 8 to "remember the days of darkness" and the stark reminder that "everything to come is *hebel*." Verse 9 almost sounds like a glib "Don't worry, be happy." Is that really how we are to deal with the onset of aging and the prospect of our death? If the advice of the first two lines in verse 9 troubles you, then look at the advice in the next two lines. "Follow the ways of your heart." What? Haven't you been told over and over again by your God-fearing parents or by your pastor not to follow your heart? And then the parallel line says to follow "whatever your eyes see." That sounds like the end of the book of Judges, where everyone did what was right in their own eyes. In fact, Numbers 15:39 tells God's people not to chase after the lusts of their own hearts and eyes. So how can the Teacher counsel us to rejoice?

As often is the case, the context helps us out. Look at the final two lines of verse 9: "But know for all these things God will bring you into judgment." What verses 9–10 ask us to do, then, is to pursue joy within the boundaries set by God. These verse are not sarcastic, saying, "Go ahead and live it up now, but you will pay in the end." Rather, it is a call to follow the desires of your heart with a healthy, full awareness of God's judgment. As C. S. Lewis says, "Our Lord finds our desires not too strong, but too weak."[1] Old Testament scholar Craig Bartholomew observes that these verses call those who are young to consider that they will have to give an account to God as to how they rejoice and live out their lives.

There is an important implication in verse 10. The Teacher says to those who are young, "Banish anxiety from your heart and cast off the troubles of your body." Why? The last line tells us: "for youth and vigor are meaningless." Again, the term is *hebel*. The idea is that youth and vigor are fleeting. They are here one moment and gone the next. I can testify to that. I still think of myself as a twenty-five-year-old, but I am more than double that, and it has gone by so quickly. Yet, this reality should not cause the young to live with anxiety. I believe that Old Testament scholar George Athas is right when he says that the Teacher "does not mean clinical anxiety, which is a health condition, but a chosen attitude that seeks to control all the variables of human life."[2] Some of us need to hear this. We want to create a life that we can script and control. But there is so much out of our control. We can fret over it. Or we can follow the counsel of verses 9–10 and pursue joy within the boundaries set by God.

All right, the Teacher describes the solution to the tunnel at the end of the light a second way in 12:1–8. In 11:9–10, his message is that we should pursue joy within the boundaries set by God. Now, in 12:1–8, he says,

> Remember your Creator
>   in the days of your youth,
> before the days of trouble come
>   and the years approach when you will say,
>   "I find no pleasure in them"—
> before the sun and the light
>   and the moon and the stars grow dark,
>   and the clouds return after the rain;
> when the keepers of the house tremble,
>   and the strong men stoop,

1. Lewis, "The Weight of Glory," 26.
2. Athas, *Ecclesiastes, Song of Songs*, 210.

when the grinders cease because they are few,
     and those looking through the windows grow dim;
when the doors to the street are closed
     and the sound of grinding fades;
when people rise up at the sound of birds,
     but all their songs grow faint;
when people are afraid of heights
     and of dangers in the streets;
when the almond tree blossoms
     and the grasshopper drags itself along
     and desire no longer is stirred.
Then people go to their eternal home
     and mourners go about the streets.

Remember him—before the silver cord is severed,
     and the golden bowl is broken;
before the pitcher is shattered at the spring,
     and the wheel broken at the well,
and the dust returns to the ground it came from,
     and the spirit returns to God who gave it.

"Meaningless! Meaningless!" says the Teacher.
     "Everything is meaningless!"

This is an exquisite poem. The vivid images force us to linger and reflect on the reality that lies ahead. Once again, the Teacher calls those who are young to "remember" (v. 1). In the Old Testament, the word "remember" is not so much a request to recall something you have forgotten as it is a call to pay attention and commit to action. Thus, remembering that God is Creator is intended to shape the way we approach life when it is fleeting and frustrating—and as we approach the years when we will say, "I find no pleasure in them." In some ways, it's hard to imagine a time when we will say, "I don't want to live any longer." But I know people who have loved and enjoyed life, and yet the sunset years of their lives have not been a beautiful sunset. Those years have been full of gloomy darkness.

This gloomy darkness is what the poetry in verses 2–7 describes. The language is metaphorical. Here the Teacher uses images associated with the "day of the LORD"—that is, what life will be like in the end times before God unleashes his judgment. I find these images chilling and sobering.

The sun and moon and stars grow dark (v. 2). Then, in verse 3, you see the effect on all classes of people, from lowly servants to the wealthy. The "keepers of the house" are likely male servants, while the "strong men" are either those of high social status or perhaps soldiers. Then "grinders" are female servants who crush grain with millstones to make flour, while "those looking through windows" are likely woman of high social status. So the wealthy and strong tremble and grow dim, while the common laborers slow down. The imagery in verse 4 is challenging. The rising up at the sound of birds may well refer to birds of prey making a commotion rather than the joyful sound of songbirds. Then the last line of verse 4 says, in the straightforward translation in the ESV, "The daughters of song are brought low." These could be professional mourners who have stopped their lament or female servants who are shut indoors. Whatever the case, the point is that all "sound"—and that word appears twice in verse 4—has disappeared.

All of this leads to the arrival of death in verse 5. Notice the descriptions. People fear the heights, from which an attack is likely to come, and the streets, where they might experience danger. Now, what are we to make of the almond tree blossoming? This is an allusion either to Jeremiah 1:9–12, where the almond tree is a sign of coming judgment, or to the idea that even a hopeful sign, like the arrival of spring, is a time when nature is in travail. That is indicated by the grasshopper dragging itself along. I understand this image. As a fly-fisher, I spend a lot of time walking the banks along rivers and streams. In the late summer months, the grasshoppers leap several feet as I walk through the grass. But I have noticed that on cold October days, they stay put or even jump only a few inches. Life is winding down for them. The next line in verse 5 is difficult. The NIV reads, "and desire no longer is stirred." Yet some translations provide a more literal reading: "and the caperberry has no effect." The caperberry was used as an aphrodisiac, or sexual stimulant, in the ancient Near East. But it fails to stir the sexual desires of those facing destruction. And then death comes. *Then people go to their eternal home and mourners go about the streets* (v. 5c).

Verses 6–7 continue the theme of death, still relating back to the command "Remember your Creator" in verse 1. This remembering should happen "before the days of trouble come" (v. 1), *before* life darkens and stops (vv. 2–7), and now *before* death occurs. All four objects in verse

6—the silver cord, the golden bowl, the pitcher, and the wheel—experience irreparable damage. Then verse 7 describes death in words that remind us of Genesis 2:7, where God forms human beings from dust and breathes life into them. Thus, the process is undone, and life is gone. Here the motto of the book, which appears in 1:2, is repeated. Literally, "*Vapor of vapors," says the Teacher. "Everything is vapor.*" Like a vapor, life is here one moment and gone the next.

The message of verses 1–8, communicated by vivid, melancholic poetry, is "Remember your Creator before you get old and die." The English writer Somerset Maugham retold "The Appointment in Samarra," an old tale about a servant who lived in Baghdad. One day, his master sent him to the market. But before long, the servant came back, pale, trembling, and said, "Master, just now when I was in the marketplace I was jostled by a woman in the crowd and when I turned I saw it was Death that jostled me. She looked at me and made a threatening gesture, now lend me your horse, and I will ride away from this city and avoid my fate. I will go to Samarra and there Death will not find me." So the merchant lent the servant his horse, and the servant galloped away to Samarra. Later in the day, the merchant ventured into the marketplace and saw Death standing in the crowd. He went over to her and asked, "Why did you make a threatening gesture to my servant when you saw him this morning?" Surprised, Death replied, "That was not a threatening gesture. . . . I was astonished to see him in Bagdad, for I had an appointment with him tonight in Samarra."[3] There is no escaping death. There is a tunnel at the end of the light, and the best way to prepare for it is to remember our Creator before we get old and die.

The joyful living, commanded in 11:9–10, is also serious living. When we hear the Teacher's words in 12:1–8 in light of the Bible's overall storyline, we remember that our response to God in this life determines whether we will live in his presence in the next. And we remember that death has been defeated by Jesus in his resurrection, and that his resurrection is the firstfruits of many resurrections to come (1 Cor. 15:20–28).

Now, there is a third way that Ecclesiastes fleshes out the solution to the reality that death is in our future, that all people die. First, in 11:9–10, his message is that we are to pursue joy within the boundaries set by God.

3. Maugham, "Appointment in Samarra."

Then, in 12:1–8, he calls us to remember our Creator before we get old and die. In 12:9–14, we arrive at the epilogue of the book. Here, the narrator speaks and summarizes the message of the entire book. He begins, though, by affirming the wise Teacher and offering us counsel about how to respond to the Teacher's words. In 12:9–12, he says,

> Not only was the Teacher wise, but he also imparted knowledge to the people. He pondered and searched out and set in order many proverbs. The Teacher searched to find just the right words, and what he wrote was upright and true.
> The words of the wise are like goads, their collected sayings like firmly embedded nails—given by one shepherd. Be warned, my son, of anything in addition to them.
> Of making many books there is no end, and much study wearies the body.

This is a glowing endorsement. The narrator claims that the Teacher was a wise observer who communicated carefully and truthfully. Then the narrator steps back a bit in verse 11 to reflect on the wisdom tradition as a whole. He likens the words of the wise to the nails in goads, or prodding sticks that were used to keep oxen moving—even though they did sting a bit. Quite frankly, wisdom can sting a bit when it confronts our way of doing life. But we ignore wisdom's prodding to our peril, especially because these words come from "one shepherd." I believe that this is a reference to God.

Verse 12 offers an important implication. Once again, this statement must be understood in its context. I don't believe the narrator is anti-intellectual or against books. The concern here is the foundation on which we build our lives. The narrator speaks as a father warning his son, and his message is "Do not wander outside the wisdom tradition that has its foundation in God our shepherd. Yes, there are many books that present another approach to life, and there will continue to be many more books published that will expound another way. But reading all these will be wearisome. Don't stray from godly wisdom."

This brings us to the concise yet profound conclusion to the book. This is what Ecclesiastes 12:13–14 says:

> Now all has been heard;
>   here is the conclusion of the matter:

> *Fear God and keep his commandments,*
> *for this is the duty of all mankind.*
> *For God will bring every deed into judgment,*
> *including every hidden thing,*
> *whether it is good or evil.*

The message is clear. Fear and obey God, who ultimately will judge your deeds. Ecclesiastes ends where wisdom begins: with the fear of the Lord. This fear is not terror, but the reverence, awe, and worship that God alone deserves. The reason to worship and obey God is that he is the Judge as well as the Creator. One day he will bring every deed into judgment— even the things that have been hidden from others. There is a wonderful irony here: if you fear God, you will not have to fear judgment. The final judgment is an important part of the Bible's storyline; it is the time when everything gets purged and remade so that we can enjoy life without the destructive and deadly effects of sin. So the message of 12:9–14 is "Fear and obey God, who ultimately will judge your deeds."

All right, we're living in a world of *hebel*. Life is a vapor that is here one moment and gone the next. And while it is here, you can't control it. Yes, life is both fleeting and frustrating. And it is spiraling toward darkness and death. As Zack Eswine says, "In Ecclesiastes, death is a piece of tornado from which no proverbial basement can shelter us."[4] So how should we live? The answer is not that we should just give in to pessimism or cynicism or despair. Nor is it that we should expect the pursuit of pleasure or wealth or education to numb the pain. Rather, the answer is that we are to enjoy life as a gift of God. Yet, according to Ecclesiastes 11:7–12:14, we enjoy that life in light of our Creator and Judge. Friends, **the best way to enjoy life when you are young is to remember your Creator, who will judge you after you are old and die.** That's what the book of Ecclesiastes leaves us to contemplate and to do.

I'm not sure what you need to hear today. Perhaps it is that you should enjoy the life God has given you while you can still enjoy it, even though it is full of frustration and is hurtling toward death. Sometimes I catch myself getting caught up in anxiety over things outside my control so that I do not enjoy the moments God has given me to enjoy. But that is not the right way to live. Or maybe you need to remember your Creator,

---

4. Eswine, *Recovering Eden*, 9.

who will judge you after you are old and die. According to Acts 17:31, God has "set a day when he will judge the world with justice by the man he has appointed. He has given proof of this to everyone by raising him from the dead." Yes, the day is coming when every knee will bow and every tongue confess that Jesus Christ is Lord (Phil. 2:10–11). But the great treasure is for those who do it now. When that day comes, those who have remembered their Creator will bow in glad submission rather than in miserable surrender.

So don't let *hebel* rob you of your youth. Don't let it rob you of the time you have left if your youth is in the rearview mirror. If you don't fear God now, you will fear judgment later. But if you fear God now, there will be no fear when you stand before him. Remember, **the best way to enjoy life when you are young is to remember your Creator, who will judge you after you are old and die.**

Appendix F

Sample Sermon on Song of Songs

This is an example of how to preach Song of Songs in one sermon by looking at key passages in the book. This sermon takes the view that Song of Songs unfolds like a drama. Because of the length of the sermon, I did not spend as much time on specific application as I would have liked. But my purpose for the sermon is for listeners to marvel at God's gift of sexual love and to believe that it should be reserved for marriage because marital love has a power that sex without boundaries does not.

The Best Love Song Ever

Song of Songs 1:1–17; 3:6–11; 8:5–14

When Priscilla and I got married, we included a couple of love songs in our wedding ceremony. One is a song exalting Christ's love. The other is a song that captures the power and delight of love by describing it with creation language. It is "Annie's Song," written by John Denver for his wife. I suppose our song choice dates us. The year was 1983—yes, over forty years ago! Our friend Dave played guitar and sang it. Sometimes, I write the lyrics of this song in an anniversary card or on a social media

213

post to Priscilla. I tell her that she still fills up my senses like the mountains in springtime and like a walk in the rain. I will express my desire to love her and invite her to fill me again. "Annie's Song" is a beautiful love song, but I have to admit that it is not the best love song ever written.

Today I want to introduce you to the best love song ever written. At least that is what it claims to be. It is a love song that uses creation language and appears in the Bible. Please find Song of Songs in your Bible or on your Bible app. It is right after Psalms, Proverbs, and Ecclesiastes.

You might be a bit shocked that we are turning to Song of Songs. This might be the first sermon you have ever heard on it. So why do we avoid Song of Songs? There are several reasons why we rarely preach or teach it. And these are the same reasons why we hurry past it when it comes up in our Bible reading plan. Here are four reasons we ignore Song of Songs.

First, the lyrics seem a bit silly to us. Years ago, Paul McCartney wrote a song called "Silly Love Songs." Song of Songs sure seems to fit that category. For example, Song of Songs 4:1 says, "How beautiful are you, my darling! Oh, how beautiful! Your eyes behind your veil are like doves. Your hair is like a flock of goats." Try telling the woman you love that her hair is like a flock of goats, especially if she thinks she is having a bad hair day!

The second reason why we avoid Song of Songs is that the lyrics are somewhat embarrassing. They are sexual, border on erotic, and may cause you to blush. For example, Song of Songs 4:5 says, "Your breasts are like two fawns, like twin fawns of a gazelle that browse among the lilies." Enough said.

Third, the lyrics are confusing. Even if they do not seem silly, even if they do not embarrass you, a lot of them do not make complete sense. The one commonality they have is that their metaphors come from creation, yet they are still confusing. For example, Song of Songs 7:2 says, "Your waist is a mound of wheat encircled by lilies." What in the world does that mean? Another reason why the lyrics are confusing is the switching between speakers. Our English translations try to help us by giving us headings like "She," "He," and "Others" or "Friends." But they don't always agree with one another.

Now, there is a final reason why we avoid Song of Songs. Not only do the lyrics seem silly, embarrassing, and confusing. The lyrics do not mention God except for a brief reference in one place near the end of the book. I will point that out in a few minutes. So this is not a book where you get a rich theology of God, like you do in 1 Samuel or Psalms or Isaiah. It does not seem like God is involved in the book except for a lone passing reference to him.

However, I will argue that this *is* a book about God, specifically about the gift of romantic love that he has created. And I believe that if we are patient with the lyrics, we will learn to appreciate, and perhaps treasure, the way they express the joy and delight and sheer ecstasy of romantic love.

Now, as we get ready to explore Song of Songs, I need to mention three other questions we have to answer in order to make sense of it. First, what is the literary strategy? Is the song a drama, a love story communicated in poetry? Or is this simply a long love poem or an anthology of love poems that celebrate love but do not necessarily tell a story? Old Testament scholars are split on this. But I view it as a drama—that is, a love song with a developing story.

Second, what is the purpose of Song of Songs? Is it an allegory of God's love for Israel or Christ's love for the church? That is how the church read it for hundreds of years. Or, is the book a marriage manual or sex manual? Or is it simply a celebration of sexual or married love? I believe it is the latter. I view Song of Songs as a celebration of the power and beauty of sexual love in a committed, exclusive relationship. The book celebrates the joy and delight of marital love—the climax to God's creation of the man and woman.

So then, I am arguing that Song of Songs is a drama—a love song with a developing story—and that it is a celebration of romantic, marital love in a committed exclusive relationship. But there is a third question we have to ask. What is the role of Solomon? Is he the groom in the story, or an idealized lover—the kind where the woman says to the groom, "You are my Solomon?" Or is Solomon the villain, or even an intruder? I believe that he is a villain or an intruder.

But wait! Isn't this the Song of Solomon? Didn't he write it? Yes, we know he messed up later in his life and became a womanizer and an idolator, but isn't it possible that he wrote this early in his married life? Look with me at Song of Songs 1:1. A straightforward reading of the Hebrew of verse 1 is "The song of songs which is to Solomon." The expression "song of songs" is like "king of kings." It is a superlative, meaning "the best song." It's the next part of verse 1 that is debated. The little preposition that I translated as "to" can mean "to"—as in "dedicated to"—or

"for" or "about" or "by." Is this a song written by Solomon, for Solomon, or about Solomon? Only the context can tell us.

When we read the book closely, I believe that the idea is that this is a song about Solomon, a song concerning him. And in this song he is not a hero. I agree with the view that says Song of Songs is a "northern kingdom satire on the reign of Solomon and his exploitation of women (ironically to his demise) and memorializing of the exemplary character of the Shulammite maiden who rejected the wooing of the king out of faithfulness to her commoner-lover."[1] Read 1 Kings 11 for the account of Solomon's downfall.

Thankfully, if you prefer to view Solomon as a "good guy," a real or idealized lover, you will still end up at the end of the book with a celebration of the power and delight of romantic love. Let's turn now to the text and look at three key scenes.

First, let's look at the opening scene in 1:2–17. In this scene, a young woman and a young man express their passionate love for each other, despite the interference of the king. The opening words that follow the title might take us by surprise. The young woman speaks, and her words are full of passion. She says, in verses 2–4, *Let him kiss me with the kisses of his mouth—for your love is more delightful than wine. Pleasing is the fragrance of your perfumes; your name is like perfume poured out. No wonder the young women love you! Take me away with you—let us hurry! Let the king bring me into his chambers. We rejoice and delight in you; we will praise your love more than wine. How right they are to adore you!* Do you feel her passion? She sounds like the kind of young woman who would write the name of the one she loves a hundred times on a piece of stationery.

However, I hear a tone of urgency as well. In verse 4, she says, "Let us hurry." And the next line tells us why. Now, I am grateful for our English versions of the Bible, but here is a place where I believe that the NIV's interpretation is not the best one. It translates her words about the king bringing her into his chambers as something she desires. But I think that the ESV and the NASB are right to translate this as, "The king has brought me into his chambers." There's nothing in the grammar of this statement to suggest that it is a wish, as the NIV and even the CSB translate it. So I

---

1. Hill and Walton, *Old Testament*, 473.

believe that this is a plea for rescue. Either the king has already brought her into his harem, or he is about to do so. The timing is not indicated by the verb and must be determined by the context. Please note, then, that I understand the king, who will be identified as Solomon as the book continues, as a separate character from the young man whose voice we will hear shortly. If you believe that the young man and the king are one and the same, then you will translate the second line in verse 4 like the NIV, as a positive statement of desire. But if the young man and the king are not the same, then you will read the second line as the problem and the reason for the plea "Let us hurry!"

Notice in the last two lines of verse 4 that we have a different speaker. Instead of references to "me," the pronoun switches to "we." This seems to be the friends speaking, and you likely have a heading in your Bible indicating this. These headings can be helpful, but remember that they are not part of the inspired text. Our translators put them there to try to help us. Occasionally, we might question their decision.

In verses 5–8, the young woman speaks up again. In fact, her speech may begin in the final line of verse 4. Notice what she says as she continues: *Dark am I, yet lovely, daughters of Jerusalem, dark like the tents of Kedar, like the tent curtains of Solomon. Do not stare at me because I am dark, because I am darkened by the sun. My mother's sons were angry with me and made me take care of the vineyards; my own vineyard I had to neglect. Tell me, you whom I love, where you graze your flock and where you rest your sheep at midday. Why should I be like a veiled woman beside the flocks of your friends? If you do not know, most beautiful of women, follow the tracks of the sheep and graze your young goats by the tents of the shepherds.* This speech is important because it informs us that this young woman is a farm girl rather than a princess, even though she is lovely. She is dark because she has been out in the sun. Our culture, unlike hers, likes a good tan, as unhealthy as it may be. But in her culture, her tan is not the sign of her loveliness but the sign of her commonness. Notice too in verse 6 that she is at odds with her brothers. We'll see why a little later in the book.

Now, how does her lover feel about her? He responds by praising her beauty. Look at verses 9–11: *I liken you, my darling, to a mare among Pharaoh's chariot horses. Your cheeks are beautiful with earrings, your neck with strings of jewels. We will make you earrings of gold, studded with silver.* Perhaps only a farmer can appreciate the young man's metaphor in verse 9, but we can all understand how he feels about her in verses 10–11. He treasures her beauty.

Let's look at one more speech in this opening scene, the woman's speech in verses 12–14: *While the king was at his table, my perfume spread its fragrance. My beloved is to me a sachet of myrrh resting between my breasts. My beloved is to me a cluster of henna blossoms from the vineyards of En Gedi.* I believe that he is contrasting her experience at a meal with the king and her strong intimate feelings for her lover. The image in verse 13 has strong sexual overtones. In Proverbs 7:17–20, myrrh is a precious substance associated with physical love, although there in the context of adultery. And the Hebrew verb translated as "rest" in verse 13 means "lodge" or "spend the night."

The opening scene, then, is a couple's longing for love. They are passionate for each other despite the interference of the king. But as you might suspect, there is trouble on the horizon. After a couple of chapters of carefree dialogue between the two lovers, even though there is physical separation between them, the song turns from a major to a minor key. Please look at the scene in Song of Songs 3:6–11, which describes the emergence of a carriage from the wilderness. The text says, *Who is this coming up from the wilderness like a column of smoke, perfumed with myrrh and incense made from all the spices of the merchant? Look! It is Solomon's carriage, escorted by sixty warriors, the noblest of Israel, all of them wearing the sword, all experienced in battle, each with his sword at his side, prepared for the terrors of the night. King Solomon made for himself the carriage; he made it of wood from Lebanon. Its posts he made of silver, its base of gold. Its seat was upholstered with purple, its interior inlaid with love. Daughters of Jerusalem, come out, and look, you daughters of Zion. Look on King Solomon wearing a crown, the crown with which his mother crowned him on the day of his wedding, the day his heart rejoiced.*

How do we understand this scene? While some read it as a description of a wedding procession, I believe that it describes Solomon driving around on his chariot-bed, like a wealthy athlete or entertainer with a tricked-out SUV or limo ready to do all kinds of things on the bed in back if he can entice a young lady. He comes in his luxurious carriage with expensive, exotic spices, and he has sixty warriors—perhaps a contrast to his father

David's thirty mighty men that we read about in 2 Samuel. Another key detail is in verse 6: Solomon's emergence from the wilderness. This is a reference to uncultivated, uncivilized land that is the opposite of the garden of Eden. I am thinking here of Isaiah 51:3, where God comforts Zion and promises to "make her deserts like Eden, her wastelands like the garden of the LORD." There certainly is irony in the reference in verse 11 to the day of his wedding, because 1 Kings 11:3 tells us that Solomon amassed seven hundred wives and three hundred concubines. So then, I believe that this scene portrays Solomon as a pathetic figure, lost in a lonely world of materialism and sexual conquest.

The drama progresses in chapters 4–7 and builds up to the final scene in 8:5–14. What will happen to this couple? The question raised in verse 5, presumably by the daughters of Jerusalem to whom she has just spoken, pictures the young woman escaping from the wilderness, leaning on her lover. The daughters of Jerusalem ask, *Who is this coming up from the wilderness, leaning on her beloved?*

Then the young woman speaks and gives a moving plea for her lover to commit to her completely because of the stunning power of love. She says, *Under the apple tree I roused you; there your mother conceived you, there she who was in labor gave you birth. Place me like a seal over your heart, like a seal on your arm; for love is as strong as death, its jealousy unyielding as the grave. It burns like blazing fire, like a mighty flame. Many waters cannot quench love; rivers cannot sweep it away. If one were to give all the wealth of one's house for love, it would be utterly scorned.*

Her words are so moving! The request for him to place her like a seal over his heart is a plea for him to belong to her intimately. She makes this plea, recognizing that "love is as strong as death." This is a surprising metaphor, but not intended negatively. Just as you cannot overcome death, so you cannot overcome love. Its power is overwhelming. Then she elaborates, describing love's "jealousy" as being as "unyielding as the grave." We usually think of jealousy as a negative emotion. Yet, in Exodus 20:5, the Lord describes himself as "jealous," and in Exodus 34:14, he says that his name is "Jealous." Jealousy is a strong desire for exclusive possession. What makes it appropriate or inappropriate is whether this jealousy is legitimate or not. Just as the Lord has a right to claim the exclusive affections of people he created and redeemed, so a spouse has the right to claim the exclusive affections of his or her spouse. This jealousy is so powerful that it "burns like a blazing fire, like a mighty flame." This expression, "a mighty flame," should stop us in our tracks, because a straightforward translation is "the flame of Yah." *Yah* is a shortened form of the Hebrew name *Yahweh*, God's memorial name, which signifies his ongoing care for his people and his willingness to act on their behalf. So this flame is "the flame of the LORD"! Although this image might seem to be destructive, the emphasis is on love's power. And what a tremendous, though subtle, reminder that the Lord stands behind it all.

Finally, in verse 7, we hear that love cannot be swept away by the powers of chaos—"many waters"—nor exchanged for wealth. That's why I believe that troubled marriages can be salvaged when God is involved. When people say, "I don't love my spouse anymore," they mean that the feeling is gone. But it can return. Feelings are always the first to go and the last to return. Yet the power of love can lead to reconciliation. During my years as a pastor, I have performed two remarriage ceremonies for couples who got divorced. But God worked beautifully in their lives, restoring their love for each other, and they chose to remarry.

Now, at this point trouble appears again. This time, it is the woman's brothers. In verses 8–9, they say, *We have a little sister, and her breasts are not yet grown. What shall we do for our sister on the day she is spoken for? If she is a wall, we will build towers of silver on her. If she is a door, we will enclose her with panels of cedar.* Verse 8 indicates that they have underestimated her maturity, and they plan to keep men away until the proper time.

Yet, in verses 10–12, she takes control of her destiny and pledges herself to her beloved rather than to Solomon. Listen to her words: *I am a wall, and my breasts are like towers. Thus I have become in his eyes like one bringing contentment. Solomon had a vineyard in Baal Hamon; he let out his vineyard to tenants. Each was to bring for its fruit a thousand shekels of silver. But my own vineyard is mine to give; the thousand shekels are for you, Solomon, and two hundred are for those who tend its fruit.* The bold language in verse 10 is not lurid, like the trappers who named those majestic mountains in Wyoming "the Tetons." Rather, this is an affirmation that she is strong and mature, and in the eyes of her lover, she brings "contentment," or "peace," since the word is *shalom*, which signifies that everything is just right as it ought to be. By contrast, she says that Solomon, who claimed her as one of his vineyards, no longer has her because her vineyard (that is, her body) is hers to give. There is a delightful play on words here. She who brings *shalom* to her lover, but rejects the advances of *shelomoh*, the Hebrew name of Solomon. So he can keep his money.

The ending to the poem is rather remarkable, ending abruptly without a torrid sex scene but rather with the lovers longing for each other. In verse 13, the young man says, *You who dwell in the gardens with friends in attendance, let me hear your voice!* Here the reply, in verse 14, which closes the book, is *Come away, my beloved, and be like a gazelle or like a young stag on the spice-laden mountains.* This is a final testimony to the power and delight of love! So what have we seen in this closing scene? Essentially, the young woman expresses the power of her love for the young man, rejects Solomon, and invites the young man to "come away" with her.

It is here that we find the message of the book. Song of Songs affirms that **marital love has a God-given power and delight that sex without boundaries can never achieve.** So then, the most delightful, breathtaking, captivating, power-of-God type of love that you can find is not in the palace of Solomon or in the Playboy mansion or on *The Bachelor*, but in the loyal love of a man and woman in an exclusive relationship, regardless of how much wealth and comfort they have or do not have. That's why we pursue loyal love in our marriages, as hard as marriage can be, with all the little foxes that can ruin the vineyard of marriage—to use the imagery of Song of Songs 2:15. To be sure, marriage is not sexual nirvana. But, pursue this kind of marriage and work for this kind of marriage.

Ultimately, the kind of love described here points us to God, because marital, sexual love is a picture of the love that God has within himself and the love that Christ has for the church. So even though we do not treat Song of Songs as an allegory, it definitely points forward to the love that Christ has for the church in dying for her, his spouse, as described in Ephesians 5:25–27. When our marriages are at their best, they point forward to the gospel—the good news that God loved us so much that while we were still sinners, he sent Christ to die for us so that our broken relationship with him can be restored. And when our marriages are at their lowest, it is only Christ's love that enables us to love our spouse—even when the feeling is gone or there are deep-seated conflicts in our relationship. Never forget that **marital love has a God-given power and delight that sex without boundaries can never achieve.**

A Categorization of the Psalms

Book 1				
1—Wisdom	10—Lament (I)	18—Confidence	26—Lament (I)	34—Praise (T)
2—Royal	11—Confidence	19—Wisdom	27—Confidence	35—Lament (I)
3—Lament (I)	12—Lament (I)	20—Royal	28—Lament (I)	36—Lament (I)
4—Lament (I)	13—Lament (I)	21—Royal	29—Praise (H)	37—Wisdom
5—Lament (I)	14—Lament (I)	22—Lament (I)	30—Praise (T)	38—Penitential
6—Penitential	15—Wisdom	23—Confidence	31—Lament (I)	39—Lament (I)
7—Lament (I)	16—Confidence	24—Royal	32—Penitential	40—Praise (T)
8—Praise (H)	17—Lament (I)	25—Lament (I)	33—Praise (H)	41—Lament (I)
9—Lament (I)				

Book 2				
42—Lament (I)	49—Wisdom	55—Lament (I)	61—Lament (I)	67—Praise (T)
43—Lament (I)	50—Prophetic	56—Lament (I)	62—Confidence	68—Praise (T)
44—Lament (C)	51—Penitential	57—Lament (I)	63—Lament (I)	69—Lament (I)
45—Royal	52—Lament (I)	58—Lament (C)	64—Lament (I)	70—Lament (I)
46—Confidence	53—Lament (I)	59—Lament (I)	65—Praise (T)	71—Lament (I)
47—Royal	54—Lament (I)	60—Lament (C)	66—Praise (T)	72—Royal
48—Praise (H)				

Book 3				
73—Wisdom	77—Lament (I)	81—Praise (H)	84—Praise (T)	87—Praise (T)
74—Lament (C)	78—Wisdom	82—Lament (C)	85—Lament (C)	88—Lament (I)
75—Praise (T)	79—Lament (C)	83—Lament (C)	86—Lament (I)	89—Royal
76—Praise (T)	80—Lament (C)			

Note: C = communal; H = hymn; I = individual; T = thanksgiving.

Book 4				
90—Lament (C)	94—Lament (C)	98—Praise (H)	101—Royal	104—Praise (T)
91—Confidence	95—Praise (H)	99—Royal	102—Penitential	105—Praise (T)
92—Praise (T)	96—Praise (H)	100—Praise (H)	103—Praise (H)	106—Praise (H)
93—Royal	97—Royal			/ Lament (C)

Book 5				
107—Praise (T)	116—Praise (T)	125—Confidence	134—Praise (H)	143—Penitential
108—Praise (T)	117—Praise (H)	126—Lament (C)	135—Praise (T)	144—Royal
109—Lament (I)	118—Praise (T)	127—Wisdom	136—Wisdom	145—Royal
110—Royal	119—Wisdom	128—Wisdom	137—Lament (C)	146—Praise (H)
111—Praise (T)	120—Lament (I)	129—Lament (C)	138—Praise (T)	147—Praise (H)
112—Wisdom	121—Confidence	130—Penitential	139—Lament (I)	148—Praise (H)
113—Praise (H)	122—Praise (T)	131—Confidence	140—Lament (I)	149—Praise (H)
114—Praise (T)	123—Lament (C)	132—Royal	141—Lament (I)	150—Praise (H)
115—Confidence	124—Praise (T)	133—Wisdom	142—Lament (I)	

Note: C = communal; H = hymn; I = individual; T = thanksgiving.

Bibliography

Alcántara, Jared E. *How to Preach Proverbs*. Dallas: Fontes, 2022.

Allen, Leslie C. ידה. In *New International Dictionary of Old Testament Theology and Exegesis*, ed. Willem A. VanGemeren, 2:405–8. Grand Rapids: Zondervan, 1997.

Allen, Ronald B. *Lord of Song: The Messiah Revealed in the Psalms*. Portland: Multnomah, 1985.

———. *Praise! A Matter of Life and Breath*. Nashville: Nelson, 1980.

Alstad, Ken. *Savvy Sayin's*. Tucson: Ken Alstad Company, 1986.

Alter, Robert. *The Art of Biblical Poetry*. New York: Basic Books, 1985.

———. *The Hebrew Bible: A Translation with Commentary*. 3 vols. New York: Norton, 2019.

Andersen, Francis I. *Job: An Introduction and Commentary*. Tyndale Old Testament Commentaries. Downers Grove, IL: IVP Academic, 2008.

Ash, Christopher. *Job: The Wisdom of the Cross*. Preaching the Word. Wheaton: Crossway, 2014.

Athas, George. *Ecclesiastes, Song of Songs*. Story of God Bible Commentary. Grand Rapids: Zondervan Academic, 2020.

Barbarisi, Daniel. "The Man Who Found Forrest Fenn's Treasure." *Outside*, May 12, 2022. https://www.outsideonline.com/2419429/forrest-fenn-treasure-jack-stuef.

Bartholomew, Craig. *Ecclesiastes*. Baker Commentary on the Old Testament Wisdom and Psalms. Grand Rapids: Baker Academic, 2009.

———. *When You Want to Yell at God: The Book of Job*. Bellingham, WA: Lexham, 2014.

Bartholomew, Craig G., and Ryan P. O'Dowd. *Old Testament Wisdom Literature: A Theological Introduction*. Downers Grove, IL: IVP Academic, 2011.

225

Bateman, Herbert W., IV, and D. Brent Sandy, eds. *Interpreting the Psalms for Teaching and Preaching*. St. Louis: Chalice, 2010.

Beale, G. K. *The Temple and the Church's Mission: A Biblical Theology of the Dwelling Place of God*. New Studies in Biblical Theology. Downers Grove, IL: InterVarsity, 2004.

Berlin, Adele. *The Dynamics of Biblical Parallelism*. Rev. ed. Grand Rapids: Eerdmans, 2008.

Brueggemann, Walter. *The Message of the Psalms: A Theological Commentary*. Minneapolis: Augsburg, 1984.

———. *The Psalms and the Life of Faith*. Edited by Patrick D. Miller. Minneapolis: Fortress, 1995.

Campbell, Stephen D., Richard G. Rohlfing Jr., and Richard S. Briggs, eds. *A New Song: Biblical Hebrew Poetry as Jewish and Christian Scripture*. Studies in Scripture and Biblical Theology. Bellingham, WA: Lexham, 2023.

Carson, D. A. "Challenges for the Twenty-First-Century Pulpit." In *Preach the Word: Essays on Expository Preaching in Honor of R. Kent Hughes*, edited by Leland Ryken and Todd Wilson, 172–89. Wheaton: Crossway, 2007.

———. *Exegetical Fallacies*. 2nd ed. Grand Rapids: Baker, 1996.

Choi, Calvin W. "Ecclesiastes." In *The Big Idea Companion for Preaching and Teaching*, edited by Matthew D. Kim and Scott M. Gibson, 239–44. Grand Rapids: Baker Academic, 2021.

Clines, David J. A. *Job 1–20*. Word Biblical Commentary 17. Grand Rapids: Zondervan Academic, 2015.

———. *Job 21–37*. Word Biblical Commentary 18A. Grand Rapids: Zondervan Academic, 2015.

———. *Job 38–42*. Word Biblical Commentary 18B. Grand Rapids: Zondervan Academic, 2015.

Craigie, Peter C. *Psalms 1–50*. Word Biblical Commentary 19. Waco: Word, 1983.

Culy, Martin M., Mikeal C. Parsons, and Joshua J. Stigall. *Luke: A Handbook on the Greek Text*. Baylor Handbook on the Greek New Testament. Waco: Baylor University Press, 2010.

Delitzsch, Franz. *Biblical Commentary on the Psalms*. Translated by Francis Bolton. 3 vols. Clark's Foreign Theological Library 4/29–31. Edinburgh: T&T Clark, 1876–77.

———. *Commentary on the Song of Songs and Ecclesiastes*. Translated by M. G. Easton. Keil and Delitzsch Commentaries on the Old Testament. Grand Rapids: Eerdmans, 1950.

Dell, Katherine J. *The Theology of the Book of Proverbs*. Old Testament Theology. Cambridge: Cambridge University Press, 2023.

Duguid, Iain M. *The Song of Songs: An Introduction and Commentary*. Tyndale Old Testament Commentaries. Downers Grove, IL: IVP Academic, 2015.

Duvall, J. Scott, and J. Daniel Hays. *God's Relational Presence: The Cohesive Center of Biblical Theology*. Grand Rapids: Baker Academic, 2019.

Eaton, Michael A. *Ecclesiastes: An Introduction and Commentary*. Tyndale Old Testament Commentaries. Downers Grove, IL: InterVarsity, 1983.

Estes, Daniel J. *Job*. Teach the Text Commentary Series. Grand Rapids: Baker Books, 2013.

Eswine, Zack. *Recovering Eden: The Gospel according to Ecclesiastes*. The Gospel according to the Old Testament. Phillipsburg, NJ: P&R, 2014.

Evans, Vyvyan. *Cognitive Linguistics: A Complete Guide*. 2nd ed. Edinburgh: Edinburgh University Press, 2019.

Firth, Jill. "The Suffering Servant in Book V of the Psalter." In *Reading the Psalms Theologically*, edited by David M. Howard Jr. and Andrew J. Schmutzer, 111–26. Bellingham, WA: Lexham Academic, 2023.

Fokkelman, J. P. *Reading Biblical Poetry: An Introductory Guide*. Translated by Ineke Smit. Louisville: Westminster John Knox, 2001.

Fox, Michael V. *Ecclesiastes*. JPS Bible Commentary. Philadelphia: Jewish Publication Society, 2004.

———. *Proverbs 1–9: A New Translation with Introduction and Commentary*. Anchor Yale Bible 18A. New Haven: Yale University Press, 2000.

———. *Proverbs 10–31: A New Translation with Introduction and Commentary*. Anchor Yale Bible 18B. New Haven: Yale University Press, 2009.

———. *The Song of Songs and the Ancient Egyptian Love Songs*. Madison: University of Wisconsin Press, 1985.

Franklin, Benjamin. *Poor Richard's Almanack*. Rye Brook, NY: Peter Pauper, 1980.

Futato, Mark D. *Interpreting the Psalms: An Exegetical Handbook*. Grand Rapids: Kregel, 2007.

Geeraerts, Dirk. *Theories of Lexical Semantics*. Oxford: Oxford University Press, 2010.

Gibson, David. *Living Life Backward: How Ecclesiastes Teaches Us to Live in Light of the End*. Wheaton: Crossway, 2017.

Glickman, Craig. *Solomon's Song of Love: Let the Song of Solomon Inspire Your Own Love Story*. West Monroe, LA: Howard, 2004.

Goldingay, John. *Proverbs*. Commentaries for Christian Formation. Grand Rapids: Eerdmans, 2023.

———. *Psalms*. 3 vols. Baker Commentary on the Old Testament Wisdom and Psalms. Grand Rapids: Baker Academic, 2006–8.

Gorman, Amanda. "& So." In *Call Us What We Carry: Poems*, 25. New York: Viking, 2021.

Greidanus, Sidney. *Preaching Christ from Ecclesiastes: Foundations for Expository Sermons*. Grand Rapids: Eerdmans, 2010.

Hartley, John E. *The Book of Job*. New International Commentary on the Old Testament. Grand Rapids: Eerdmans, 1988.

Heim, Knut Martin. *Ecclesiastes: An Introduction and Commentary*. Tyndale Old Testament Commentaries. Downers Grove, IL: IVP Academic, 2015.

Held, Shai. "'With Fists Flailing at the Gates of Heaven': Wrestling with Psalm 88, a Psalm for Chronic Illness." In *A New Song: Biblical Hebrew Poetry as Jewish and Christian Scripture*, edited by Stephen D. Campbell, Richard G. Rohlfing Jr., and Richard S. Briggs, 142–55. Bellingham, WA: Lexham Academic, 2023.

Hernández, Dominick S. *Engaging the Old Testament: How to Read Biblical Narrative, Poetry, and Prophecy Well*. Grand Rapids: Baker Academic, 2023.

Hess, Richard S. *Song of Songs*. Baker Commentary on the Old Testament Wisdom and Psalms. Grand Rapids: Baker Academic, 2005.

Hill, Andrew E., and John H. Walton. *A Survey of the Old Testament*. 3rd ed. Grand Rapids: Zondervan, 2009.

Hill, Robert Charles, trans. *St. John Chrysostom Commentary on the Psalms*. 2 vols. Brookline, MA: Holy Cross Orthodox Press, 1998.

Howard, David M., Jr., and Andrew J. Schmutzer, eds. *Reading the Psalms Thologically*. Studies in Scripture and Biblical Theology. Bellingham, WA: Lexham, 2023.

Hubbard, Robert L., Jr. "גאל." In *New International Dictionary of Old Testament Theology and Exegesis*, edited by Willem A. VanGemeren, 1:789–94. Grand Rapids: Zondervan, 1997.

Imes, Carmen Joy. *Praying the Psalms with Augustine and Friends*. Sacred Roots Spiritual Classics 1. Witchita: TUMI, 2021.

Jacoby, Matthew. *Deeper Places: Experiencing God in the Psalms*. Grand Rapids: Baker Books, 2013.

Jaeger, Marietta. *The Lost Child*. Grand Rapids: Zondervan, 1983.

Jeanty, Edner A., and O. Carl Brown. *999 Haitian Proverbs in Creole and English*. Port-au-Prince: Editions Learning Center, 1976.

Johnson, John E. "An Analysis of Proverbs 1:1–7." *Bibliotheca Sacra* 144 (1987): 419–32.

Keel, Othmar. *The Song of Songs*. Translated by Frederick J. Gaiser. Continental Commentaries. Minneapolis: Fortress, 1994.

Keller, Timothy. *Preaching: Communicating Faith in an Age of Skepticism*. New York: Viking, 2015.

Keller, Timothy, and Kathy Keller. *God's Wisdom for Navigating Life: A Year of Daily Devotions in the Book of Proverbs*. New York: Viking, 2017.

———. *The Songs of Jesus: A Year of Daily Devotions in the Psalms*. New York: Viking, 2015.

Kidner, Derek. *Proverbs*. Kidner Classic Commentaries. Downers Grove, IL: InterVarsity, 2018.

———. *Proverbs: An Introduction and Commentary*. Tyndale Old Testament Commentaries. Downers Grove, IL: InterVarsity, 2008.

———. *Psalms 1–72: An Introduction and Commentary on Books I and II of the Psalms*. Tyndale Old Testament Commentaries. Downers Grove, IL: InterVarsity, 1973.

———. *Psalms 73–150: A Commentary on Books III–V of the Psalms*. Tyndale Old Testament Commentaries. Downers Grove, IL: InterVarsity, 1975.

King, Philip J., and Lawrence E. Stager. *Life in Biblical Israel*. Louisville: Westminster John Knox, 2001.

Kline, Jonathan G. *A Proverb a Day in Biblical Hebrew*. Peabody, MA: Hendrickson, 2019.

Knight, Michelle. "The Rational Poet: Appealing to the Heart and the Mind in the Book of Judges." Center for Hebraic Thought. *The Biblical Mind*, August 12, 2020. https://hebraicthought.org/book-of-judges-poetic-appeal-heart-mind/.

Koptak, Paul E. *Proverbs*. NIV Application Commentary. Grand Rapids: Zondervan, 2003.

Kuta, Sarah. "You Can Own a Piece of Forrest Fenn's Treasure." *Smithsonian Magazine*, November 28, 2022. https://www.smithsonianmag.com/smart-news/forrest-fenn-treasure-auction-180981183/.

Kynes, Bill, and Will Kynes. *Wrestling with Job: Defiant Faith in the Face of Suffering*. Downers Grove, IL: IVP Academic, 2022.

Kynes, Will. *An Obituary for "Wisdom Literature": The Birth, Death, and Intertextual Reintegration of a Biblical Corpus*. Oxford: Oxford University Press, 2019.

Langley, Kenneth. "Psalms." In *The Big Idea Companion for Preaching and Teaching*, edited by Matthew D. Kim and Scott M. Gibson, 199–220. Grand Rapids: Baker Academic, 2021.

Lewis, C. S. *A Grief Observed*. San Francisco: HarperOne, 2015.

———. "The Weight of Glory." In *The Weight of Glory: And Other Addresses*, 25–46. San Francisco: HarperSanFrancisco, 2001.

Lloyd-Jones, D. Martyn. *Preaching and Preachers*. Grand Rapids: Zondervan, 1971.

Longman, Tremper, III. *The Book of Ecclesiastes*. The New International Commentary on the Old Testament. Grand Rapids: Eerdmans, 1998.

———. *The Fear of the Lord Is Wisdom: A Theological Introduction to Wisdom in Israel*. Grand Rapids: Baker Academic, 2017.

———. *How to Read the Psalms*. Downers Grove, IL: InterVarsity, 1988.

———. *Job*. Baker Commentary on the Old Testament Wisdom and Psalms. Grand Rapids: Baker Academic, 2012.

———. *Proverbs*. Baker Commentary on the Old Testament Wisdom and Psalms. Grand Rapids: Baker Academic, 2006.

———. *Psalms: An Introduction and Commentary*. Tyndale Old Testament Commentaries. Downers Grove, IL: IVP Academic, 2014.

———. *The Song of Songs*. The New International Commentary on the Old Testament. Grand Rapids: Eerdmans, 2001.

MacLeish, Archibald. *J. B.* Boston: Houghton Mifflin Company, 1958.

Mathewson, Steven D. *The Art of Preaching Old Testament Narrative.* 2nd ed. Grand Rapids: Baker Academic, 2021.

———. "Let the Big Idea Live! A Response to Abraham Kuruvilla." *Journal of the Evangelical Homiletics Society* 19, no. 1 (2019): 33–41.

———. "Proverbs." In *The Big Idea Companion for Preaching and Teaching*, edited by Matthew D. Kim and Scott M. Gibson, 221–38. Grand Rapids: Baker Academic, 2021.

Maugham, W. Somerset. "The Appointment in Samarra." Accessed April 19, 2024. https://www.k-state.edu/english/baker/english320/Maugham-AS.htm.

Morales, L. Michael. *Who Shall Ascend the Mountain of the Lord? A Biblical Theology of the Book of Leviticus.* Downers Grove, IL: InterVarsity, 2015.

Neusner, Jacob. *The Mishnah: A New Translation.* New Haven: Yale University Press, 1988.

O'Donnell, Douglas S. *The Song of Solomon: An Invitation to Intimacy.* Preaching the Word. Wheaton: Crossway, 2012.

O'Dowd, Ryan P. *Proverbs.* Story of God Bible Commentary. Grand Rapids: Zondervan, 2017.

Ortlund, Eric. "The Wisdom of the Song of Songs: A Pastoral Guide for Preaching and Teaching." *Themelios* 45 (2020): 494–514.

Ortlund, Raymond C., Jr. *Proverbs: Wisdom That Works.* Preaching the Word. Wheaton: Crossway, 2012.

Pehlke, Helmuth. "Metallurgy." In *Dictionary of Daily Life in Biblical and Post-Biblical Antiquity*, edited by Edwin M. Yamauchi and Marvin R. Wilson, 3:300–337. Peabody, MA: Hendrickson, 2016.

Pennington, Jonathan T. *Jesus the Great Philosopher: Rediscovering the Wisdom Needed for the Good Life.* Grand Rapids: Brazos, 2020.

Peterson, Eugene. *A Long Obedience in the Same Direction: Discipleship in an Instant Society.* 20th anniversary ed. Downers Grove, IL: InterVarsity, 2000.

Peterson, Justin Alan. "Toward a Collaborative Sermon Preparation Process: The Necessity and Benefit of Team Sermon Prep." DMin diss., Western Seminary, 2022.

Phillips, Elaine A. *An Introduction to Reading Biblical Wisdom Texts.* Peabody, MA: Hendrickson, 2017.

Postell, Seth D. "Does the Book of Psalms Present a Divine Messiah?" In *Reading the Psalms Theologically*, edited by David M. Howard Jr. and Andrew J. Schmutzer, 96–110. Bellingham, WA: Lexham Academic, 2023.

Pritchard, James B., ed. *The Ancient Near East.* Vol. 1, *An Anthology of Texts and Pictures.* Princeton: Princeton University Press, 1958.

Provan, Iain. *Ecclesiastes, Song of Songs*. NIV Application Commentary. Grand Rapids: Zondervan, 2001.

Robinson, Haddon W. *Biblical Preaching: The Development and Delivery of Expository Messages*. 3rd ed. Grand Rapids: Baker Academic, 2014.

Ross, Allen P. *A Commentary on the Psalms*. 3 vols. Kregel Exegetical Library. Grand Rapids: Kregel Academic, 2011–16.

———. *Proverbs*. Edited by Tremper Longman III and David E. Garland. Rev. ed. Expositor's Bible Commentary. Grand Rapids: Zondervan, 2017.

Ryken, Leland. *Sweeter Than Honey, Richer Than Gold: A Guided Study of Biblical Poetry*. Reading the Bible as Literature. Wooster, OH: Weaver, 2015.

———. *Worldly Saints: The Puritans as They Really Were*. Grand Rapids: Academie Books, 1986.

Ryken, Philip G. *Ecclesiastes: Why Everything Matters*. Preaching the Word. Wheaton: Crossway, 2014.

———. *The Love of Loves in the Song of Songs*. Wheaton: Crossway, 2019.

Schreiner, Patrick. *Acts*. Christian Standard Commentary. Nashville: Holman Bible Publishers, 2021.

Seow, C. L. *Job 1–21: Interpretation and Commentary*. Illuminations. Grand Rapids: Eerdmans, 2013.

Shigematsu, Ken. *Job*. In *The Big Idea Companion for Preaching and Teaching*, edited by Matthew D. Kim and Scott M. Gibson, 192–98. Grand Rapids: Baker Academic, 2021.

Steinbeck, John. *East of Eden*. New York: Viking, 2003.

Tully, Eric J. *Reading the Prophets as Christian Scripture: A Literary, Canonical, and Theological Introduction*. Grand Rapids: Baker Academic, 2022.

Van der Merwe, Christo H. J., Jacobus A. Naudé, and Jan H. Kroeze. *A Biblical Hebrew Reference Grammar*. 2nd ed. London: Bloomsbury, 2017.

VanGemeren, Willem A. *Psalms*. Edited by Tremper Longman III and David E. Garland. Rev. ed. Expositor's Bible Commentary. Grand Rapids: Zondervan, 2008.

Van Wolde, Ellen. *Reframing Biblical Studies: When Language and Text Meet Culture, Cognition, and Context*. Winona Lake, IN: Eisenbrauns, 2009.

Vermeulen, Karolien, and Elizabeth R. Hayes. *How We Read the Bible: A Guide to Scripture's Style and Meaning*. Grand Rapids: Eerdmans, 2022.

Vroegop, Mark. *Dark Clouds, Deep Mercy: Discovering the Grace of Lament*. Wheaton: Crossway, 2019.

Waltke, Bruce K. *The Book of Proverbs: Chapters 1–15*. New International Commentary on the Old Testament. Grand Rapids: Eerdmans, 2004.

———. *The Book of Proverbs: Chapters 15–31*. New International Commentary on the Old Testament. Grand Rapids: Eerdmans, 2005.

———. "Old Testament Interpretation Issues for Big Idea Preaching: Problematic Sources, Poetics, and Preaching the Old Testament, An Exposition of Proverbs 26:1–12." In *The Big Idea of Biblical Preaching: Connecting the Bible to People*, edited by Keith Willhite and Scott M. Gibson, 41–52. Festschrift for Haddon W. Robinson. Grand Rapids: Baker, 1998.

———. *An Old Testament Theology: An Exegetical, Canonical, and Thematic Approach*. Grand Rapids: Zondervan, 2007.

———. "Proverbs 10:1–16: A Coherent Collection?" In *Reading and Hearing the Word of God: From Text to Sermon*, edited by Arie C. Leder, 161–80. Grand Rapids: CRC Publications, 1998.

Waltke, Bruce K., and Ivan D. V. De Silva. *Proverbs: A Shorter Commentary*. Grand Rapids: Eerdmans, 2021.

Waltke, Bruce K., and James M. Houston. *The Psalms as Christian Worship: A Historical Commentary*. With Erika Moore. Grand Rapids: Eerdmans, 2010.

Waltke, Bruce K., and Fred G. Zaspel. *How to Read and Understand the Psalms*. Wheaton: Crossway, 2023.

Walton, John H. *Job*. NIV Application Commentary. Grand Rapids: Zondervan, 2012.

Walton, John H., and Tremper Longman III. *How to Read Job*. Downers Grove, IL: IVP Academic, 2015.

Webb, Barry G. *Five Festal Garments: Christian Reflections on the Song of Songs, Ruth, Lamentations, Ecclesiastes, Esther*. New Studies in Biblical Theology 10. Downers Grove, IL: InterVarsity, 2000.

———. *Job*. Evangelical Biblical Theology Commentary. Bellingham, WA: Lexham Academic, 2023.

Westermann, Claus. *The Psalms: Structure, Content, and Message*. Translated by Ralph D. Gerhrke. Minneapolis: Augsburg, 1980.

Wiesel, Elie. *Messengers of God: Biblical Portraits and Legends*. Translated by Marion Wiesel. New York: Random House, 1976.

Wilson, Gerald Henry. *The Editing of the Hebrew Psalter*. Society of Biblical Literature Dissertation Series 76. Chico, CA: Scholars Press, 1985.

———. *Psalms*. Vol. 1. NIV Application Commentary. Grand Rapids: Zondervan, 2002.

Wilson, Lindsay. *Proverbs: An Introduction and Commentary*. Tyndale Old Testament Commentaries. Downers Grove, IL: InterVarsity, 2018.

Scripture Index

233

Subject Index